THE HOME BOOK

SECOND NATIONAL EDITION

A Complete Guide to Homeowner and Homebuilder Responsibilities

Includes:

- Construction Performance Guidelines
- Important Maintenance Items
- Information on Green Home Construction

David E. MacLellan
George E. Wolfson, AIA
Douglas Hansen

Published by:
The Building Standards Institute
Washington, D.C.
Walnut Creek, California

The Home Book is published by The Building Standards Institute, a private non-profit corporation under license from MacLellan Media, Inc. This book is not a publication of any state or other government agency.

First Printing: January 2014
Second Printing: May 2016

The Building Standards Institute, 1030 15th St. NW, B-1 Floor, Suite 368, Washington, D.C. 20005
The Building Standards Institute, P.O. Box 2456, Walnut Creek, CA 94595
www.buildingstandardsinstitute.org

Publisher's Cataloging-In-Publication Data
(Prepared by The Donohue Group, Inc.)

Names: MacLellan, David E. | Wolfson, George E. | Hansen, Douglas. | Ortegon, Eunice, illustrator. | Bologna, Joe, illustrator. | Martin, Glen, 1958- | Daiker, Stacy.
Title: The home book : a complete guide to homeowner and homebuilder responsibilities / David E. MacLellan, George E. Wolfson, AIA, Douglas Hansen ; illustrations: Eunice Ortegon, Joe Bologna, AIA.
Description: Second national edition / revisions were completed by Glen Martin and Stacy Daiker. | Washington, D.C. ; Walnut Creek, California : The Building Standards Institute, [2016] | "Includes: Construction Performance Guidelines, Important Maintenance Items, Information on Green Home Construction." | "Includes 380 residential workmanship guidelines"--Cover. | Includes bibliographical references and index.
Identifiers: LCCN 2016939845 | ISBN 978-0-692-69169-4
Subjects: LCSH: House construction--United States--Handbooks, manuals, etc. | Dwellings--Maintenance and repair--Handbooks, manuals, etc. | Home ownership--United States--Handbooks, manuals, etc. | Ecological houses--Design and construction--Handbooks, manuals, etc.
Classification: LCC TH4813 .T46 2016 | DDC 690.837--dc23

The Home Book, Second National Edition was reformatted and revised by the Publisher, The Building Standards Institute. Second National Edition revisions were completed by Glen Martin and Stacy Daiker.

Illustrations: Eunice Ortegon, Joe Bologna, AIA
Cover Design: George Foster
Graphic Design: David Grandin
Editorial Assistance: Leanne Hamaji, Sarah Huson

Printed in the United States of America.

TABLE OF CONTENTS

Chapter Four: Roofs

Chapter Five: Exterior Components

Chapter Six: Interior Components

The Home Book

Preface

Despite a significant need, uniform standards for performance and workmanship in the homebuilding industry do not exist. While numerous books have been written about construction quality, few books, publications, or other materials dealing with building performance standards or guidelines have been published. The various *building codes*, adopted and modified by governing agencies in all states in the country, cover building, plumbing, electrical, mechanical and other Home component systems. They derive their language from a health and safety viewpoint, and not necessarily from a construction quality or workmanship standard.

Historically, the definition of quality in homebuilding has been largely a matter of personal opinion. One person's "minimum quality standards" may be another person's "overbuilding". When disputes arise regarding construction quality and workmanship, both homeowners and builders are often frustrated by the absence of a written, unbiased reference to deal with these issues. The intent of this Manual is to provide that written reference.

The Home Book is available as a primary reference to both qualify and quantify residential construction issues. The authors have taken steps to prepare this Manual in a style that is easily understood by a typical Homeowner. The book is not a technical manual written for the construction industry, nor is it a "how to do it" manual describing specific methods to build or repair a Home. A similar manual for California was first published in 2002 and has been updated three times since then. This book expands the previous publications and represents three years of research into national standards and practices. Also included is feedback from the users of the earlier manuals. Several reference books are noted in the Bibliography.

INTRODUCING
HANDY HAMMER
AND YOUR
NEW OR
REMODELED HOME

Introduction

The Purpose of This Manual

The primary purpose of this Manual is to provide the reader with reliable guidelines to evaluate the performance of his or her Home. The authors have been engaged in the business of research and analysis of construction practices for the past 30 years. The Performance Guidelines flow from their own knowledge and from construction industry data and publications. (Refer to Preface: "**Limitation on Liability**", page 15.) The authors have attempted to quantify nearly all of the possible conditions arising from new Home or remodel construction and then apply a Performance Guideline to each condition. To put it simply, a guideline for construction is nothing more than the consensus of those persons or trade groups involved in the homebuilding business who have agreed upon a set of "rules" for fit and finish of Homes. To accomplish the purpose of reasonable uniformity of guidelines, the authors have incorporated comments and changes from more than 70 industry professionals, including homebuilders, specialty contractors, architects and engineers. Further reviews of the manuscript were conducted by government *building officials*, trade organizations and consumer interest groups. Several law firms, whose practices range from representing homebuilders to representing homeowners, have provided review and comments on this Manual.

A secondary purpose of the Manual is to set forth a guide for the Homeowner to perform certain essential maintenance tasks at his or her Home. The Builder may provide this Manual to a Homeowner as part of an express limited warranty connected with the purchase contract. Accordingly, the purchase contract may also require that the Homeowner perform certain maintenance items as a condition of keeping the warranty in good standing. Homeowners should check to see if (and what) maintenance is expected of them to maintain their warranty, and if any conditions in this Manual are specifically excluded from their Builder's limited warranty.

If this Manual is given by the Builder to the Homeowner as part of a limited warranty document, the Homeowner is likely to have the right to contact the Builder regarding an unacceptable condition and use this Manual as a point of reference. This Manual does not track with any particular home warranty program, and in fact, warranties provided by homebuilding companies to their customers may specifically exclude or modify certain items covered in this Manual.

This Manual is organized by descriptions of common Home construction problems, the components of the Home possibly affected by the condition, the appropriate Performance Guideline, the Builder's Responsibility, and the Homeowner's Responsibility. If a Homeowner believes that a particular component or system of the Home may not meet the Performance Guideline, the condition is likely to be found either in the chapter relating to that component of the Home, or in the Index at the end of the Manual.

Codes

Many years ago, governmental officials decided it was appropriate for builders of Homes to adhere to certain construction standards that affected the health, safety and welfare of the general populace. As a result, the *Uniform Building Code* was published in 1927 and it was primarily adopted by the western states. Similarly, two other regional codes were widely adopted. In the Midwest the BOCA *National Building Code*, authored by BOCA (the Building Officials and Code Administrators International, Inc.) and in the South, the *Standard Building Code*, authored by SBCCI (the Southern Building Code Congress International, Inc.) was used. The three agencies collaborated on a nationwide residential code known as the CABO *One and Two Family Dwelling Code*. The three code-authoring agencies merged in the late 1990's to become the International Code Council (ICC). In 2000, they published the first edition of the *International Residential Code* (IRC), which succeeded the CABO code. Since then, new editions of the IRC are published every three years. These Codes, in the past, present and future, are the minimum building requirement to which the Builder must build. As stated previously, the codes typically deal with health, safety and energy conservation issues in construction and do not deal with "fit and finish" or maintenance. The authors have been careful in producing the subject matter of this Manual, so as not to create a conflict between any applicable codes and the following Performance Guidelines. Codes are continuously changing. If there are any conflicts between this Manual and the standards set forth in any current or future codes or other building standards adopted by any governmental agency, the codes and standards shall take precedence.

Definitions

The following definitions apply in this Manual:

- **After-Market Contractor:** A person or company who constructs features and structures at the Home after the Builder has completed his work. Examples of after-market work are: swimming pools, landscaping, sidewalks, *patios*, decks, fences, trellises and retaining walls. In a multifamily project such as a townhouse or *condominium*, the Builder typically performs this work; in a single-family development, this work is usually performed by after-market contractors who likely have no business relationship with the Builder.
- **Builder (Contractor):** A person or company who has the primary responsibility for the construction or remodeling of the Home. This person or company typically has entered into a contract to build or remodel the Home for the Homeowner. The Builder may use other trades to perform specialty work, and these trades are called subcontractors. Licensing requirements for

contractors vary from state-to-state and it is up to the Homeowner to verify that a license is required for the work performed. It is the responsibility of the Builder to obtain the necessary licenses (but not necessarily the building permit) to perform work for the Homeowner. A list of state agencies that oversee or regulate contractors is found at page 6 of this Manual.

HANDY HAMMER
READY TO MAINTAIN THE HOUSE

- **Home:** Any single-family dwelling including a stand-alone single-family Home, a condominium, or attached townhouse. Specifically excluded from this definition are apartments and mobile homes.
- **Homeowner:** A person or entity that purchases a Home from the Builder or may also be a person or entity that subsequently purchases a Home from a previous Homeowner. It may also be a person who enters into a remodeling contract for an existing Home, or a contract with a Builder to build a Home on land that a Homeowner already owns.
- **Homeowners Association:** A mutual benefit association (usually a non-profit corporation) of owners of residential property (most often a condominium or townhouse) who wish to have their common ownership interests managed according to their financial and maintenance objectives. The association is governed by an elected board of directors, and each member (Homeowner) pays regular, periodic fees to the association in exchange for financial and maintenance services.
- **Maintenance:** Work to be performed by Homeowners and/or Homeowner Associations to preserve the integrity of buildings and grounds so that neither shall fall into disrepair.
- **Performance Guideline:** A tolerance or level of reasonable expectation for the components of a Home to be constructed so as to meet certain objectives relating to their appearance, function, and longevity.
- **Warranty (Limited):** A contract or pledge given by the Builder to a Homeowner or Homeowners Association that describes, among other things, the covered components, the standards to which the Home was built, what the Builder will do if the standards are not met, how long the standards will apply, and what the Homeowner must do in the form of maintenance to keep the warranty intact. Some components are not warranted by the Builder but may have the component manufacturer's warranty assigned to the Homeowner. Most warranties are limited and not all inclusive. The Homeowner should read the warranty carefully to understand its limitations. This Manual intentionally does not describe warranty time periods. That is up to the Builder and any governmental regulations that may affect warranties.
- **Weather (Normal and Extreme):** Long-term average ("normal") weather conditions can be determined by NOAA (National Oceanic and Atmospheric Administration) from most stations reported in NOAA's publications, Climatological Data or Local Climatological Data. The great diversity of climate contrasts is not fully represented by NOAA sites, and may require supplemental data and information determined to be suitable by NOAA and state experts in climate and hydrology.

For purposes of this Manual, extreme weather conditions shall have these two characteristics:

1) The local weather event shall be classified as extreme by NOAA according to data taken from the nearest (to the occurrence) and most representative reporting weather station deemed suitable and reliable by the National Weather Service and other NOAA climate experts; and
2) The local weather event shall also be classified as a 25-year return interval for the particular event in question (for example, wind, precipitation, snowfall or snow depth, temperature) at that locale.

Reports can be obtained from the NOAA website: www.ncdc.noaa.gov

Other industry terms appear in this Manual in *blue* and *italicized* type. Definitions for these terms and phrases are found in the Glossary.

Contractor Regulation and Oversight Agencies

State	Organization/Contact	Purpose of State Organization	State License Req'd	Local License Req'd	Comments
Alabama	*License Board for General Contractors* *www.genconbd.state.al.us*	*License and regulation*	*Yes*	*No*	*State contractor's license required for residential projects over $50,000. License required for electrician, electrical, HVAC, plumber, asbestos and lead abatement, and gas fitters.*
Alaska	*Division of Corporations, Business and Professional Licensing as well as Department of Community and Economic Development:* *https://www.commerce.alaska.gov/web/cbpl/ProfessionalLicensing/ConstructionContractors.aspx*	*License, registration, and regulation*	*Yes (partial)*	*No*	*Requires that contractors register with the Dept. of Community and Economic Development. Contractors must be licensed and have proof of bonding and liability insurance for jobs over $10,000. License required for electrical, plumbing, mechanical, HVAC, refrigeration and asbestos abatement.*
Arizona	*Arizona Registrar of Contractors:* *www.azroc.gov*	*License & regulation*	*Yes*	*No*	*State contractor's license required. License required for every trade involved in residential construction. Contractors must have proof of bonding for jobs over $150,000.*
Arkansas	*Arkansas Contractors License Board:* *www.state.ar.us/clb/*	*License & regulation*	*Yes*	*No*	*State contractor's license required for projects over $20,000. License required for electricians, plumbers, HVAC, refrigeration, asbestos and lead abatement, boiler sales & installation, and alarm system installation.*
California	*Contractors State Licensing Board:* *www.cslb.ca.gov*	*License and regulation*	*Yes*	*No*	*State contractor's license required. License required for every trade involved in residential construction and remodeling.*
Colorado	*Department of Regulatory Agencies:* *www.dora.state.co.us/registrations*	*License verification*	*Yes (partial)*	*Yes*	*No state contractor's license required. Regulated at city or county level. License required for electrical, plumbing.*
Connecticut	*Department of Consumer Protection:* *www.ct.gov/dcp*	*Certification and registration*	*Yes (partial)*	*No*	*No state contractor's license required. New home contractors must be certified and register with Dept. of Consumer Protection, and pay into the New Home Construction Guaranty Fund. General contractors must register with the State. State license required for electrical, plumbing, HVAC, asbestos, and lead abatement, well drilling, spa/pool maintenance, glaziers, and fire protection.*
Delaware	*Division of Revenue:* *http://revenue.delaware.gov/services/Business_Tax/Cont_New.shtml*	*Business license registration*	*Yes*	*No*	*Contractor's license required for projects over $50,000. All businesses must register with the Division of Revenue. State license required for HVAC, electrical, plumbing, asbestos removal.*
Florida	*Construction Industry Licensing Board:* *http://www.myfloridalicense.com/dbpr/pro/cilb/*	*License, registration, and regulation*	*Yes (partial)*	*Yes*	*State contractor's need registration and certification. License required for electrical, asbestos abatement, building code administration, and inspectors.*
Georgia	*State Licensing Board of Residential and General Contractors:* *http://sos.ga.gov/index.php/licensing/plb/46*	*License and regulation*	*Yes*	*No*	*State general or residential contractor's license required. License required for electrical, plumbing, and air conditioning.*
Hawaii	*Department of Commerce and Consumer Affairs Licensing Area:* *http://cca.hawaii.gov/rico/licensedcontractor/*	*Provides licensing & registration information with State*	*Yes*	*No*	*State contractor's license required for contractors, electrical, plumbing, asbestos, and lead abatement.*

State	Organization/Contact	Purpose of State Organization	State License Req'd	Local License Req'd	Comments
Idaho	*Idaho Contractors Board: http://ibol.idaho.gov/IBOL/BoardPage.aspx?Bureau=CON*	*Registration*	*No*	*Yes*	*Residential contractors register at the local level. State license required for electrical, plumbers, and sprinkler contractors, and fire protection.*
Illinois	*Attorney General, Consumer Protection Division: www.illinoisattorneygeneral.gov/consumers/homerepair_construction.html Illinois Department of Financial and Professional Regulation: www.Idfpr.com*	*Protect consumers*	*No*	*Yes*	*No state license required for general contractors. License required for roofing and plumbing.*
Indiana	*Attorney General, Consumer Services Division: www.in.gov/attorneygeneral/*	*Protect consumers Specialty license and regulation*	*No*	*Yes*	*No state license required for general contractors. License required for plumbing, asbestos and lead abatement. All other licenses are issued at the local / county level.*
Iowa	*Iowa Workforce Labor Services Division: www.iowaworkforce.org/labor*	*Registration*	*No*	*Yes*	*No state license required for general contractors. Contractors must register with the state. License required for electrical, plumbing, HVAC, asbestos and lead abatement.*
Kansas	*Department of Revenue: www.ksrevenue.org*	*Registration with Department of Revenue*	*No*	*Yes*	*No state license for general contractors. All businesses must register with the Department of Revenue.*
Kentucky	*Public Protection Cabinet: http://dhbc.ky.gov*	*Specialty license and regulation*	*No*	*Yes*	*No state license for general contractors. License required for electrical, HVAC, plumbing, asbestos and lead abatement.*
Louisiana	*Louisiana State Licensing Board for Contractors: www.lslbc.louisiana.gov*	*Regulation and ensures compliance with license requirement*	*Yes*	*No*	*State license required for general contractors. License required for plumbing, and asbestos and lead abatement. Home improvement contractors must register with the state.*
Maine	*Dept. of Professional and Financial Registration Office of Professional and Occupational Regulation: www.maine.gov/pfr/professionallicensing/*	*Specialty license and regulation*	*Yes (partial)*	*No*	*No state license required for general contractors. License required for electrical and plumbing. Home repair contractors must register with the state.*
Maryland	*Department of Labor, Licensing and Regulation: www.dllr.state.md.us*	*Specialty license and regulation*	*No*	*Yes*	*Contractors must register with the state Attorney General office. Local licenses are required, however if licensed in one county, contractor may also conduct business in other counties. License required for electrical, plumbing, HVAC, home improvement, asbestos and lead abatement.*
Massachu-setts	*Division of Professional Licensure: www.mass.gov/dpl*	*License and regulation*	*Yes*	*No*	*State license required for construction supervisor, electrical, plumbing, home improvement trades and asbestos and lead abatement.*
Michigan	*Department of Licensing & Regulatory Affairs: www.michigan.gov/lara*	*License and regulation*	*Yes*	*No*	*Residential Contractor license required as well as electrical, plumbing, and asbestos and lead abatement.*
Minnesota	*Department of Labor & Industry: www.doli.state.mn.us*	*License and regulation*	*Yes*	*No*	*Residential Contractor license required. Licenses for electrical and plumbing licensed through separate departments.*

State	Organization/Contact	Purpose of State Organization	State License Req'd	Local License Req'd	Comments
Mississippi	*Mississippi State Board of Contractors* *www.msboc.us*	*License and regulation*	*Yes*	*No*	*State contractor's license required for projects exceeding $50,000 or remodels over $10,000.*
Missouri	*Official State Website:* *www.mo.gov*	*Contractor registration*	*No*	*Yes*	*No state license required for contractors. License required for asbestos and lead abatement.*
Montana	*Department of Labor & Industry:* *http://erd.dli.mt.gov*	*Contractor registration*	*No*	*No*	*No state contractor's license required. Contractors must register if they have employees. License required for electrical and plumbing.*
Nebraska	*Department of Labor:* *www.dol.nebraska.gov*	*Allows and confirms contractor registration*	*No*	*Yes*	*No state contractor's license required. Non-resident contractors must register with the Secretary of State. License required for electrical and plumbing. Counties with populations over 100,000 require and issue licenses.*
Nevada	*Nevada State Contractors Board:* *www.nscb.state.nv.us*	*License and regulation*	*Yes*	*No*	*State contractor's license required for every trade involved in residential construction. License required for asbestos abatement.*
New Hampshire	*Department of Health & Human Services:* *www.state.nh.us*	*Specialty license and regulation*	*Yes (partial)*	*No*	*No state license required for general contractors. License required for electrical, plumbing, asbestos and lead abatement.*
New Jersey	*Department of Labor & Workforce Development:* *http://lwd.dol.state.nj.us*	*License, registration, and regulation*	*Yes (partial)*	*No*	*New home builders and home improvement contractors must register with state. License required for electrical, plumbing, and home improvement contractors.*
New Mexico	*Regulation & Licensing Department:* *www.rld.state.nm.us/construction/constructions-industries-overview.aspx*	*License and regulation*	*Yes*	*No*	*State contractor's license is required.*
New York	*New York State Attorney General:* *www.oag.state.ny.us*	*License & regulation*	*Yes (partial)*	*Yes*	*Except for asbestos abatement, construction work regulated at the local level. License required for asbestos abatement.*
North Carolina	*Licensing Board for General Construction:* *www.nclbgc.org*	*License and regulation*	*Yes*	*No*	*State contractor's license required for jobs over $30,000. License required for electrical, plumbing, heating, fire sprinklers, refrigeration and asbestos and lead abatement.*
North Dakota	*Secretary of State Contractor Licensing:* *www.nd.gov/sos/licensing*	*License and regulation*	*Yes*	*No*	*State contractor's license required for jobs over $4,000. License required for electrical, plumbing, heating and asbestos and lead abatement.*
Ohio	*Ohio Construction Industry Licensing Board (OCILB):* *www.com.state.oh.us*	*License and regulation*	*Yes (partial)*	*Yes*	*License may be required at local level. Licensing requirements vary between cities and counties. State license required for electrical, plumbing, HVAC, asbestos and lead abatement, refrigeration, and hydronics.*
Oklahoma	*Construction Industries Board:* *www.cib.state.ok.us*	*License and regulation*	*Yes (partial)*	*No*	*No state license for general contractors. License required for electrical, plumbing, and mechanical.*
Oregon	*Construction Contractors Board:* *www.oregon.gov/ccb*	*License, registration, and regulation*	*Yes*	*No*	*State contractor's license required. License required for electrical, plumbing, asbestos and lead abatement, and boiler trade.*

State	Organization/Contact	Purpose of State Organization	State License Req'd	Local License Req'd	Comments
Pennsylvania	*Pennsylvania Attorney General: www.attorneygeneral.gov*	*License and regulation*	*No*	*No*	*General contractors must register with the Attorney General's office. License required at local levels. License required for asbestos and lead abatement.*
Rhode Island	*Contractors' Registration & Licensing Board: www.crb.state.ri.us*	*License and regulation*	*Yes (partial)*	*No*	*Contractors must register. License required for electrical, plumbing, and asbestos.*
South Carolina	*Department. of Labor, Licensing and Regulation: www.llr.state.sc.us/pol/residentialbuilders*	*License and regulation*	*Yes*	*No*	*State contractor's license required for projects over $200. State issues Contractor and Residential contractor licenses. License required for asbestos and lead abatement, and HVAC.*
South Dakota	*Department of Labor & Regulation: http://dol.sd.gov/bdcomm*	*License and regulation*	*Yes (partial)*	*No*	*No state license required for general contractors. License required for electrical, plumbing. Certificates required for asbestos abatement.*
Tennessee	*Board for Licensing Contractors: http://tn.gov/commerce/section/contractors-home-improvement*	*License and regulation*	*Yes*	*No*	*State contractor's license required for projects over $25,000. License required for electrical, plumbing, HVAC, and mechanical.*
Texas	*Department of Licensing & Regulation: www.license.state.tx.us*	*License and regulation*	*Yes (partial)*	*Yes*	*No state license required for general contractors. Permits issued at the local level. License required for electrical, plumbing, HVAC, fire sprinkler, and well drilling.*
Utah	*Division of Occupational & Professional Licensing: www.dopl.utah.gov/index.html*	*License and regulation*	*Yes*	*No*	*State license required for general contractors, electrical, and plumbing.*
Vermont	*Official State Website: www.Vermont.gov/portal/business/*	*License and regulation*	*Yes (partial)*	*Yes*	*No state license required for general contractors. License required for electrical, plumbing. Certification required for asbestos and lead abatement.*
Virginia	*Department of Professional and Occupational Regulation: www.dpor.virginia.gov*	*License and regulation*	*Yes*	*No*	*State license required for general contractors, electrical, plumbing, HVAC, gas fitting and asbestos and lead abatement.*
Washington	*Department of Labor and Industries Contractor: www.Lni.wa.gov*	*Contractor registration*	*Yes (partial)*	*No*	*Contractors must register with the Dept. of Labor and Industries. License required for electrical and plumbing.*
West Virginia	*West Virginia Division of Labor: www.wvlabor.com/newwebsite/Pages/index.html*	*License and regulation*	*Yes*	*No*	*State license required for general contractors, electrical, asbestos, and lead abatement.*
Wisconsin	*Department of Safety & Professional Services: http://dsps.wi.gov*	*License, and regulation*	*Yes (partial)*	*No*	*Residential contractors must have credential, general liability insurance, and attend continuing education. State license required for electrical, plumbing, HVAC, and asbestos and lead abatement.*
Wyoming	*Association of Municipalities www.wyoming.govoffice.com*	*License and regulation*	*Yes (partial)*	*Yes*	*State license required for electrical contractors. All other contactors licensed at the city or county level.*

State regulations and requirements might change. Reader should verify requirements with applicable state agency.

The Authors

David E. MacLellan

David MacLellan has been a homebuilder since 1969. He has constructed nearly all types of housing including apartments, condominiums, townhouses, mobile home parks, planned unit developments, semi-custom homes, and custom homes. Mr. MacLellan is an engineering graduate from Penn State University with both bachelor's and master's degrees. He is licensed in California and Oregon as a general and specialty building contractor. As a frequent speaker on the subject of construction problems and their remedies, Mr. MacLellan has lectured to numerous professional groups, including the Pacific Coast Builders Conference, the North Carolina Homebuilders Association and the Homebuilders Association of Bucks County, Pennsylvania. He has founded 17 homeowner associations, and he served for nine years as President of the homeowner's association in the community where he lives. He has provided testimony in more than 300 lawsuits or disputes involving construction problems. Mr. MacLellan has been appointed as a Superior Court Referee concerning matters of land use and construction defects. His consulting firm, Pacific InterWest Building Consultants, Inc. operates in California, Oregon and Washington. In June 2011, Mr. MacLellan was inducted into the California Homebuilding Foundation Hall of Fame.

George E. Wolfson, AIA

George Wolfson is a licensed architect, general building contractor, and real estate broker whose professional career spans more than three decades. Mr. Wolfson holds both bachelor's and master's degrees in architecture from the University of Houston and Columbia University respectively. His professional interest area within The American Institute of Architects includes Codes and Practices. As a principal in the consulting firm, Builders Protective Network, Mr. Wolfson has engaged in over 300 operations including field investigations, destructive testing, providing remedial architectural drawings and mediating disputes between owners and builders. He has co-authored three industry publications with David MacLellan: the ***California Building Performance Guidelines for Residential Construction, The National Home Maintenance Manual,*** and ***The Handbook of Specifications and Scopes of Work for Trade Contractors.***

Douglas Hansen

Douglas Hansen is the principal author of the ***Code Check*** series of field guides to building codes, with over 1 million copies in print. Mr. Hansen sits on the technical committee for Electrical Systems Maintenance of the National Fire Protection Association. The committee is responsible for NFPA 73 – The Standard for Electrical Inspection of Existing Dwellings. Mr. Hansen conducts seminars throughout the country to inspectors, building departments, and electricians on building and electrical codes, construction defects, and inspection techniques. He has authored dozens of magazine articles and books. Mr. Hansen holds a general contractor's license and several International Code Council inspection certifications. He also serves as an expert witness in cases involving contractor and inspector standard of care, building codes, construction defects, and disclosure issues.

Acknowledgements

To complete the preparation of this Manual, the authors were assisted by four knowledgeable and well-respected persons in the homebuilding field. These persons include: James Russell, a nationally known building code consultant; Fred Herman, retired Chief Building Official of the City of Palo Alto, California and Life Director of the International Code Council; Richard T. Edwards, a codes and standards expert who sits on two ASTM Committees and holds 13 specialty certifications from the International Code Council; and Robert Rivinius, retired Chief Administrative Officer of the California Building Industry Association, who created the marketing strategy for this book.

In addition, the authors wish to thank each of the contributors and the following reviewers for their thorough and detailed efforts:

- Karen Ackland, ForeWord Reviews
- Tyler Berding, Esq., Berding and Weil
- Builders Association of Northern Nevada
- Building Industry Association of Hawaii
- California Building Industry Association
- Kelly Carrell, The Super HandyMom, *The Super Handyman*, King Features Syndicated columnist
- Florida Home Builders Association
- Steven Holland, Esq., Ring Hunter Holland and Schenone
- Home Builders and Remodelers of Connecticut
- Oklahoma State Home Builders Association
- Oregon Home Builders Association
- Robert Raymer, P.E.
- Texas Association of Builders

How to Measure for Performance Guidelines

If a Homeowner believes a condition exists in his or her Home that does not meet a Performance Guideline set forth in this Manual, the Homeowner should first make a measurement. In order to make the measurement, the following measuring tools and devices are needed:

1. A tape measure that has at least 1/16 inch markings and is 25 feet or longer;
2. Dividers (this tool looks like a compass except it has a point at both ends). Dividers can be purchased at most stationery or drafting supply stores;
3. A carpenter's level at least 3 feet long;
4. A *plumb* bob and string at least 10 feet long;
5. A straight edge that is 8 feet long.

TOOLS TO MEASURE FOR PERFORMANCE STANDARDS

Items 1, 3, and 4 can be purchased at any hardware store. Item 5 can be any piece of material that is 8 feet long and perfectly straight. A piece of dry, ¾ inch thick plywood that is 6 inches wide and 8 feet long will make a good straight edge. Make sure the factory or mill cut edge is the side used for measurement. Avoid using a piece of scrap that someone has cut with their own saw. CAUTION: Do not use a standard 8 foot 2 x 4 *stud* for this purpose because studs can warp and still appear straight, but are not truly straight. If measurement of small cracks becomes necessary (such as separations of hardwood flooring), a good measurement tool is a set of feeler gauges. These can be purchased at any automotive supply store.

Examples of Measurement

- ***Concrete* crack**: look at the crack and locate the widest point. Take the points of the dividers and place them just inside the edges of the crack. Without opening or closing the arms of the dividers, transfer the measurement to the tape measure and write it down.
- **Wall out of plumb**: make a loop about 8 feet down the string attached to the plumb bob (this assumes the wall being measured is 8 feet high). For walls of greater or lesser height, adjust the loop to the height of the wall. Using a nail or small screw, tack the string tight to the ceiling 2 inches out from the wall/ceiling intersection. Let the plumb bob hang freely so it almost touches the floor. When the plumb bob stops swinging, measure the largest gap along the string using the dividers. Use a tape measure to determine the distance. Deduct 2 inches plus the thickness of the string. The difference is the amount the wall is out of plumb. For walls that tilt out, tack the plumb bob string to the ceiling and let the side of the plumb bob barely touch the wall near the floor. Measure from the point of the plumb bob to the wall.

Responsibility of the Builder

Builders have the legal obligation to build a home in conformity with the representations, or promises, that are made to the Homeowner in writing and those that are required or implied by law. Representations are usually contained in a Builder's warranty and may be subject to terms and conditions such as the time periods, Homeowner responsibilities, and the occurrence of naturally caused conditions. The law may also imply the Home be constructed within certain performance tolerances, such as those contained in *building codes* and other standards.

This Manual will assist the Homeowner in identifying common conditions sometimes found in new home construction and remodeling, and help in the resolution of disputes over the performance of new homes. In general, the Builder wants to work with the Homeowner to assure many years of problem-free ownership. This is why Builders and other industry professionals have assisted the authors of this book to define these Performance Guidelines.

If a deviation from the Performance Guidelines is established, either by acknowledgment of the Builder or through the various steps in a dispute resolution process set forth in the Homeowner's warranty, the Builder should correct the unacceptable condition in a manner that brings the condition into conformance with the Performance Guidelines.

Responsibility of the Homeowner

This Manual will help the Homeowner understand their new Home or remodeled portions of an existing Home; conditions under which they can get help from the Builder; the difference between normal and unacceptable performance of their Home, and what their responsibilities are to provide proper maintenance and use.

A Home is a complex structure. It is important that the Homeowner and the Builder work together in a cooperative fashion to prolong the performance of the Home. If any condition that appears to be unusual or threatening regarding construction is observed, the Homeowner has a duty to notify the Builder immediately. Further, if the condition is an emergency and a potential life safety situation, and the Builder cannot be contacted (such as a weekend or holiday), the Homeowner has a duty to mitigate his or her damages. That is to say, rather than allow the condition to continue, and possibly worsen because the Builder could not be reached, the Homeowner must contract with others to make temporary emergency repairs. Many Builders offer 24-hour emergency repair numbers for this purpose. Failure to provide timely notification could lead to a worsening condition for which the Builder may not be responsible. This is especially important for Homes undergoing remodeling where part of the Home may be occupied.

The Homeowner also has a duty to maintain the surrounding grounds and structures, whether or not they were installed by the Builder. Maintenance should be performed in accordance with the maintenance manual provided by the Builder with the warranty, or in the absence of a maintenance manual, in accordance with generally accepted homeowner maintenance procedures, several of which are included in this Manual.

The Walkthrough

The *walkthrough* is the event where the Builder delivers and demonstrates the new Home or the remodeled section to the Homeowner. The walkthrough is sometimes referred to as "taking delivery" of the Home. The walkthrough is one of the single most important events that require participation by the Homeowner. Adequate time must be reserved by both the Builder and Homeowner so that the Homeowner can be advised about the care, maintenance, and use of the Home, as well as to inspect the condition and "fit and finish" of the Home.

THE WALKTHROUGH IS ONE OF THE MOST IMPORTANT STEPS IN TAKING DELIVERY OF THE HOUSE.

A general rule of thumb is that one-hour of walkthrough time should be allowed for every 1,000 square feet of the Home within a four hour maximum. Taking the time to make a comprehensive walkthrough is especially important to the Homeowner because unacceptable conditions that are readily observable during the walkthrough may become the Homeowner's responsibility if they are not noted at the time of walkthrough. Typically, areas such as countertops, finish flooring, *doors*, walls, windows, and mirrors are subject to being damaged with scrapes, scratches, and mars resulting from moving household goods. It should be noted that most Builders do not allow early walkthroughs or partial walkthroughs prior to the completion of the Home for the following reasons:

1) Potential liability resulting from construction conditions;
2) Last minute items will be completed as part of the normal "punch list" process; and
3) Disruption to the production schedule of the Builder.

Limitation on Liability

The Home Book published herein provides information for use by homeowners, homebuilders, subcontractors, and governmental entities in dealing with matters of residential construction, particularly issues regarding workmanship. The performance guidelines are based upon research and reports obtained by the authors and the publisher, The Building Standards Institute. The Building Standards Institute, MacLellan Media, Inc., and the authors assume no liability for the design, scheduling, or manner of construction utilized by any users of this publication, whether in compliance or not with this publication. Each user should consult with his or her own design professionals for incorporation of any performance guidelines or designs in their product. Further, if this publication is given by the Builder to a Homeowner or Homeowners Association as part of a limited warranty offered by the Builder, the Builder assumes no liability for the content of this publication other than to incorporate this publication by reference and to be bound by some or all of the performance guidelines as more particularly stated in the Builder's warranty. The authors and publisher are not engaged in rendering design, legal, investigative, accounting, or related professional services or advice.

The authors have attempted to diligently research and quantify conditions commonly known in residential construction. In addition to their own experience, the authors consulted with numerous homebuilding industry organizations and technical support groups. Persons interested in providing additional content are invited to express their comments to the authors at the e-mail address: info@buildingstandardsinstitute.org for possible inclusions in future editions of this Manual. It is important to note that the performance guidelines set forth in this Manual are effective only beginning with the first date of publication.

The following subjects are intentionally not covered in this Manual because of their specialized characteristics:

1) Swimming Pools;
2) Home Theaters;
3) Photovoltaic Systems and Solar Heating;
4) Electronic Home Management and Security Systems;
5) Vegetated Roofs;
6) Computer and Fiber Optic Systems;
7) Regulations of the Americans with Disabilities Act (ADA).

After-Market Contractors

During the time a subdivision of new homes nears completion and Homeowners begin to occupy the new homes, business opportunities arise for after-market contractors. Typically, these contractors have no relationship with the Builder or the Builder's subcontractors. After-market contractors often provide goods and services such as swimming pools, security systems, landscaping, fencing, deck, patio and masonry work. After-market contractors can perform valuable services that may add to the beauty and enjoyment of the Home. Since these contractors are generally not involved in the original design and construction of the Home, it is important that special attention is paid to the work performed by these contractors. If the after-market work is not carefully integrated into the original construction, problems may arise that could potentially lead to unsatisfactory performance of the new Home or voiding the Builder's warranty.

Contractor licensing requirements vary by state and/or local jurisdiction. Some after-market contractors may not retain the correct licensing required. (Refer to "**Contractor Regulation and Oversight Agencies**" for contractor licensing requirements, page 6.) The most efficient way for a Homeowner to investigate a contractor is to request at least three references of work that the contractor has completed over the preceding six months (exclude any relatives of the contractor). Arrange a visit to the home references to inspect the work. Ask the following questions:

1. Did the contractor show up on time and perform as agreed?
2. Did the contractor constantly ask for more money?
3. Did the contractor leave his work clean and orderly?
4. Did the owner receive any liens from unpaid subcontractors and suppliers?

WARNING

Often an after-market contractor's pitch to a new Homeowner is:

- ☒ A license is not needed for the work that we do (Refer to "**Contractor Regulation and Oversight Agencies**" for contractor licensing requirements, page 6);
- ☒ We can do it cheaper because we're not licensed;
- ☒ No building permit is needed for this work.

The lure of a cheap price often results in shoddy and incomplete workmanship. An unlicensed contractor often carries no insurance and does not pay payroll taxes. Further, it is a misdemeanor in many states for any person (such as a new Homeowner) to enter into a contract, either oral or written, with an unlicensed contractor. This is called aiding and abetting.

Ten Most Common Mistakes Made by New Homeowners

1. **Altering Finished Grades.** Alteration of finished *grades* by the Homeowner or an after-market contractor results in some of the most costly claims made in the construction defect disputes. Unlike a *condominium* or planned unit development where the Builder customarily installs the *walkways*, patios, landscaping, and drainage systems (and thus may become liable for their performance), a single-family residence is often delivered without any of these items except a *driveway*. At a very minimum, *building codes* require that the Home be delivered to the Homeowner with the surrounding bare lot sloped away from the Home at a 2% *slope*. A slight V-shaped impression, called a *swale*, is sometimes cut in the lot. Rainwater is intended to flow away from the Home, to the swale, and then eventually to the street or some other approved storm water collection system. Unfortunately, the Homeowner or an after-market contractor will often pour the sidewalks and patios directly on top of the finished grade. This alters the water flow by trapping it between the walkway and the Home. Swimming pool contractors have been known to set their decks and coping too high, causing water to flow back toward the Home. Often, the net effect of altering the storm water flow around the Home causes water to seep under the *foundation*. Many soils that are high in clay content will not permit water to drain readily. The wet, clay soil can then swell (expand) to up to 30% of its dry volume. The swelling soil can actually lift the Home foundation upward causing extensive interior and exterior damage.

THIS NEW WALK INVITES WATER TO FLOW UNDER THE HOUSE, CAUSING CRACKS, FOUNDATION MOVEMENT, OR MOLD FORMATION!
MOISTURE PATHWAY
ORIGINAL 2% SLOPE AWAY FROM HOUSE

DO NOT ALTER ORIGINAL SITE DRAINAGE!

2. **Pouring a Concrete Patio Too High.** In addition to being poured with a 2% slope, a *concrete* patio or deck should be poured at least 2 inches below *door thresholds* and stucco *weep screeds* (a weep screed is the metal band at the bottom of the *stucco* just above the ground). The weep screed allows water that may be behind the stucco to "weep" out and run onto the patio *slab*. The same requirement applies when other types of *cladding* are used, such as lap *siding*, panel siding, or brick. Pouring the patio or deck too high can also result in rainwater being drawn back up into the exterior cladding of the Home. As a result, decay of the structure may occur and can

create a route for termites to enter the building. Since the finished grade should be maintained 6 inches below the Home slab or finished floor, any installed concrete work should not trap water against the *foundation*. In addition, planters should not be allowed to fill above the required grade.

3. **Improperly Attaching a Deck Trellis, Sunscreen, or Lanai Structure to the Home.** There are many proper ways to create a watertight connection between the Home and a deck trellis or lanai structure. Unfortunately, these "add on structures" are often just nailed or bolted directly to the outside wall of the Home. Inevitably, rainwater finds its way into the penetrations and the *dry rot* process begins. It is critical that the deck *ledger* (the board that is placed up against the side of the Home) be flashed with metal *flashing* in an industry-approved manner. If bolts are used to attach the ledger board to the Home, the bolt holes should be filled with *caulk*. **Note: Local government agencies often require a building permit to construct a trellis or lanai attached to a Home.** A building permit is often required, because a trellis or lanai is considered a structure that could fall and cause injury. Decks which are attached to the Home or which are larger than 200 square feet, or which are over 30 inches above the adjacent grade within 3 feet, often require a building permit. Patio covers may also require a building permit. Check with the local building department before starting work.

4. **Allowing Irrigation Sprinkler Heads to Spray Against the Home.** Irrigation sprinkler heads that spray against the panel or lap *siding*, masonry, or *stucco* walls of a Home can lead to rotted walls and leaching of color from the siding, masonry or stucco. Exterior walls are not constructed to withstand constant exposure to direct landscape irrigation. In addition, irrigation water that ponds at the base of a foundation can lead to upward movement of the foundation. It is important that all irrigation spray be directed away from the Home rather than towards the Home. Spray heads should be checked regularly during the irrigation season to make sure that they have not turned and point toward the Home. As landscaping grows, spray heads should be raised, relocated, or in some cases eliminated to keep moisture away from the side of the Home. *Posts* supporting overhead decks that have shrubbery growing closely around them are particularly vulnerable to irrigation spray.

5. **Disconnecting or Not Using Bathroom and Laundry Vent Fans.** Bathrooms and laundries are areas of high humidity. Bathroom and laundry fans should never be disconnected (even though the noise may bother the occupant). The fan should always be turned on during use of the room. Failure to use the vent fans can result in water vapor getting into the *drywall*, the

electrical outlets and even the framing members. Over time, mold, mildew and fungi may grow in these areas. Water vapor that condenses on walls and windows can eventually find its way into the walls of the Home and weaken the structure through dry rot. Rooms where humidifiers are used should also be well ventilated.

6. **Walking on the Roof.** A Homeowner should never walk on the roof. Walking on the roof can be a slip and fall hazard. Untrained persons are likely to break or scuff the roof covering and cause roof leaks. Most Homes built today have one of three types of *roof covers*: composition *shingles*, concrete or clay *tiles*, or *wood shakes* or shingles. A few Homes are constructed with "flat" roofs, sometimes known as *built-up roofs*. Often custom homes have slate or metal roof coverings. Cleaning *gutters* should be done from a ladder and not by standing on the roof. If an object is thrown on the roof, such as a child's toy, it should be retrieved using a ladder and a telescoping pole, rather than by walking on the roof. Most residential warranties exclude damage resulting from unauthorized persons walking on roofs.

7. **Overloading Upper Cabinets.** While lower cabinets rest on the floor, upper cabinets are hung from a wall using screws or nails. By stacking heavy dishes and glassware in an upper cabinet, a Homeowner can load the cabinet beyond its capacity. This can result in sagging shelves, or worse yet, detachment of the cabinet from the wall. Heavy china and cookware should always be placed in the lower cabinets. Do not overload cabinet drawers with heavy items and take care to not pull drawers out too far. This action results in the plastic guide being snapped off at the back of the cabinet drawer.

8. **Overloading the Floor System.** Builders have the option of many wooden floor systems to use when building homes. Regardless of the choice, all systems must meet the *building code* minimum requirements for floor deflection (up and down movement). Many Homeowners are surprised to learn that the building code permits more deflection than that which they may be comfortable. Household items such as waterbeds, pool tables, and weight lifting equipment can cause significant floor deflection, even if the Home was built in accordance with the code. Many Homes have a concrete *slab* first floor and a wooden second floor. It is best to keep heavy items on the first floor, if possible, particularly if the first floor is a concrete slab.

9. **Storing Household Goods on Garage and Attic Trusses.** Garage and *attic trusses* are designed to support the weight of the roof and ceiling and not the weight of anything else. Unfortunately, many Homeowners view the space in the attic and above the garage ceiling as

additional storage space. Storing household goods in these areas can result in sagging and even a possible collapse of the roof structure. If a Homeowner wishes to use this space for storage, a structural engineer should be consulted to determine if additional reinforcement is necessary.

10. **Tinting Dual Pane Windows.** Many new homes are constructed with *dual pane* windows (also known as double-glazed windows or insulating windows). The two panes of glass are separated by a spacer up to 5/8 inch in thickness. The air space between the dual panes is "dead air". This area is so tightly sealed that air can neither enter nor leave the space. By placing a tinting film on the inside of the window, the sun's rays are reflected back into the dead air space. The temperature in this space can become so hot that it may cause the elastic seal to rupture, causing the insulating value of the window to be lost. Windows with broken or ruptured seals are easy to identify: they have moisture between the panes of glass. Homeowners should never tint a dual pane window on the inside unless it is specifically approved by the window manufacturer.

DO NOT USE ATTIC FOR STORAGE
IT WASN'T DESIGNED FOR THAT USE!

Additional Problems to be Avoided by New Homeowners

☒ **Hanging a Ceiling Fan from a Light Fixture Box.**
Light fixture boxes in the ceiling are not designed to carry the weight of a ceiling fan. Ceiling fans have a special mounting box different from a typical light fixture box. If a ceiling fan is hung from a light fixture box, the vibration and the weight of the fan may cause the box to rip out of the ceiling. Ceiling fans also have special electrical connection requirements that differ from ordinary light fixtures.

☒ **Placing Plastic Deflectors over Heating Vents.**
These *vents*, known as heating air supply grills, are often placed in front of a window or sliding *door* (either in the floor or ceiling). They are designed to sweep the air from these areas and mix it with the air in the center of the room. By placing deflectors over the grills, the Homeowner creates a space of stagnant air with high humidity during rainy periods. Moisture condenses on windows and often rots windowsills and structural members inside the wall. Mold and mildew are likely to grow in these areas. Plastic deflectors should never be used on warm air supply grills.

☒ **Cracking Fireplace Linings.**
Generally, all fuel fireplace linings are of two types: a cast panel of simulated brick or real brick with *mortar* between each brick. All fireplaces require a series of low heat fires to "*cure*" the fireplace lining. By initially building a very hot fire (such as burning sawdust, wax logs, newspapers, or gift wrap), intense heat can generate and cause the fireplace lining to crack. Never burn paper or chemically treated wood products in the fireplace. Be certain to follow the manufacturer's instructions at all times.

☒ **Placing Rugs or Non-breathable Coverings over Wood and Synthetic Decks.**
Decks need to breathe, even decks constructed of synthetic materials. By placing non-breathable coverings (such as indoor/outdoor carpeting) over wood and synthetic decks, moisture will be trapped between the bottom of the covering and the top of the deck. This can result in fungus growth, rot and premature failure of the deck.

☒ **Incorrectly Installing a Security Alarm / Penetration of Windows and Walls.**
If an after-market alarm is installed by the Homeowner or by a contractor who has not been hired by the Builder, great care should be taken to seal all penetrations through windows and walls to avoid future *dry rot*. Never drill into the bottom track of a window or door to install an alarm contact.

☒ **Nailing Fences to Home Walls.**
Nailing any part of a fence to a Home wall invites two problems: 1) trapping rainwater between the fence post and the Home wall, and 2) the invasion of termites through the fence into the Home structure. The terminating fence post should be placed in the ground beside the *foundation* and should not be attached to or come in contact with the Home.

☒ **Applying Vinyl Wallpaper Over Drywall**
Drywall needs to breathe. By placing non-breathable vinyl wallpaper over drywall moisture will be trapped within the wall cavity. This can result in fungus rot and mold grown in the wall cavity.

Performance Guidelines

The following nine chapters cover more than 380 Performance Guidelines for residential construction. When reading a section of particular interest, the following hints are offered to avoid misinterpretation and misunderstanding:

- Is the condition identified in this Manual*? Check the Index if the condition is not listed in the Table of Contents.
- If a measurement is necessary to determine the Guideline, was it measured accurately? See "**How to Measure for Performance Guidelines**" on page 12.
- Was the condition allowed to get worse before the Builder was notified?
- Is the condition covered under the Builder's limited warranty or excluded from the Builder's limited warranty? Check the limited warranty for exclusions and expirations before notifying the Builder.
- Is the condition the result of insufficient or improper Homeowner maintenance? For example, the *eave* leaks because the *gutters* were not cleaned.
- Is the condition caused by the Homeowner? For example, the roof leaks because the Homeowner broke roof tiles while installing holiday lights.

(*) If the condition is not identified in this Manual, describe it in an e-mail to The Building Standards Institute. Contact The Building Standards Institute from their website: www.buildingstandardsinstitute.org. In most cases, The Building Standards Institute will be able to provide clarifying information. Please note that The Building Standards Institute does not furnish legal advice.

Use of This Manual in All 50 States

This Manual is intended for use by Homeowners and Builders (including home remodelers) in all 50 states. The authors and publisher conducted research into the codes, standards, and workmanship guidelines, to the extent they existed, for each state in the country. While there are some geographical differences in construction methods, the authors and their reference associates have diligently described fair and equitable workmanship guidelines whether a Home is built in Alaska or Florida. Further, no attempt has been made to identify or quantify certain local building practices. If a guideline appears in this Manual, it is applicable nationally.

Chapter One

FOUNDATIONS

includes:

Slab On Grade

Grade Beam, Pier, and "T" Footings

Basements and Other Below Grade Structures

Landslides, Sinkholes and Other Soil Movement

References for this chapter:

- *Concrete Performance Standards & Maintenance Guidelines,* 2001
- *Residential Construction Performance Guidelines, 3rd ed.*, NAHB 2011
- *Code Check 3rd ed.*, Taunton Press
- *California Building Code 2013,* California Building Standards Commission
- *Residential Water Problems*, by Alvin Sacks
- *Residential & Light Commercial Construction Standards*, by Don Reynolds
- *International Building Code 2012,* International Code Council
- *International Residential Code 2012,* International Code Council
- *Indiana Quality Assurance Builder Standards 2009,* Indiana Builders Association
- *New Home Warranty Program 2010*, New Jersey Department of Community Affairs
- *South Carolina Residential Construction Standards 1997,* Residential Builders Commission of the South Carolina Department of Labor
- *Standard Specifications for Tolerances for Concrete Construction and Materials* (ACI 117-10)
- *Workmanship Standards for Licensed Contractors 2009,* Arizona Registrar of Contractors
- *NASCLA Residential Construction Standards 2009,* National Association of State Contracting Licensing Agencies
- *Homeowner Handbook 2003,* Greater Atlanta Home Builders Association

A comprehensive list of references by author and publisher is found in the Bibliography section.

Chapter One

Foundations

General Subject Information: In certain areas of the country, many new Homes are built on *slab foundations*. These foundations consist of reinforced *concrete* that is poured on a prepared *grade*. Reinforcing can consist of steel rods called *rebar*, welded wire mesh or cables that are stretched tight after pouring the concrete. A reinforced concrete foundation like this is also known as a post-tensioned slab. Another popular type of foundation is known as the *grade beam* and *pier* system, also known as *crawl space* foundations or *post* and beam in some geographic areas. This system consists of piers drilled into the ground and filled with reinforcing steel and concrete. The piers are connected to low concrete perimeter and interior walls called grade beams. In many geographic areas of the country, the soils are strong enough to use grade beams only, without installing piers. Often the cross section of the grade beam will be thicker at the bottom and resemble an inverted "T". A third type of foundation, known as the *basement* foundation, is commonly installed in homes in the East and Midwest. Some older homes and custom built homes have basements that consist of a room or rooms below the ground level. Also, depending upon the topography of the lot, a Home can have a hybrid foundation of two or more of the types described above.

Slab on Grade

Condition #1: Concrete Slab On Grade Foundation Is Cracked

Potentially Impacting:

- *Slab foundations*
- Garage floors
- *Basement* floors
- Structural integrity

Performance Guideline

Cracks that occur in slab on grade floors should not exceed 3/16 inch in width or 1/8 inch in vertical displacement for more than 12 inches in length. For slab floors that are to be covered with vinyl flooring or similar material, cracks should not be visible in the finish floor at a distance of 6 feet under normal daylight conditions.

Comments: *Concrete* cracks for many reasons. Cracking is inherent in the nature of a *cement* product. Among the worst cracks are those caused by expansive, clay like soils that shrink or expand based upon water content in the soil. Cracks related to soil expansion usually appear as vertical displacement rather than horizontal cracks in the same plane. No matter how careful the Builder is concrete will still crack.

Builder Responsibility: Because some concrete cracking is inevitable, the Builder cannot be held responsible for all cracks. However, if the slab on grade cracks are greater than the acceptable Guideline, the Builder should repair the concrete in a manner that will conform to the Performance Guideline. One of the repair methods consists of filling the crack with latex fortified cement mixture or epoxy filler.

Homeowner Responsibility: ***Maintenance Alert!*** The finished grade along the foundation must *slope* away from the foundation to allow for proper drainage. Slope must be a minimum of ¼ inch per 1 foot for concrete walks and *patios* and 6 inches within 10 feet for soil.

- It is recommended that the Homeowner install *drip irrigation* along the foundation for better water control. This will eliminate any over-spray onto the Home or concrete foundation.
- Periodic inspections of the irrigation system, materials, and slopes are necessary for proper maintenance.
- If rain is forecast, the Homeowner should put the irrigation controller on "RAIN" setting.
- If the Builder has not installed *gutters* and *downspouts*, it is highly recommended that a gutter and downspout system be installed by the Homeowner. Some jurisdictions require that collected water must be filtered on site. Check the current regulations of your jurisdiction.

Condition #2: Concrete Slab Is Not Level

Potentially Impacting:

- *Slab* floors
- *Basement* floors

Performance Guideline

The slab should be level and any deviations should not exceed ½ inch of vertical change in 20 feet of length. For distances greater than 20 feet the deviation tolerance is ½ inches per foot to a maximum of 1 inch. This Guideline does not apply to multistory buildings with post-tension concrete floors. See additional Comments after Condition #3 below.

Comments: Concrete floors poured in an area that will ultimately be covered with another material should be poured as flat as possible. Some adjustments can be made when setting tile and marble and installing hardwood flooring. Basement slabs may have *drains* in them and it is proper for the Builder to *slope* the slab toward the drains. Garage slabs are intentionally sloped from the inside wall toward the *garage door* to allow water from wet cars to drain toward the garage door.

Builder Responsibility: The Builder should conduct an investigation to determine the cause of the condition. If the condition is a result of improper construction and not a result of improper use or lack of maintenance by the Homeowner, the Builder should perform repairs to bring the slab back into conformance with the Performance Guideline.

Homeowner Responsibility: None.

Condition #3: Concrete Slab Is Uneven

Potentially Impacting:

- *Foundation slab*
- *Basement slab*

Performance Guideline

Concrete floors should not have areas of unevenness of more than ¼ inch over a horizontal distance of 10 feet. This Guideline does not apply to multistory buildings with post-tension concrete floors. See Comments below.

Comments: Except for floors that are specifically designed to slope to drains (such as basement floors or certain decks), unevenness in concrete, known as undulations or "wows", should be avoided when finishing the slab. Smoothing an uneven concrete slab is not difficult. Many remedies are available.

Builder Responsibility: If the Performance Guideline is exceeded, the Builder should, using a recognized industry-accepted method, repair the floor to conform to the Guideline.

Homeowner Responsibility: None.

Additional Comments: The guidelines for levelness and unevenness in concrete floors of mid-rise and high-rise residential buildings are very technical and complex. Because of numerous factors, it is beyond the scope of this Manual for interpretation. There are two technical publications that address these issues: The American Concrete Institute Publication, ACI 302.1R-04 entitled "Guide for Concrete Floor and Slab Construction" and ASTM International Publication E1155 describing the relationship between floor levelness and floor flatness. If issues arise regarding floor levelness and floor unevenness in mid-rise and high-rise residential structures, the two above-mentioned publications should serve as appropriate references.

Grade Beam, Pier, and "T" Footings

Condition #1: Exterior Foundation Grade Beam Is Out of Level

Potentially Impacting:
- Floor
- Walls
- Roof structure

Performance Guideline

Over 40 feet of length, the top surface of the grade beam should be no more than 1 inch lower than the highest point, and no more than 1 inch higher than the lowest point. If the length of measurement is shorter, the allowable deviation is reduced proportionately.

Comments: A "benchmark" is a given height for which the Builder and/or designer have agreed for the height of the grade beam to be installed. The term "level" is actually a comparison above and below a theoretical elevation, for example, benchmarks.

Builder Responsibility: The Builder should furnish and install a level foundation for the Home. The Builder should adjust the foundation or mudsill to conform to the Guideline.

Homeowner Responsibility: None.

Condition #2: Foundation Grade Beam Is Out of Square

Potentially Impacting:

- The installation of finish materials such as cabinets, tiles, countertops, or anything square or rectangular.

Performance Guideline

If measuring the top of the grade beam: from the corner, measure one direction 12 feet. From the original starting point of the wall, measure 90 degrees the other direction 16 feet (12 feet and 16 feet from the corner should be at a 90 degree angle to one another). The diagonal distance should be 20 feet plus or minus 1 inch.

Comments: A grade beam that is out of square typically does not compromise the Home structurally; however, it may become an appearance issue and create extra work to custom fit the finish materials.

Builder Responsibility: If the *foundation* is out of square more than the Performance Guideline and this materially affects the performance of the residence, the Builder should correct the out of square foundation by making proper adjustments, most likely in the *frame*. If the Builder is remodeling a Home whose existing foundation is out of square, it is acceptable for the Builder, with agreement from the Homeowner, to "match" the out of square portion of the existing foundation with the new foundation.

Homeowner Responsibility: None.

Condition #3: Wood Scraps or Cardboard Left around Piers or Grade Beams

Potentially Impacting:

- Integrity of the wood structure

Performance Guideline

The Home should be completed with all wood or paper/cardboard removed from the crawl space and around the grade beam and piers. The only exception to this is cardboard that is wax treated and used to create a void under the grade beam as part of the construction process. Unless wood is pressure treated or foundation grade redwood, it cannot be placed within 6 inches of the ground.

Comments: Wood material attracts termites and encourages infestation within the structure of the Home.

Builder Responsibility: If building practices resulted in wood or paper materials left in the crawl space and near the grade beams, the Builder should remove those materials.

Homeowner Responsibility: ***Maintenance Alert!*** The Homeowner should avoid placing wood or paper products beneath the Home, in the crawl space, and/or near the foundation. The Homeowner should not attach anything wooden to the Home if it makes contact with the earth (such as a fence post).

Condition #4: Tree Stumps Left in, around, and under Foundation

Potentially Impacting:

- Structural integrity of the Home
- Insect infestation

Performance Guideline

Trees that are slated to be removed in preparation for the foundation shall have their stumps removed also. All stumps within at least 5 feet of the foundation shall be removed. Under no circumstances should foundations be constructed over tree stumps or large (3 inch diameter) roots.

Builder Responsibility: The Builder should conform to the Performance Guideline.

Homeowner Responsibility: None.

Condition #5: Efflorescence (White Powder) Appears on Concrete Surfaces

Potentially Impacting:

- Garage floors
- *Driveways* and walks
- *Foundation* walls

Performance Guideline

Efflorescence on concrete surfaces is considered acceptable. This condition often occurs when one of the ingredients in the cement reacts with moist air. The exception to this Guideline is where efflorescence appears only at cracks in concrete walls or floors. This condition is a sign of excessive moisture entering the wall or floor from behind or underneath the finished surface.

Builder Responsibility: None, if efflorescence is observed overall on surfaces. If significant efflorescence is observed at cracks, an investigation should be conducted to determine if water is passing through the concrete from behind.

Homeowner Responsibility: If the efflorescence is considered unsightly, the Homeowner can remove it with a brush and water. More stubborn areas can be brushed with a mixture of one cup of white vinegar to a bucket of water.

Condition #6: Concrete Appears To Be Deteriorating or Disintegrating (Sulfates)

Potentially Impacting:

- *Concrete/foundation slab* integrity
- Moisture levels inside structure

Performance Guideline

Minimum Performance Guidelines are met by following general International Building Code requirements regarding sulfates and concrete mix design.

General Subject Information: The effect of sulfates in the soil on concrete has been researched and debated for more than 70 years and is still not totally understood. Sulfate exposure can be a result of an external or internal source. External sources are the naturally occurring sulfates in the environment. Another external source is sulfates that are a product of industrial processes or various human activities, for example, fertilizers used in landscaping. A third external source is excessive groundwater combined with minerals in surrounding soils that are incompatible with the concrete mix. Internal sources of sulfates may include the sulfates introduced in the concrete, for example, "dirty *aggregate*" (rock) from which concrete is made. Despite multiple sources, the potential that sulfate will cause structural problems is extremely small.

Comments: The time to eliminate and/or reduce sulfate exposure is during the design and construction phase. Studies have shown that sulfate attack can be greatly reduced by: 1) Conducting lab analysis on soils for specific minerals, for example sulfides and sulfates; 2) Incorporating sulfate resistant concrete in the design; 3) Insuring that good clean aggregate is used; and 4) By following the water-*cement* ratio of the mix design during the pour. These steps will help reduce and/or eliminate the potential for sulfate exposure.

ONLY USE SULFATE-FREE FERTILIZER NEAR THE HOUSE

Builder Responsibility: The Builder should conduct adequate testing of the soils to determine the mineral content of the existing soils and their compatibility with the concrete mix being used. If it is determined that the soil contains sulfates, the Builder must use (per code) a concrete mix with a water-cement ratio that limits the sulfate's potential for attack. The Builder is responsible for concrete installed on soils that have not been thoroughly tested for minerals containing sulfates.

Homeowner Responsibility: *Maintenance Alert!* The Homeowner should not use fertilizers that are high in sulfates in and/or around foundations. Watering around concrete, specifically foundations should be kept to a minimum. Do not flood areas adjacent to foundations. Excessive irrigation by the Homeowner will cause problems and is not the Builder's responsibility. Maintaining adequate drainage away from building foundations is a Homeowner maintenance responsibility. (Refer to Preface: "**Ten Most Common Mistakes Made by New Homeowners**", page 17, item #1.)

Basements and Other Below Grade Structures

General Subject Information: A *basement* is the portion of the Home that extends below the surrounding *grade*. Basements can be partial (usually found in Homes built on hillsides) or full (completely under the first floor). Full basements are often found in new homes built in certain areas of the country such as the East and Midwest. Some custom builders include basements regardless of geographic location. Additionally, below grade structures such as garages are common in mid-rise and high-rise multifamily projects. *Crawl spaces* do not qualify as basements. Basements are usually constructed for two distinct uses: utility or habitability. Examples of utility are storage, workshop, laundry, and location of mechanical equipment. Examples of habitability are bonus rooms, bedrooms, home theaters, and arts and crafts rooms. It is important to distinguish between the two uses when applying Performance Guidelines.

Typically, basements consist of poured *concrete* walls or concrete block walls and a concrete *slab* floor. Because the basement is below grade, care must be taken during construction and after construction by the Homeowner to limit moisture intrusion. An exterior *foundation* drainage system is typically necessary and this system may include a *sump pump*. A basement that is built and marketed as habitable space (or future habitable space) is likely to have finished wall and floor coverings placed over the concrete surfaces. Code-approved heating and ventilation must be installed. The Performance Guidelines that apply to basements intended for habitable use are the same Performance Guidelines that apply to the rest of the Home. In other words, the slab of habitable basement floor is considered the same as a *slab on grade* floor; habitable basement walls are considered the same as upstairs walls.

The following are Performance Guidelines for basement and garage spaces built for utility purposes with poured concrete walls or concrete block walls and poured concrete floors.

Condition #1: Basement/Garage Walls or Floors Leak

Potentially Impacting:

- Usability of the space
- Condition of stored goods
- Moisture levels in habitable areas
- Indoor air quality

Performance Guideline

Water should not trickle or seep through basement or garage walls or floors.

Comments: Because basements are built below *grade*, they can be damp in winter months. Basements built for utility purposes do not have the same requirements for heating, cooling, and ventilation as habitable basements. Condensation on walls should not be confused with an actual leak from the outside.

Builder Responsibility: Assuming that the finished grades have not been negatively altered, the Homeowner did not install items such as planter beds, *flatwork*, irrigation that altered the flow of water, or the Homeowner has not damaged any installed *waterproofing* system, the Builder should perform repairs to keep water from trickling or seeping through basement walls or floors. Condensate on walls is not acceptable in habitable spaces.

Homeowner Responsibility:
The Homeowner should avoid making changes to the surrounding grades that would cause rain or irrigation water to flow down or collect at the outside of the basement walls. This includes over-watering, constructing planter beds without independent drainage, building "dams" between *foundations* and raised *walkways* and failure to keep *swales* and *yard drains* cleaned out. If basement dampness is an issue, the Homeowner should install a dehumidifier. In no event should the waterproof coating on the outside of the basement wall be damaged when planting or installing irrigation.

DOWNSPOUT DISCHARGE TOO CLOSE TO FOUNDATION
IMPROPER IRRIGATION SPRINKLER
SUB-SURFACE WATER CAN CAUSE A FLOODED CRAWLSPACE OR UPLIFTED SLAB
DO NOT ALTER THE DRAINAGE!

Condition #2: Water Leaks into Basement through Plumbing and Electrical Penetrations in the Wall

Potentially Impacting:
- Usability of the space
- Condition of stored goods
- Moisture levels in habitable areas

Performance Guideline

Water should not pass into the basement through penetrations in the basement walls.

Comments: Penetrations in basement walls should be filled or sealed with a waterproof sealant or mastic on the outside of the wall before backfilling. The sealant or mastic should be approved for below-grade use.

Builder Responsibility: The Builder should perform repairs to eliminate the leakage.

Homeowner Responsibility: If walls are leaking, the Homeowner should notify the Builder at once to prevent further damage.

Condition #3: Crawl Space Has Standing Water

Potentially Impacting:
- *Foundation* integrity
- Hardwood flooring movement
- Mold and mildew growth

Performance Guideline

There should not be any standing water in crawl spaces for more than 48 hours after cessation of rain.

Comments: Depending on the location of the Home and the type of soil underneath, water in the crawl spaces has been a historic issue. In such locations, after the foundation is poured, the most effective step is to *slope* the soil inside the crawl space so there are no depressed areas. The next most effective step is to keep water from entering the crawl space by sloping the outside *grade* away from the foundation walls and by making sure that no *downspouts* discharge at the foundation wall. Some local codes require the installation of crawl space *drains*.

Builder Responsibility: If standing water is present more than 48 hours after cessation of rain, and the Performance Guidelines have been met, the Builder should re-grade the crawl space or install a perimeter drain system to eliminate the standing water.

Homeowners Responsibility: The Homeowner should be careful not to alter the slope away from the foundation during the placement of *concrete* work for walks, *patios* and landscaping. If the crawl space has a drain, be sure that it is free flowing.

Condition #4: Basement or *Concrete* Garage Walls Are Not *Plumb*

Potentially Impacting:
- Appearance
- Structural integrity

Performance Guideline

Basement walls are considered out of plumb if they exceed more than 1 inch in 8 vertical feet.

Builder Responsibility: The Builder should take corrective action to conform to the Guideline.

Homeowner Responsibility: None.

Condition #5: Basement or *Concrete* Garage Walls Are Bowed

Potentially Impacting:
- Appearance
- Structural integrity

Performance Guideline

Walls should not bow more than 1 inch in 8 feet (measured either horizontally or vertically).

Builder Responsibility: The Builder should take corrective action to conform to the Guideline.

Homeowner Responsibility: None.

Condition #6: Basement Walls or Floors Have Cracks or Holes

Potentially Impacting:

- Appearance
- Watertightness

Performance Guideline

Cracks in basement walls should not exceed ¼ inch in width. Voids or honeycombs should not exceed 1 inch in diameter and 1 inch in depth. Cracks in basement floors should not exceed ¼ inch in width and 3/16 inch in vertical displacement.

Builder Responsibility: Assuming cracks and voids do not leak, the Builder should make cosmetic repairs, such as patching, to conform to the Performance Guideline.

Homeowner Responsibility: None.

Condition #7: Garage Slab Has Separated from Adjacent Foundation Wall

Potentially Impacting:

- Appearance
- Insect infestation

Performance Guideline

Garage slabs should not separate from the adjacent foundation wall by more than an average of ½ inch as measured along its length. If more than 50% of the slab has pulled away or separated from the adjacent wall, the condition is unacceptable.

Comments: Typically, garage slabs are poured independent of the foundation walls. A felt or foam strip is placed between the edge of the garage slab and the adjacent wall. This strip serves as a cushion between the slab and the wall. Since the slab and wall are not connected, some movement and separation can be expected.

Builder Responsibility: Assuming the separation does not leak, if the condition exceeds the Performance Guideline, the Builder should make cosmetic repairs (such as filling with an *elastomeric caulk*) to conform to the Performance Guideline.

Homeowner Responsibility: None.

Landslides, Sinkholes and Other Soil Movement

Comments: Landslides, sinkholes and other soil movement, together called *subsidence*, are mentioned in the Foundations Chapter because *foundations* are the first Home component likely to be affected by subsidence. However, other components of the Home can also be adversely affected, such as the *frame*, cladding, plumbing, *drywall* and window and *door* operations.

Landslides, sinkholes and settling soil are occurrences that begin beneath the soil surface, as opposed to erosion, which is a surface activity. Much of the soil in certain geographic areas of the country is subject to movement. Subsidence may be caused by construction practices including poor drainage, improper compaction of trenches and foundation *pads*, building on land that was once a lake bottom or tidal estuary, cutting hillsides, or by other geologic activities that occur deep within the earth. Soil movement can also be related to after-market construction such as *patios* and landscaping improvements, by overwatering or by drainage changes. Soil movement and drainage should be part of every Homeowner's concern during maintenance or when making after-market improvements to their home.

RETAINING WALLS

HELP PREVENT
SOIL MOVEMENT

Problems that arise from soil subsidence are complex issues and not within the scope of this Manual. These issues are best referred to geotechnical consultants. If a Homeowner notices abnormal soil movement activity or its result (such as hill slippage, excessive trench or foundation settlement, or large cracks in the foundation, *slab*, *stucco*, or drywall), the Builder should be notified promptly. It is very likely that the Builder has retained a geotechnical consultant as part of the project approval process and may be able to quickly assess whether or not the movement is cause for concern.

Chapter Two

FLOORS & CEILINGS

includes:

Floor Squeaks

Wood Subfloors and Ceilings

Wood Beams and Posts

References for this chapter:

- *Residential Construction Performance Guidelines*, NAHB 2011 ed.
- *Residential & Light Commercial Construction Standards*, by Don Reynolds
- *Code Check Building 3rd ed.*, Taunton Press
- *International Building Code 2012,* International Code Council
- *International Residential Code 2012,* International Code Council
- *Indiana Quality Assurance Builder Standards 2009,* Indiana Builders Association
- *NASCLA Residential Construction Standards, 2009,* National Association of State Contracting Licensing Agencies
- *Workmanship Standards for Licensed Contractors 2009,* Arizona Registrar of Contractors
- *New Home Warranty Program 2010,* State of New Jersey Department of Community Affairs
- *California Building Code 2013,* California Building Standards Commission
- *Homeowner Handbook 2003,* Greater Atlanta Home Builders Association
- *South Carolina Residential Construction Standards 1997,* Residential Builders Commission of the South Carolina Department of Labor, et.al.

A comprehensive list of references by author and publisher is found in the Bibliography section.

Chapter Two

Floors and Ceilings

General Subject Information: Floors and ceilings begin their formation during the 'rough' carpentry stage of Home construction. Rough carpentry or 'framing' generally deals with the structural portion of a building that supports floors, ceilings, walls and *roofs*. Finish floor coverings are discussed in **Chapter Six—Interior Components**. Usually the rough carpentry floors and walls are covered by an assortment of interior and exterior finishes including, but not limited to *drywall*, *plaster*, paneling, *stucco*, *siding*, brick *veneer*, and floor coverings (for example, carpet, vinyl and hardwood.)

Floor Squeaks

Condition #1: Floor Squeaks

Potentially Impacting:

- Occupant comfort

Performance Guideline

Squeaks that are caused by loose subfloors, for example, plywood floor sheathing, loose nails or fasteners, may be considered unacceptable if the floor squeaks noticeably and continuously. NOTE: A squeak-proof floor cannot be guaranteed due to seasonal weather conditions that cause the Home frame to expand and contract.

Comments: The best method of installation is to glue the subfloor to the *joists* and then screw the subfloor to the joists. A wood subfloor can squeak as a result of an underlying joist coming loose from the plywood *sheathing*. This may cause a squeak as a result of a nail or fastener becoming loose. As a person steps onto the plywood sheathing, for example in a location where the plywood has lost its bond with the floor joist, the plywood may rub up and down on the nail causing a squeak. Squeaks can also be a result of the plywood flexing.

Builder Responsibility: The Builder should perform repairs of wood sub-flooring that does not conform to the Performance Guideline and is a direct result of an improperly installed floor joist, fastener and/or sheathing. Installing a screw into the wood floor joist through the plywood floor sheathing will generally eliminate a floor squeak.

Homeowner Responsibility: The Homeowner should be aware that floor squeaks will most likely occur with seasonal weather changes and they are considered a maintenance item.

Wood Subfloors and Ceilings

Condition #1: Wood Subfloors or Ceilings Are Not Flat

Potentially Impacting:

- Flooring
- Appearance

Performance Guideline

Any floor or ceiling that exceeds ¼ inch depression or ridge in a 32 inch by 32 inch area is considered unacceptable.

Comments: Because wood is a natural product, some minor framing imperfections can and should be expected.

Builder Responsibility: The Builder should perform repairs to structured *subfloor* or finish materials to conform to the Performance Guideline.

Homeowner Responsibility: None.

Condition #2: Wood Subfloors Are Out of Level

Potentially Impacting:
- Occupant comfort
- Furniture placement

Performance Guideline

No point on the surface of a wood subfloor should be more than ½ inch higher or lower than any other point on that same surface within 20 feet.

Comments: This Performance Guideline applies to all wood floors in living spaces only. Decks or other floors that have a predetermined *slope* for drains and/or drainage are excluded from this Performance Guideline.

Builder Responsibility: The Builder should perform repairs to conform to the Performance Guideline.

Homeowner Responsibility: The Homeowner should not store excessively heavy objects on a wood subfloor. (Refer to Preface: "**Ten Most Common Mistakes Made by New Homeowners**", page 19, item #8.)

Condition #3: Wood Subfloors Have "Springiness" or Bounce

Potentially Impacting:
- Furniture placement
- Occupant comfort

Performance Guideline

All floor joists should meet the required size and rating set forth in the applicable building code for the township, parish, city or county in effect at the time the Home was constructed. If manufactured floor trusses are used, the span and spacing should conform to the manufacturer's engineered calculations and recommendations.

Comments: Floors that are over-spanned or inadequately supported by wood floor joists or blocking may exhibit unacceptable bounce or deflection. This can affect the structural integrity of the *subfloor* as well as become a nuisance to the Homeowner. Long spanned floors can exhibit this tendency even if they meet deflection standards permitted in the building code.

Builder Responsibility: If the floors are over-spanned for the *grade* of lumber permitted or if the truss manufacturer's span recommendations were not followed, the Builder should reinforce and/or correct the noted deficiency to make the condition conform to the Performance Guideline.

Homeowner Responsibility: None.

Condition #4: Subfloor Is Out of Square

Potentially Impacting:

- Finish flooring

Performance Guideline

The diagonal of a triangle cannot be any greater or less than 1 inch out of proportion of a triangle with right angle legs of 12 feet and 16 feet. Example: If a room measures 12 feet one direction and 16 feet in the other direction, a perfect diagonal measurement would be 20 feet. The Performance Guideline does not allow the length of the diagonal to be greater or less than 1 inch within 20 feet. Applying this Guideline to rooms of different sizes, the tolerance of the length of the third leg of the triangle (hypotenuse) cannot be more or less than 0.42% of its diagonal length. An exception is an addition or remodel of an existing Home where the Builder and the Homeowner agree that it is practical to accept the existing out-of-square floor condition.

Comments: Squareness should be checked before pouring the foundation and again during the *frame* layout. Out-of-square conditions can more easily be corrected before the framing process begins.

Builder Responsibility: If *subfloors* (or *slab foundations*) are far enough out of square that the frame members do not adequately bear on them, the Builder should perform repairs to the foundation or frame to conform to the Performance Guideline. If wood subfloors are out of square to an extent that subcontractors installing finish material such as tile, marble or pattern vinyl cannot compensate and a pattern line or *grout* line is more than ½ inch out of square in 6 feet of length, the Builder should adjust the adjacent wall to bring the out of square condition to conform to the Performance Guideline.

Homeowner Responsibility: None.

Wood Beams and Posts

Condition #1: Exterior Wood Beams or Posts Are Warped, Checked, or Split

Potentially Impacting:

- Appearance
- Structural integrity

Performance Guideline

Exposed wood beams or posts that have splits that exceed ½ inch in width and 6 inches in length are considered excessive and are unacceptable.

Comments: Wood posts and beams are a natural material and are thus subject to splitting. This is considered normal. All lumber is *grade* stamped as to its level of quality. If the lumber is free from *heart* material, it will most likely resist splitting. The typical material used for posts and beams meet structural requirements, and not necessarily concerns regarding appearance. It should be noted that exposed lumber is subject to moisture and will expand and contract accordingly. Splitting is usually not considered a structural concern but more of an appearance issue. If it is the intent of the Builder to create a wood beam that is free of splits or checks, composite or architectural grade laminated beams should be used. Otherwise, conforming splits can be filled with an appropriate wood filler.

Builder Responsibility: The Builder should replace or repair posts or beams that do not conform to the Performance Guideline.

Homeowner Responsibility: The Homeowner should conduct annual inspections of all exterior wood materials. ***Maintenance Alert!*** If the observed condition is less than the Performance Guideline, the Homeowner can fill the split with any number of commercially available wood fillers. If significant *dry rot* is observed, a structural specialist should be consulted to see if the beam or post needs replacing. Dry rot can be detected by using a sharp probe, such as an ice pick, to check the softness of wood at joints and along boards that are closest to the ground.

Condition #2: Wood Beams or Posts Are Twisted or *Cupped*

Potentially Impacting:

- Appearance
- Structural integrity
- Watertightness

Performance Guideline

Any beam or post that twists more than ¾ inch in an 8 foot length is considered unacceptable. Cups exceeding ½ inch in 12 inches of beam height are considered unacceptable.

Comments: When beams or posts twist in an amount that does not exceed the Performance Guideline they generally do not create structural problems. However, if a beam ties into a wall and twisting occurs, it may create a condition for water intrusion.

Builder Responsibility: The Builder should repair unacceptable wood beams or posts to conform to the Performance Guideline.

Homeowner Responsibility: The Homeowner should inspect all exterior lumber annually for any *caulking* separation or paint peeling. The Homeowner should repair observed conditions immediately in order to prevent future problems.

Chapter Three

WALLS

includes:

Stucco Walls

Siding
Hardboard
Panel
Vinyl and Aluminum
Cement Board
General

Exterior Trim

Interior Walls

Shear Walls

References for this chapter:

- *Handbook of Construction Tolerances*, by David Kent Ballast
- *Residential Construction Performance Guidelines*, NAHB 2011 ed.
- *Code Check Building 3rd ed.*, Taunton Press
- *Residential & Light Commercial Construction Standards*, by Don Reynolds
- *International Building Code 2012*, International Code Council
- *International Residential Code 2012*, International Code Council
- *Workmanship Standards for Licensed Contractors 2009,* Arizona Registrar of Contractors
- *NASCLA Residential Construction Standards 2009,* National Association of State Contracting Licensing Agencies
- *Indiana Quality Assurance Builder Standards 2009,* Indiana Builders Association
- *New Home Warranty Program 2010,* New Jersey Department of Community Affairs
- *California Building Code 2013,* California Buildings Standards Commission
- *South Carolina Residential Construction Standards 1997,* Residential Builders Commission of the South Carolina Department of Labor, et. al.
- *Homeowner Handbook 2003,* Greater Atlanta Home Builders Association

A comprehensive list of references by author and publisher is found in the Bibliography section.

Chapter Three

Walls

Stucco Walls

General Subject Information: Stucco is a coating material that is applied to the exterior of the Home. It traces its origin to both Europe and the American Southwest where a crude mixture of adobe clay, sand and water was applied over adobe bricks. By the 1920s, stucco consisted of portland cement, sand, and water. It was applied by hand troweling and later by hose nozzles. Wood or metal lath held the stucco to the vertical walls. It was applied in three coats known as scratch, brown, and finish or color coat. Unless otherwise noted in this Manual, the term "stucco" refers to the above-described portland cement three-coat process.

A second finish system, known as the one-coat system, has gained popularity in recent years. This method of exterior finish consists of foam boards applied to the studs or sheathing of the Home frame. Next, metal wire lath is stapled through the foam boards to the studs and a fiber cement product is applied with trowels or by spraying. Lastly, a finish coat consisting of colored stucco or paint specifically manufactured to penetrate stucco is applied. The thickness of the one-coat is about 3/8 inch plus the thickness of the foam board.

A third system, known as Exterior Insulation and Finish Systems (EIFS) was introduced to the United States in the late 1970s. EIFS are a type of cladding for exterior building walls that provide a surface (resembling stucco) in an integrated composite system. EIFS typically consist of a foam board adhesively and/or mechanically attached over a continuous rigid undersurface board-like material, continuous fiberglass mesh embedded in a polymer-based basecoat. This is followed by a finish or color coat made of a 100% acrylic paint-like material, which provides color and texture. Early EIFS construction used moisture barrier systems that are no longer allowed in residential construction. Newer EIFS assemblies have a drainage plane and must be installed in exact conformity to the manufacturer's instructions. EIFS is not covered in this edition of the Manual.

Condition #1: Stucco Walls Have Cracks

Potentially Impacting:

- Appearance
- Watertightness
- Structural integrity

Performance Guideline

All exterior stucco covered walls, soffits and/or garden walls should not have any cracks that exceed 1/8 inch in width or 1/8 inch in adjacent surface displacement. However, cracks less than 1/8 inch covering more than 33% of a 1 foot square area of a dry surface wall (similar to a spider web pattern and often referred to as "map cracking") are unacceptable. If the wall is wet, it will show a disproportionate number of surface irregularities and cracks. This Guideline applies to walls measured when dry.

Comments: Why does stucco crack? When new Homes are built, the wood framing materials contain up to 19% moisture. As the lumber dries, the wood shrinks, causing stress to the stucco system. As the Home ages, components expand and contract at different rates, causing stress on the weaker materials. Expansion and contraction is an inherent characteristic of a wood structure. Many times, a wood *door* that sometimes sticks will open and close smoothly at other times. That is because the wood expands and contracts as a result of moisture content in the air. When the building structure expands and contracts during the settling period, stucco is certain to crack in predictable locations. This condition should be expected and is considered normal. Stucco can also crack during the application process if it *cures* too quickly or if it is not allowed to cure between coats. Cracking is very common at the corners of door and window frames and/or anywhere there is a hinging effect within the rough framing of the structure. These particular areas are considered "hinge points" in the framing and induce stress to the hard, brittle stucco finish. If and/or when cracks appear in the walls and soffits, it is not something to necessarily be alarmed about. Always remember: stucco will always crack, the question is "How much cracking can occur before it becomes unacceptable?"

Builder Responsibility: The Builder has a duty to provide a Home that is free from excessive cracking. If cracks exceed the Performance Guideline, the Builder should conduct an investigation, determine the actual cause of cracking, and perform repairs (if cracks are determined to be a result of improper construction and not from misuse by the Homeowner).

Homeowner Responsibility: The Homeowner should not alter the finished *grades* around the perimeter of the Home. Wet soil that is not properly drained can cause foundation movement which could result in stucco cracking. Normal cracking in stucco should be expected. If cracks exceed the Performance Guideline, the Homeowner should notify the Builder.

Condition #2: Walls Have Water Stains or Water Damage

Potentially Impacting:

- Appearance
- Watertightness
- Structural integrity

Performance Guideline

All lath, building paper, and plaster cladding should be installed in such a manner that will ensure the Home to be watertight and free from any exterior water intrusion.

Builder Responsibility: Upon notification of water intrusion, the Builder should conduct a thorough investigation, determine the exact cause, and then complete the subject repairs as necessary.

Homeowner Responsibility: ***Maintenance Alert!*** If the Home has wood *trim* around the windows and *exterior doors*, the Homeowner should inspect the trim for gaps and should apply *caulking* annually. If a leak appears, the Homeowner should notify the Builder immediately.

Condition #3: Color Coat Repair Work Does Not Match Existing Color

Potentially Impacting:

- Appearance

Performance Guideline

A poor color match is defined as a visible patch or area that can be seen by a layperson at a distance of 6 feet in indirect light. Any repair work that is necessary should be re-colored from one corner to the other corner at full height, or properly "fogged" to acceptably blend the color coats.

Comments: Trying to match color coats on *stucco* is almost impossible. The manufacturer runs a batch of color compound, which is then labeled according to that lot number. Each lot will have a slight difference to its final color. Other factors, such as temperature and humidity, may cause the same lot, applied on different days, to have noticeable variations in color.

Builder Responsibility: The Builder should match the existing color as closely as possible and perform repairs by re-coloring repaired walls "corner to corner".

Homeowner Responsibility: None.

Condition #4: Weep Screed Flashing Is Rusting or Rust Marks Appear on Numerous Places on the Surface of the Outside Walls

Potentially Impacting:

- Appearance
- Watertightness

Performance Guideline

Weep screeds should not become rusted to the point of deterioration. Rust marks on the surface of walls are considered unacceptable if more than 5 marks measuring over 1 inch long occur per 100 square feet.

Comments: Over time, weep screeds may rust. Unlike *roof flashing* and other exterior flashing, the weep screed typically is not primed and/or painted to allow for future protection from the elements. Weep screeds serve three purposes: 1) as a gauge for the thickness of the *stucco*, 2) to allow the application of the stucco to be in a straight line and 3) to provide an avenue for moisture that is trapped behind the stucco to exit at the base of the wall. Rust marks on weep screeds usually indicate a *bleed through* of rusted lath or nails in the stucco. Some rust marks are inevitable.

Builder Responsibility: If the weep screed becomes rusted and deteriorated to the point that it no longer serves the purpose for which it was intended, the Builder should replace the weep screed. If the frequency of rust marks exceeds the Performance Guideline, the Builder should seal the rusted areas and re-color the wall.

Homeowner Responsibility: The Homeowner should prevent irrigation water from spraying against the stucco and vegetation from overgrowing into the screed area.

Condition #5: Stucco Color Coat Is Separating from the Underneath Coat

Potentially Impacting:

- Appearance
- *Useful life* of exterior coating

Performance Guideline

Stucco color should not separate from the underneath coat.

Comments: Stucco, very simply, is a *cement* and sand application that is comprised of three coats: scratch, brown and color coat, and is approximately 7/8 inch thick. First, a water-resistant *building paper* is applied directly to the framing. A "chicken wire mesh", also known as *lath*, is then applied directly over the building paper. The first coat (scratch coat) is applied to the wall and embeds the wire mesh. The brown coat is applied next, and then finally the color coat. Stucco is mixed at the job site and requires certain ratios of sand, cement and water. If the sand or water ratio is too high, the integrity of the product will be compromised causing the system to fail. All three coats must be mixed with the proper ratios. It is important that the stucco be allowed to "*cure*" between coats.

Builder Responsibility: The Builder should perform repairs in areas where the coatings have separated.

Homeowner Responsibility: ***Maintenance Alert!*** The Homeowner should not fasten any objects to the exterior walls and *soffits* that are not properly *flashed, counter flashed* and sealed. The Homeowner should inspect and perform necessary maintenance in the following areas:

?!!
Z Z Z Z
Z Z
AVOID THIS NIGHTMARE, MOUNTING SATELLITE DISHES CAN CAUSE WALL LEAKS

- Around the foundation, the Homeowner should maintain a minimum clearance of 6 inches from finished *grade* to *weep screed* and a 2 inch minimum clearance between *concrete*/asphalt and the weep screed.
- The Homeowner should maintain a minimum *slope* of ¼ inch per foot away from the Home (foundation) on both soil and hard surfaces.
- The Homeowner should not permit irrigation sprinklers to spray on any stucco surfaces.

Condition #6: Wet Spots Remain on Stucco Walls after a Rain Storm

Potentially Impacting:

- ♦ Appearance

Performance Guideline

This condition is normal and acceptable.

Comments: *Stucco* is a semi-porous material and will retain water after a storm. The special paper that is behind stucco acts as a water-resistant member to prevent moisture from entering the Home. The rate of drying of the wall is not uniform.

Builder Responsibility: None.

Homeowner Responsibility: None.

Condition #7: Lath Is Visible through the Stucco

Potentially Impacting:

- *Useful life* of exterior coating
- Appearance

Performance Guideline

Lath should not be visible through stucco, nor should any portion of the lath protrude through stucco.

Builder Responsibility: The Builder should perform repairs so that lath is not visible or protruding through stucco.

Homeowner Responsibility: None.

Condition #8: Foam Board Is Visible through the Stucco

Potentially Impacting:

- *Useful life* of the exterior coating
- Watertightness

Performance Guideline

Foam boards should not be visible at any surface area of the one-coat system. All foam boards should be covered by at least 3/8 inch of combined base and finish coat.

Comments: The areas where foam boards butt against exterior openings, such as window and *door trim*, are often areas where the foam boards do not get completely covered by one-coat *stucco*. Apart from opportunities for water intrusion, foam will break down when exposed to prolonged sunlight.

Builder Responsibility: The Builder should perform repairs to recoat any exposed foam.

Homeowner Responsibility: None.

Condition #9: Stud Locations Are Telegraphed through the Stucco

Potentially Impacting:

- Appearance

Performance Guideline

Stud locations should not be visible through the stucco under normal daylight conditions.

Builder Responsibility: The Builder should perform repairs to recoat any walls exhibiting *telegraphing*.

Homeowner Responsibility: None.

Condition #10: White Powdery Substance (Efflorescence) Appears on Stucco Walls in Winter Months

Potentially Impacting:

- Appearance

Performance Guideline

The white powdery substance known as efflorescence that appears on stucco walls and bare concrete slabs during the rainy season is caused by lime in the cement reacting with moist air. It is considered acceptable and can easily be removed with water and a brush.

Builder Responsibility: None.

Homeowner Responsibility: The Homeowner should remove efflorescence with a mixture of water and diluted white vinegar, and a brush.

Condition #11: Wood Trim Is Embedded in Stucco

Potentially Impacting:

- Appearance
- Watertightness

Performance Guideline

Wood trim embedded in stucco is considered acceptable. Water- resistant building paper must run continuously behind the embedded wood to prevent moisture from entering the wall cavity. Wood will shrink as it dries out (especially large beams) and a gap may develop between the wood and the stucco. If the gap exceeds ¼ inch at any part or warps more than ¼ inch away from the face of the building, it is considered unacceptable.

Comments: Wood trim is often placed around *exterior doors* and windows as part of the architectural features of the Home. Beams and other structural members are embedded into stucco for the same reason. Much of the trim wood is "keyed" by having the stucco side beveled back or grooved to accept a tight fit between stucco and wood. It is good practice during construction to *primer* paint the back of the wood trim before applying, to lengthen its life. Another good practice is to counterflash (see *flashing*) the head (top) of the window and *patio door* with sheet metal to avoid water intrusion at this vulnerable point.

Builder Responsibility: The Builder should repair or replace excessively gapped or warped wood trim and any other pieces exhibiting the same problems.

Homeowner Responsibility: ***Maintenance Alert!*** After the first year of occupancy, it is very important for the Homeowner to inspect for gaps. The Homeowner should completely remove any old *caulking* before re-caulking the area and then caulk around all wood members with a 25-year rated outdoor caulk.

Condition #12: Stucco Wall Appears "Wavy" during Sunset Hours or When Illuminated with Landscaping Lights

Potentially Impacting:

- Appearance

Performance Guideline

Stucco walls that exhibit a wavy characteristic under low light or artificial light are acceptable.

Comments: It is normal for stucco walls to have a wavy appearance under low light or artificial lighting. Stucco is a cement mixture that is applied to walls with a trowel or spray gun. The final finish may not be perfectly flat.

Builder Responsibility: None.

Homeowner Responsibility: None.

Condition #13: Plywood behind Stucco Is Delaminating or Splitting

Potentially Impacting:

- Appearance
- Watertightness

Performance Guideline

Any sub-surface plywood, for example plywood that is installed behind wood siding or stucco, that warps or splits excessively is unacceptable and should be replaced. For this Guideline, "excessive" means that the laminations can be easily separated using hammer claws. This also applies to OSB (Oriented Strand Board) that has become swollen from rain water.

Comments: If plywood or OSB has expanded, swelled or is *delaminating*, this generally means that water has migrated to the backside of the exterior finish. The sub-surface *sheathing* will need to be replaced and the source of water intrusion needs to be determined.

Builder Responsibility: The Builder should locate and seal the source of water intrusion, as well as repair and/or replace any plywood or OSB that does not conform to the Performance Guideline. The Builder should replace any finishes that have been damaged and/or removed.

Homeowner Responsibility: The Homeowner should conduct periodic maintenance, including *caulking* and painting to prevent potential problems described above.

Hardboard Siding

General Subject Information: There are a number of *siding* products on the market made of wood fiber materials. It is impractical to cover them all individually. The information that follows is generally applicable to these types of products. This section concentrates primarily on siding made of wood particles or other wood based products that are mixed with a resin to bind them together. Most of these siding systems are intended to look like horizontal wood siding and are often embossed with a wood *grain* finish.

Condition #1: Exterior Surface of Siding Is Buckled

Potentially Impacting:

- Appearance
- Watertightness

Performance Guideline

Hardboard siding should not warp or buckle more than 3/16 inch out of plane when nailed to studs placed at 16 inches on center.

Builder Responsibility: If the Performance Guideline is not met during original construction, the Builder should perform the necessary repairs. There are several conditions that can cause buckling that the Builder can control. The Builder should ensure that the following conditions are met: correct fastener spacing; adequate space for expansion between pieces; protective *flashing*; appropriate *vapor barriers* as recommended by the manufacturer; and protection from moisture during on-site storage and prior to installation.

Homeowner Responsibility: ***Maintenance Alert!*** The Homeowner is responsible for maintaining the siding system in a sound, water-resisting condition. Among other things, this involves painting the siding on a regular schedule (as provided in the manufacturer's recommendations), re-*caulking* joints annually, and making sure that exposure to earth, paved surfaces, and water are properly controlled.

Condition #2: Drip Edge of Lap Siding Is Swollen or Split

Potentially Impacting:

- *Useful life* of *siding*
- Appearance

Performance Guideline

Swelling should not exceed approximately 10% of the original thickness of the drip edge, causing the material to crack and separate.

Comments: Siding materials are subject to swelling at the lower or "drip" edge of each lap when the core material is exposed to and absorbs excessive moisture. This swelling is commonly known as "brooming." In order to avoid "brooming", it is essential to prevent moisture from entering the *hardboard* material at the drip edge. This can only be done if the drip edge is properly coated with

100% acrylic paint. This coating should be maintained by the Homeowner as part of a scheduled maintenance program. Additional drip edge performance and protection information is available from siding manufacturers.

Builder Responsibility: The Builder should paint siding systems in accordance with the material and workmanship requirements published by the manufacturer, paying special attention to the complete coating of all drip edges. Drip edges that have deteriorated due to abuse or lack of Homeowner maintenance are not the responsibility of the Builder.

Homeowner Responsibility: ***Maintenance Alert!*** It is important for the Homeowner to observe the condition of painted siding surfaces on a periodic basis. An annual inspection is recommended. When paint begins to show signs of wear, this often first occurs in limited areas. Undertaking maintenance and touch up painting before paint degradation proceeds too far will significantly extend the life of the siding system. The Homeowner should also prevent irrigation heads from spraying onto siding.

Condition #3: Siding Material Is Swollen or Split around Nails

Potentially Impacting:

- *Useful life* of *siding*
- Appearance
- Watertightness

Performance Guideline

Siding should not visibly swell around nails. The usual pattern of unacceptable swelling is a "donut" shaped thickening of the siding material around the nail head. Nail heads should not be driven deeper than the surface of the siding.

Comments: Swelling around nails often occurs when the nails are driven too deeply ("overset"), damaging the surface of the siding and creating a path for the entry of water into the siding material. Another cause may be the use of improper nails that deteriorate in the presence of moisture, which can also lead to undesirable water intrusion into the siding material.

Builder Responsibility: The Builder should ensure that nails are not overset and that the proper types of nails (as recommended by the siding manufacturer) are used in the installation of siding. If nail heads are not driven more than halfway through the siding, *caulking* and painting is an acceptable repair. If the nail is driven into more than half the thickness of the siding, another nail must be properly driven in an adjacent location, and the original nail should be caulked and painted.

Homeowner Responsibility: The Homeowner's maintenance of siding surfaces, including an appropriate painting schedule, will significantly extend the life of the siding and limit the tendency of swelling around nails.

Condition #4: Siding Splits, Softens, and Rots at the Base of Walls

Potentially Impacting:

- Appearance
- *Useful life* of *siding*
- Integrity of underlying structural components

Performance Guideline

Siding should not split, soften or rot.

Comments: This condition is often a result of the following situations: 1) siding that terminates less than 6 inches above earth; 2) siding that terminates less than 2 inches above paved surfaces; 3) siding that is in direct contact with storm water flows; and 4) siding that is subjected to direct spray from landscape irrigation systems. Siding may also be damaged by improper after-market improvements or by improper maintenance.

Builder Responsibility: The Builder should not permit the construction of any condition that will result in siding deterioration at the base of walls. If such conditions exist, the Builder should perform the necessary repairs.

Homeowner Responsibility: *Maintenance Alert!* The Homeowner must guard against introducing conditions that could result in deterioration of siding. For example, the Homeowner must maintain appropriate clearances between siding and earth or paving. When landscape improvements are installed, care should be taken to maintain the original clearances. The Homeowner is also responsible for proper maintenance of systems that can adversely affect siding. Check sprinkler head spray patterns periodically to make sure irrigation water isn't spraying directly onto siding.

Condition #5: Siding Butt Joints Are Too Wide

Potentially Impacting:

- Appearance

Performance Guideline

Butt joints (the gaps between the ends of each board) should not be wider than 3/16 inch.

Comments: Nearly all *siding* manufacturers require gaps at the butt joints as part of proper installation. The siding boards need to expand and contract with seasonal changes in temperature and humidity. If there is no gap, the boards will often buckle. Butt joints should be covered with a plastic or metal spacer, or *caulked* and painted in accordance with the manufacturer's installation instructions.

Builder Responsibility: The Builder should prepare butt joints to conform to the Performance Guideline.

Homeowner Responsibility: The Homeowner should re-caulk per the maintenance schedule.

Condition #6: Siding Is Crooked

Potentially Impacting:

- Appearance

Performance Guideline

Siding boards should be within ¼ inch of level over 10 feet of length.

Builder Responsibility: The Builder should reinstall unacceptable siding to conform to the Performance Guideline.

Homeowner Responsibility: None.

Condition #7: Siding Is Soft and Rotting at Window and Door Trim, Railings, and Other Locations

Potentially Impacting:

- Appearance
- *Useful life* of *siding*
- Integrity of underlying structural components

Performance Guideline

Siding should not rot, be soft, or deteriorate. Joints between adjacent pieces of siding, siding and trim, siding and rail caps, and other such components should be assembled in such a way that siding deterioration resulting from water intrusion does not occur.

Comments: Water intrusion occurs for two principal reasons: 1) the materials and assembly methods used in the original installation are not correctly selected and integrated into a weather-tight system and 2) joints and other potential water entry points are not adequately maintained by the Homeowner. Where *caulked* joints are used, manufacturers generally specify joints 3/16 inch wide and approximately as deep as the width. Smaller joints are difficult to caulk effectively and the caulk in larger joints will dry up, separate and deteriorate more rapidly. It is a good practice during construction to protect vertical transitions from one type of material to another with metal *flashing*.

INSPECT THESE AREAS:
HEAD
SIDES
LOOK FOR GAPS
CHECK FOR GAPS IN WINDOW TRIM CAULKING

Builder Responsibility: The Builder should install siding-to-siding and siding-to-trim joints in a sound, waterproof manner that readily sheds water. The Builder should repair unacceptable conditions resulting from improper construction.

Homeowner Responsibility: ***Maintenance Alert!*** The Homeowner is responsible for periodic maintenance of items such as caulked joints that are essential to preventing unwanted water in the siding system. (Refer to "**Homeowner Maintenance Summary—Trim and Siding**", page 258.)

Condition #8: Siding Has Raised Nail Heads

Potentially Impacting:

- Appearance
- *Useful life* of *siding*

Performance Guideline

Nails should be set with the bottom of the nail head flush with the surface of the siding. Use only nails recommended by the siding manufacturer.

Builder Responsibility: The Builder should ensure that nailing is performed in accordance with the requirements of the manufacturer. Nails that protrude at the outset of installation are a result of poor nailing techniques. Nails that protrude progressively over time may be the result of using the wrong types of nails or installation into framing lumber with high moisture content.

Homeowner Responsibility: None.

Panel Siding

General Subject Information: Panel *siding* is typically plywood or *hardboard* that is installed in pieces that are 4 feet x 4 feet or 4 feet x 8 or 9 feet. Often the outer surface of the plywood sheet has been "textured" by re-sawing or embossing. Also, the surface may have grooves cut into it to simulate boards or wide channels to simulate *battens*. This type of siding is often found on the sides and back of the Home.

Condition #1: Joints at Panel Edges Are Excessively Wide or Raised

Potentially Impacting:

- Appearance

Performance Guideline

Joints at panel edges should not exceed 3/16 inch in width or 3/16 inch out of plane from the adjacent panel.

Builder Responsibility: The Builder should repair or replace any non-conforming panels to conform to the Performance Guideline.

Homeowner Responsibility: None.

Condition #2: Panels Are Delaminating

Potentially Impacting:

- Appearance
- Structural integrity

Performance Guideline

Siding panels should not delaminate.

Builder Responsibility: The Builder should repair or replace any non-conforming panels.

Homeowner Responsibility: None.

Condition #3: Panels Are Bowed

Potentially Impacting:

- Appearance

Performance Guideline

Panel bows in excess of ¼ inch between studs at 16 inches on center are unacceptable.

Builder Responsibility: The Builder should adjust the building *frame* or the individual panel to conform to the Performance Guideline.

Homeowner Responsibility: None.

Vinyl and Aluminum Siding

General Subject Information: Vinyl and aluminum *siding* are popular alternatives to *hardboard* siding. Vinyl and aluminum siding are lightweight, non-wood products that are manufactured with baked on or integral color and are resistant to wood destroying insects. Embossed aluminum panels are often used to manufacture siding that looks like sawn wood. Many of these panels and siding products can be painted. One disadvantage of aluminum siding is it will dent when hit with objects such as a baseball. The repair involves filling with automotive body filler, sanding, and repainting. If the siding or panel is embossed with a wood *grain* finish, it most likely will have to be replaced.

Condition #1: Vinyl or Aluminum Siding Is Bowed

Potentially Impacting:

- Appearance

Performance Guideline

Bows in vinyl or aluminum siding should not exceed ¼ inch between studs placed at 16 inches on center.

Builder Responsibility: The Builder should make the repairs necessary to conform to the Performance Guideline.

Homeowner Responsibility: None.

Condition #2: Vinyl or Aluminum Siding Is Faded or Blotched

Potentially Impacting:

- Appearance

Performance Guideline

Over a period of years, most vinyl and factory finished aluminum siding will fade uniformly. Non-uniform fading (or blotching) is considered unacceptable. Most vinyl and aluminum siding manufacturers warrant their product against fading and non-uniform discoloration.

Builder Responsibility: If the vinyl or aluminum siding condition does not meet the manufacturer's warranty standard, the Builder should assist the Homeowner in arranging repair or replacement of the non-conforming siding from the manufacturer.

Homeowner Responsibility: The Homeowner should refer to the manufacturer's warranty information on vinyl and aluminum siding for recommended use and maintenance procedures.

Cement Board Siding

General Subject Information: Cement board *siding* is another popular siding material. Cement board siding offers the advantages of being fire resistant, moisture resistant, and resistant to wood destroying insects. The disadvantage to cement board siding is that because of the physical properties of the cement binder, it is prone to cracking if not properly installed.

Condition #1: Cement Board Siding Is Cracked or Chipped

Potentially Impacting:

- Appearance
- Watertightness

Performance Guideline

Any cracks in cement board siding less than 2 inches in length or 1/8 inch in width are considered acceptable. Cracks in excess of this Guideline are unacceptable. Chips or full breaks in excess of ½ inch in radius are unacceptable.

Builder Responsibility: The Builder should *caulk* and paint cracks or chips that measure within the Performance Guideline. The Builder should replace the unacceptable boards if cracks or chips exceed the Performance Guideline. Staples shall not be used to apply cement board siding.

Homeowner Responsibility: None.

Siding (General)

Condition #1: Nails Have Stained Siding

Potentially Impacting:

- Appearance

Performance Guideline

Stains that discolor siding for more than ½ inch in length or if visible from a distance of 20 feet under normal daylight conditions are unacceptable.

Builder Responsibility: If conditions are a result of improper installation, the Builder should perform repairs to conform to the Performance Guideline.

Homeowner Responsibility: ***Maintenance Alert!*** The Homeowner should inspect siding nails annually. Bleeds can be sealed with a clear aerosol sealer. The Homeowner should follow an exterior painting schedule to ensure proper maintenance.

Brick and Masonry

Brick and Masonry is covered in **Chapter Five—Exterior Components, Brick and Masonry**, page 126.

Exterior Trim

General Subject Information: Exterior *trim* is the wood or wood-like material that often surrounds windows, *doors*, *gutter fascia*, garage doorjambs, columns and *water tables*. It can be smooth or rough sawn. In order to preserve the wood trim, it needs to be *caulked* and painted more frequently than the *siding*. Another type of trim that is often associated with stucco applications is referred to as *plant ons*. These are foam pieces that are glued to the stucco prior to the *finish coat*. Then they are textured and coated with the stucco body. This trim provides architectural relief to the stucco around doors, windows and corners. Wood trim is discussed in this section.

Condition #1: There Are Gaps between the Home Body and the Exterior Trim

Potentially Impacting:
- Appearance
- Watertightness

Performance Guideline

Within the first year or longer, if the warranty states, there shall be no gap larger than 3/8 inch between any trim piece and the Home siding or stucco, or ¼ inch between butt joints or miter joints of the trim pieces themselves. Water shall not be allowed to intrude into any part of the wall cavity or column system.

Builder Responsibility: Within the warranty period, the Builder should correct any gaps in wood trim that are in excess of 3/8 inch. Caulking is acceptable unless the gap is greater than 3/8 inch. For gaps in excess of 3/8 inch, the Builder should replace the trim piece.

Homeowner Responsibility: The Homeowner should notify the Builder if gaps appear within the warranty period and before conditions get worse.

Condition #2: Exterior Trim Board Is Split, Bowed, Twisted, or Cupped

Potentially Impacting:

- Appearance

Performance Guideline

Splits wider than 3/8 inch in 3 inches of length are unacceptable. Bows and twists in excess of 3/8 inches in 6 feet of length are unacceptable. Cups that exceed 3/16 inch in 4 inches of width are unacceptable.

Comments: Wood *trim* is a material that requires more frequent maintenance for the first three years of the Home's life. Typical maintenance includes resetting nails, *caulking* and painting. Trim on south and west facing walls will require considerably more attention than the same trim on east and north facing walls. In recent years there have been advances in trim technology such as reconstituted wood pieces bonded together that produce a more durable trim product.

Builder Responsibility: The Builder should replace trim to conform to the Performance Guideline.

Homeowner Responsibility: The Homeowner does not have any responsibility within the warranty period (usually the first year), but is responsible for maintenance of the trim from year two forward. The warranty period may vary state to state.

Interior Walls

Condition #1: Walls Are Out of Plumb

Potentially Impacting:

- Door swing and fit
- Appearance

Performance Guideline

Walls are considered out of plumb if there is more than a 3/8 inch offset in any 32 inches of vertical measurement or if an offset exceeds ½ inch in 8 foot cumulative vertical measurement. An exception is an addition or remodel of an existing Home, where the Builder and the Homeowner agree that it is practical to match the existing out of plumb wall (provided that the out of plumb wall does not pose a structural threat).

Comments: Walls that are out of plumb can especially affect door performance, such as fit and *swing*. If a door will not hang without swinging either in or out, the wall is probably out of plumb. It should be noted that any wall that exceeds 2 inches out of plumb in 8 feet might indicate a structural problem with the potential for the wall to collapse.

Builder Responsibility: The Builder should perform repairs to conform to the Performance Guideline.

Homeowner Responsibility: None.

Condition #2: Walls Are Bowed

Potentially Impacting:
- Appearance of interior finishes
- *Door* swing and fit

Performance Guideline

The allowable tolerance for "rough framed walls" that are bowed should not be greater than ¼ inch in a 32 inch horizontal or vertical measurement, not to exceed ½ inch in 8 feet of length or height.

Comments: Walls that are bowed are generally more an appearance issue and tend not to compromise the structural integrity of the Home.

Builder Responsibility: The Builder should repair walls to conform to the Performance Guideline. The Builder should replace all finishes as necessary to complete said repairs.

Homeowner Responsibility: None.

Condition #3: Interior Wall Intersections Are Not Perpendicular on Walls Designed or Intended to Meet at 90 Degree Angles

Potentially Impacting:
- Appearance

Performance Guideline

The tolerance for interior walls designed to meet perpendicularly should conform to the tolerance of ¼ inch for the first 10 feet in length. After 10 feet, the rate of deviation shall not exceed ½ inch in 20 feet or more of wall length.

Comments: This condition is purely a cosmetic issue. For example, if square pattern floor covering such as tile or vinyl is applied, the deviation from perpendicular can become quite noticeable and aesthetically unacceptable.

Builder Responsibility: Depending upon the degree of deviation from perpendicular, the Builder should either move the wall or *furr out* the wall to conform to the Guideline.

Homeowner Responsibility: None.

Shear Walls

General Subject Information: *Shear walls* are specialty walls that are found at the exterior and interior of almost every Home. A shear wall is a structurally reinforced wall that restrains the Home from moving back and forth excessively in a catastrophic event such as an earthquake or an intensive wind storm. For the most part, shear walls are made by nailing structural *grade* plywood or oriented strand board (*OSB*) to the *studs* (or screwed in the case of steel studs). The nailing specification is provided by a licensed structural engineer or licensed architect. Most Homes today, particularly those of two stories or more, have shear walls because of *building code* requirements. When completed shear walls do not look any differently from non-shear walls because they are covered with *drywall*, *stucco*, *siding* or other finish material.

Condition #1: Shear Walls Are Inadequate

Potentially Impacting:
- Structural integrity

Performance Guideline

The structural integrity of any shear wall cannot fall below the values set forth in the applicable building code. (It is important to note that structural engineers often design shear walls that exceed building code requirements.)

Comments: Inadequate shear wall claims most often fall into one of the following five categories: 1) wrong size nails used; 2) wrong type of nails used; 3) nails are overdriven; 4) nailing schedule (how far apart) not followed; and 5) wrong *grade* of plywood or *OSB* used.

Builder Responsibility: The Builder should repair the wall to meet building code and structural design requirements. If the Builder believes that the wall has been designed in excess of code requirements, the Builder may obtain the opinion of a licensed structural engineer to determine if the wall in its present condition meets the requirements of the building code.

Homeowner Responsibility: None.

Condition #2: Shear Walls or Hold Downs Are Missing

Potentially Impacting:
- Structural integrity

Performance Guideline

Shear walls and hold downs, shown on the structural drawings approved by the local governing agency that issues the building permit, must be installed as shown.

Builder Responsibility: The Builder must meet the *building code* requirements using one of the following methods: 1) retrofit installation of shear walls and/or hold downs as shown on the approved plans, or 2) provide an alternate (and presumably less invasive) plan of repair from a licensed structural engineer that will meet building code requirements.

Homeowner Responsibility: None.

Green Tip! Proper *insulation* minimizes heat loss in winter and heat gain in summer.

LOOK FOR THE
GREEN HOME
MAINTENANCE
TIPS THOUGHOUT
THIS MANUAL

Chapter Four

ROOFS

includes:

Roof Structural Components

Slate, Concrete and Clay Tiles

Composition Asphalt Shingles

Wood Shakes and Shingles

Composite or Synthetic Roof System

Built-Up Roofing and Other Low Slope Roofs

Roof Ventilation

Flashing

Eaves

References for this chapter:

- *NRCA Roofing and Waterproofing Manual,* National Roofing Contractors Assoc. 2009-2011
- *Residential Construction Performance Guidelines*, NAHB 2011 ed.
- *Residential Water Problems*, by Alvin Sacks
- *Residential & Light Commercial Construction Standards*, by Don Reynolds
- *Concrete and Clay Tile Installation Manual,* Tile Roofing Institute
- *International Building Code 2012,* International Code Council
- *International Residential Code 2012,* International Code Council
- *Homeowner Handbook 2003,* Greater Atlanta Home Builders Association
- *Indiana Quality Assurance Builder Standards 2009,* Indiana Builders Association
- *NASCLA Residential Construction Standards 2009,* National Association of State Contracting Licensing Agencies
- *New Home Warranty Program 2010,* State of New Jersey Department of Community Affairs
- *Workmanship Standards for Licensed Contractors 2009,* Arizona Registrar of Contractors
- *South Carolina Residential Construction Standards 1997,* Residential Builders Commission of the South Carolina Department of Labor
- *California Building Code 2013,* California Building Standards Commission

A comprehensive list of references by author and publisher is found in the Bibliography section.

Chapter Four

Roofs

General Subject Information: Many different materials are available for application to residential *roofs*. The reasons for choosing a particular material include: geographic location of the structure, typical anticipated climatic conditions, *slope* (angle of incline) of the roof, appearance, and desired life span of the roof system. Community regulations can also play a role in the selection of roofing materials. All of the different materials encompass a range of performance characteristics, as well as anticipated life spans. Information regarding recommended configurations, installation methods, maintenance practices, and repair procedures, as well as typical anticipated life spans, can usually be obtained from the material manufacturer or from a recognized industry association shown in the references for this chapter.

Roofs can generally be separated into two broad categories: low-slope (often referred to as "flat" roofs), and steep slope (generally having a slope with more than 3 inches of rise per foot of slope). Steep slope roofs are typically fitted with water shedding roof covering systems, such as asphalt shingles, clay or *concrete tile*, slate, wood or composite shakes or shingles, or sheet metal panels. Low-slope roofs are typically covered with a waterproof *membrane* roof system, such as hot asphalt *built-up roofs* (BUR), ter-polymer-olefin (TPO) or polyvinyl-chloride (*PVC*). BUR roofs are surfaced with gravel, embedded mineral granules, or field-applied coatings, modified asphalt roof membranes, and single-ply roof membranes (which are typically smooth surfaced and have water tight, sealed seams). TPO and PVC roofs are thick membrane sheets that are cold-welded (glued) together.

BY FOLLOWING SIMPLE MAINTENANCE TIPS, YOU MAY DOUBLE THE LIFE EXPECTANCY OF YOUR ROOF.

Except for desert locations and urban *condominiums*, residential roofs are usually built as steep slope, water shedding systems. At slopes less than 3 inches per foot, special consideration should be given to design and installation of water shedding roof covering materials.

Roof Structural Components

Condition #1: Roof Ridge Sags

Potentially Impacting:

- Structural system supporting the roof
- Interior finishes
- Appearance

Performance Guideline

Roof ridge deflection should not exceed 1 inch in 20 feet of length.

Comments: Roofing materials and the roof structure should be compatible. Use of roofing material that is too heavy for the roof structure can cause excessive deflection and possible structural damage. Snow loads must be calculated into the structural design of the roof frame. Snow loads may cause the roof to deflect beyond acceptable tolerances if the roof is not built according to the plans.

Builder Responsibility: The Builder should repair any condition caused during original construction that does not conform to the Performance Guideline.

Homeowner Responsibility: The Homeowner should not install and/or fasten any products or materials on the roof. Homeowner installation of materials or products may void any warranty work by the Builder. The Homeowner should consult with the Builder prior to the installation of any "add-on" materials or products. This includes, but is not limited to, the installation of solar panels and TV antenna dishes. *Concrete* and clay *tile* roofs are susceptible to breakage and only persons qualified to walk on roofs should perform any installation of "add-on" products. The Builder will assume no responsibility for the roof systems when the Homeowner installs anything on the roof or makes any modifications without the approval of the Builder. (Refer to Preface: "**Ten Most Common Mistakes Made by New Homeowners**", page 18, item #3.)

NOTE: The addition of photovoltaic (solar) panels on roofs is a great green tip; however, great care must be used by an installer when making a retrofit to a roof. The additional weight to the roof should be checked by a structural engineer and any penetrations through the roof must be carefully considered.

Condition #2: Roof Sheathing Is Bowed

Potentially Impacting:
- Structural integrity of the roof
- Interior finishes
- Appearance

Performance Guideline

Roof sheathing should have a maximum deflection of 3/8 inch up or down in 2 feet of length. Roof sheathing should conform to the recommendations of the roofing material manufacturer, as well as the specifications of the building designer and the minimum requirements of the building code.

Builder Responsibility: The Builder should perform repairs to conform to the Performance Guideline.

Homeowner Responsibility: None.

Slate, Concrete and Clay Tiles

Condition #1: Roof Leaks

Potentially Impacting:
- Structural *frame*
- Interior finishes
- Interior furnishings

Performance Guideline

*All roof systems should be installed in a watertight fashion and should not allow water intrusion under normal inclement weather conditions; "normal" meaning what is typical for that particular geographic region. (Refer to expanded definition of "**Weather—Normal and Extreme**", page 4.)*

Comments: Roof *tiles* and slate are generally not considered the *waterproofing* component of the roof system. Roof tiles serve three purposes: 1) complimenting the architectural design of the Home, 2) shedding water down their overlapping courses and into a *gutter* or off the edge of the roof overhang, and 3) protecting the waterproofing *membrane*. The felt below the roof tiles, metal *flashings*, and the tiles themselves comprise the entire roof weatherproofing system. However, under extreme weather conditions (out of the normal), for example, wind-driven rains (rains that are driven horizontally), snow and/or ice build-up, the roof system is more susceptible to water intrusion, especially on lower *slope* and flat roofs. Under extreme weather conditions water intrusion is not considered to be defective construction.

Builder Responsibility: If the roof leaks under normal weather conditions, the Builder should correct any verified roof or flashing leaks, as well as repair damage that is a result of the subject leak. The Builder is not responsible for leaks caused by extreme weather conditions or by Homeowner negligence, such as improper fastenings and/or penetrations through the roof.

Homeowner Responsibility: ***Maintenance Alert!*** The Homeowner is responsible for periodic maintenance. For example, clearing *roof drains*, gutters and *downspouts* of leaves and other foreign debris and checking all areas that have a *caulking* or sealant type material such as *vents*, pipe penetrations, and sheet metal flashing for cracked sealant, etc. NOTE: Because *concrete* and clay tiles are subject to breaking, Homeowners should not walk on roof tiles (including slate). Generalized inspections can be done by the Homeowner from the ground, from ladders set at the edge of the roof and from adjacent properties. Binoculars are often helpful. If more detailed inspections are necessary, it is advisable to hire a qualified and properly insured roof inspection contractor. Homeowners should be extremely careful when installing products on the roof (such as solar panels) or fastening items to the roof (such as holiday lights). All after-market items attached to a roof should be installed by a qualified contractor. The original roof warranty may be voided when someone other than the original contractor makes an addition or alteration to the roof.

DO THIS...
NOT THIS!
INSPECTING THE ROOF

Condition #2: Tile or Slate Is Loose or Falling

Potentially Impacting:

- Safety issues related to falling objects
- *Underlayment* (*waterproofing membrane*) integrity

Performance Guideline

Tiles should not be loose or fall from the roof. They should be fastened in accordance with the manufacturer's published attachment schedule.

Comments: Tiles are often loose where the roof meets a wall. Since tiles should not be fastened with nails through sheet metal *flashing*, roofers may secure the tiles with roofing *cement* or other manufacturer recommended installation material. In some climate regions not all of the tiles require fastening and are hung from *battens*. All tiles should have uniform *exposure*.

Builder Responsibility: The Builder should remove and/or refasten the unacceptable tiles if caused during original installation. Tiles should be securely attached to the roof by approved methods based upon codes and the manufacturer's installation requirements.

Homeowner Responsibility: The Homeowner should conduct periodic inspections along all roof-to-wall intersections and look for loose or slipping tiles. A preliminary assessment can most often be accomplished with a visual inspection from the ground or from an elevated portion of the structure. More complete inspections should be done only by qualified roofing specialists.

Condition #3: Tile or Slate Is Chipped or Broken

Potentially Impacting:

- Safety issues related to falling objects
- *Underlayment* (*waterproofing membrane*) integrity

Performance Guideline

All cracked and broken tiles and slate are considered unacceptable, if installed in that condition. Chips smaller than ¾ inch are acceptable, providing that the total number of chipped tiles or slate does not exceed more than 10% of the square footage of the plane (face) of the roof. Tile or slate with chipped edges that are placed under sheet metal flashing are considered acceptable.

Comments: Roof tiles made of *concrete*, clay, or slate are fragile and may break. The Homeowner and the Builder should conduct a thorough inspection as early as possible in the ownership process (at the *walkthrough*). The Builder is not responsible for any breakage and/or damage caused by the Homeowner's negligence. The Homeowner should not walk on *roof valleys* or *crickets*. These areas will not support the weight and can cause penetration through the material.

Builder Responsibility: The Builder should replace any missing, broken, cracked or excessively chipped tiles or slate, which are a result of the Builder's work.

Homeowner Responsibility: ***Maintenance Alert!*** The Homeowner should inspect the roof for any cracked and/or broken tiles or slate pieces within the first month of occupancy. Homeowners should not walk on the roof, make any roof penetrations, or fasten any objects to the roof. If the Homeowner cannot inspect the roof with a ladder or by observation from a safe higher vantage point, it is strongly advised that the Homeowner hire a qualified roofing inspector to perform the inspection.

Condition #4: Tile or Slate Has Improper Exposure, Lapping or Spacing

Potentially Impacting:

- *Useful life* of the roof system
- Appearance

Performance Guideline

Exposure should not exceed that of the manufacturer's installation recommendations or building code standards.

Comments: Generally speaking, roof *tiles* and slate are probably "over exposed" if nails are visible and if not installed per the manufacturer's installation recommendations. The exception to this are the *rake* tiles along the edge of the roof, which often have exposed nails.

Builder Responsibility: If the tiles or slate have exposed nails, the Builder should perform repairs to meet code standards or the manufacturer's installation requirements.

Homeowner Responsibility: None.

Condition #5: Roof Tile Lacks Adequate Nailing

Potentially Impacting:

- Safety issue related to falling objects
- *Underlayment* integrity
- Watertightness of structure

Performance Guideline

All roof tiles and slate should be fastened according to the manufacturer's recommendations as well as to building code standards.

Comments: Different regions may require different fastening methods. Areas subject to high winds or snow conditions require different fastening or nailing schedules than those with more moderate environments.

Builder Responsibility: If there is a lack of appropriate fastening or nailing, the Builder should perform repairs to conform to the Performance Guideline.

Homeowner Responsibility: None.

Condition #6: Efflorescence (Appearance of Light Colored Deposits) on Concrete Tiles

Potentially Impacting:

- Appearance of roof surface

Performance Guideline

Concrete roof tiles should be uniform in color and free from extensive efflorescence. Minor efflorescence is considered normal and acceptable.

Comments: Water migrating through cracked or porous concrete can carry minerals to the surface of the tile where evaporation results in minerals being deposited on the tile surface. This is generally not a significant problem; it is mainly an appearance issue.

Builder Responsibility: None.

Homeowner Responsibility: None.

Composition Asphalt Shingles

Condition #1: Roof Leaks

Potentially Impacting:

- Structural *frame*
- Interior finishes
- Interior furnishings

Performance Guideline

*All roof systems should be installed in a watertight fashion and should not allow water intrusion under normal inclement weather conditions; "normal" meaning what is typical for that particular geographic region. (Refer to expanded definition of "**Weather—Normal and Extreme**", page 4.)*

Comments: *Asphalt composition* shingles are the water shedding cover on top of the *underlayment* material of the roof system. Shingles serve two purposes: 1) to compliment the architectural design of the building, and 2) shed water down their overlapping courses and into a *gutter* or off the edge of the roof. However, under extreme weather conditions, for example high wind-driven rains (*rains that are driven horizontally*) and snow and/or ice build-up, the roof system is more susceptible to water intrusion especially on low *slope* and flat roofs. Under extreme conditions water intrusion may be unavoidable.

Builder Responsibility: If the roof leaks under normal weather conditions, the Builder should correct any verified roof or *flashing* leaks and repair damage that is a result of the leak. The Builder is not responsible for leaks caused by the Homeowner's negligence, such as improper fastening to, installations on, or penetrations of the roof.

Homeowner Responsibility: ***Maintenance Alert!*** The Homeowner is responsible for annual maintenance, for example cleaning of all *roof drains*, valleys, chimney crickets, gutters and downspouts of leaves and/or other foreign debris; checking areas that have a sealant type material, for example vents, pipe penetrations, and inspecting all sheet metal flashing for deteriorated sealant, etc. The Homeowner should also avoid installing products on and/or fastening items to or through the roof. The Homeowner should not walk on roof valleys or crickets. These areas will not support the weight and can cause penetration through the material.

Condition #2: Shingles Have Blown Off

Potentially Impacting:

- Watertightness
- Appearance

Performance Guideline

Shingles should not suffer damage under normal wind loads for a particular geographic region as set forth in wind design guidelines. All asphalt composition shingles should be installed according to the manufacturer's installation recommendations and local code requirements.

Builder Responsibility: If shingles are damaged by wind and wind loads are within the wind design standards of the manufacturer, the Builder should make all the necessary repairs to conform to the Performance Guideline. The Builder is not responsible for conditions caused by the Homeowner's misuse or improper maintenance.

Homeowner Responsibility: ***Maintenance Alert!*** The Homeowner is responsible for periodic maintenance, for example, cleaning of all *roof drains*, *gutters* and downspouts of leaves and/or other foreign debris, checking all areas that have a sealant type material, for example, vents, pipe penetrations, and inspecting all sheet metal *flashing* for deteriorated sealant, etc. The Homeowner should also avoid installing products on and/or fastening items to the roof.

Condition #3: Shingles Are Not Horizontally Aligned

Potentially Impacting:

- Appearance

Performance Guideline

Unless the Builder is trying to achieve a special architectural effect by staggering the ends or rows of the shingles, shingles should be reasonably straight with even courses. The courses shall not deviate by more than 1 inch exposure to the weather in 20 feet.

Comments: Exposure is an industry term that indicates how much of each shingle or shake can be exposed to the weather. If the courses are under exposed, the integrity of the roof should not be affected. It should be noted that under exposure might void some manufacturer's material warranties. Conversely, if the shingle is over exposed, this may decrease the life expectancy of the roof system.

Builder Responsibility: If the courses are over or under exposed, as determined by the manufacturer's installation recommendations, the Builder should perform repairs necessary to conform to the installation recommendations.

Homeowner Responsibility: None.

Condition #4: Shingles Are Curled or Cupped at Edges and Corners

Potentially Impacting:

- Roof appearance
- *Useful life* of roof

Performance Guideline

Asphalt shingle edges and corners do not need to be flat, but they should not curl or cup in excess of ½ inch. Fastener heads should not be exposed. The appearance of shingles should be within manufacturer's standards or specifications.

Comments: Between the two types of asphalt shingles (organic and fiberglass shingles), organic shingles have a history of curling and *cupping*, while some fiberglass shingles have a tendency to crack more easily than organic ones. Cupping and curling shingles can also be caused by inadequate *attic* ventilation.

Builder Responsibility: If the curling and cupping becomes widespread and are beyond the manufacturer's tolerances, the Builder should replace shingles to conform to the manufacturer's tolerances.

Homeowner Responsibility: As a roof ages, the Homeowner should pay particular attention to the condition of curled and cupped shingles. The Homeowner should schedule an occasional "tune-up" by a qualified roofing contractor or consultant to significantly extend the life of the roof. Typically, a tune up involves inspecting *flashings* and shingles, replacing torn or loose shingles, and cleaning the *valleys*.

Condition #5: Shingles Overhang Edges of Roof Too Far or Too Little

Potentially Impacting:

- Integrity of eaves
- Watertightness of eaves

Performance Guideline

Composition shingles should overhang the roof edges no less than ¼ inch and not more than ¾ inch unless the manufacturer's standards and specifications indicate otherwise.

Builder Responsibility: The Builder should replace improperly installed shingles that do not conform to the Performance Guideline.

Homeowner Responsibility: ***Maintenance Alert!*** The Homeowner is responsible for periodic maintenance including clearing leaves and debris from *roof drains*, *gutters* and downspouts.

Condition #6: Asphalt Shingles Have Developed Surface Buckling

Potentially Impacting:

- Roof appearance

Performance Guideline

Buckling that exceeds 3/8 inch in height is considered unacceptable.

Comments: The *shingle* surface does not need to be absolutely flat. In fact, some manufacturers create surface irregularities to enhance the overall appearance of the roof. The determination between buckling and an intended irregular surface is that with a buckling condition, the rest of the roof will be flat with only the affected areas buckled. Buckling is sometimes the result of inadequate ventilation or trapped moisture in the *membrane*.

Builder Responsibility: The Builder should repair asphalt shingle buckling to conform to the Performance Guideline.

Homeowner Responsibility: None.

Condition #7: Shingles Have a Shading or Shadowing Pattern

Potentially Impacting:
- Roof appearance

Performance Guideline

Shading or shadowing is considered acceptable. Shingles that are not uniform in color are acceptable.

Comments: Shading or shadowing is a visual phenomenon that does not affect the performance or longevity of the roofing system. Many manufacturers try to give a "*wood shake* look" to their composition shingles. The manufacturing operation intentionally produces slight variations in the surface texture. These different textures simply affect the way the surface reflects light, thus creating shadows.

Builder Responsibility: None.

Homeowner Responsibility: None.

Condition #8: Shingle Surfacing Materials Are Eroding

Potentially Impacting:
- *Useful life* of surfacing material
- Fire resistance of the roof
- Reflectivity of the roof
- Appearance

Performance Guideline

At the time of installation, mineral granules should remain adhered to the surface of the shingles and no bare spots should be visible when looking down at the roof. During the first year after installation, a number of the granules may flow or be blown down into the gutters. This sloughing of the granules is considered normal as long as there are no bare spots.

Comments: Loss of mineral granules from the shingle surface can occur as a result of 1) rooftop traffic (such as during installation of adjacent roofing materials or other building materials), 2) servicing of rooftop mounted heating and cooling equipment, and 3) as a result of natural weathering of the roof surface. Mineral granule loss can also be a result of poor ventilation or manufacturing defects. Minor loss of granules can be expected over the life span of the roof, and generally will not significantly impact the performance or life of the roof. However, excessive granule loss can cause premature breakdown of the *membrane* within the shingle.

Builder Responsibility: The Builder should provide adequate protection to finished roof surfaces during subsequent construction (for example masonry, *siding*, etc.) to prevent undue abrasion of mineral granules. The Builder should refer occurrences of significant mineral granule loss to the manufacturer as this is likely a manufacturing defect.

Homeowner Responsibility: The Homeowner should not permit excessive access to the roof. When access is required, adequate protection, such as wearing soft-sole, laced up shoes, should be adopted to prevent loss of mineral granules.

Condition #9: Shingle Tabs Are Unsealed

Potentially Impacting:

- Wind uplift resistance

Performance Guideline

Shingles or shingle tabs should be adhered to underlying shingles.

Comments: Adhesion of shingles to the underlying shingles can be reduced by a number of factors: contamination of the asphalt seal strips by dust or construction debris, insufficiently driven fasteners, cold air temperatures immediately following shingle application, and improper seal strip manufacture.

Builder Responsibility: The Builder should fasten shingles in conformance to recommendations published by the shingle manufacturer, and/or standards published by recognized industry associations such as the National Roofing Contractors Association. Unacceptable installations should be corrected.

Homeowner Responsibility: The Homeowner should retain a qualified roofing professional to perform any addition or repair involving asphalt shingle roofs, hand-tabbing newly installed shingles if necessary to achieve a proper seal to the underlying courses.

Wood Shakes and Shingles

General Subject Information: *Wood shakes* and *shingles* have been traditional roof coverings (particularly in the West) for decades. Cedar is the primary wood used. The basic difference between a shingle and a shake is the thickness. Shakes are thicker and are often made by splitting cedar logs with a sharp tool similar to an ax. Additionally, both wood shakes and shingles can be manufactured by cutting the cedar log with a saw. Shakes are typically longer than shingles and more of the shake is exposed to the weather. Unless they are chemically treated, wood shakes and shingles can pose a significant fire hazard. Some local jurisdictions have prohibited the installation of untreated shingles and shakes. Roof tile and composition shingles are gradually taking the place of *wood shingles* and shakes in new homes.

Condition #1: Roof Leaks

Potentially Impacting:

- Structural *frame*
- Interior finishes
- Interior furnishings

Performance Guideline

*All roof systems should be installed in a watertight fashion and should not allow water intrusion under normal inclement weather conditions; "normal" meaning what is typical for that particular geographic region. (Refer to expanded definition of "**Weather—Normal and Extreme**", page 4.)*

Comments: Proper maintenance of a *wood shake* or *wood shingle* roof can substantially extend the expected life of a roof. (Refer to **Maintenance Alert** below, under **Homeowner Responsibility**.)

Builder Responsibility: The Builder should construct a roof that is watertight. If the Home does not conform to the Performance Guideline and the leak is not caused by the negligence of the Homeowner or extreme weather, the Builder should make necessary repairs to conform to the Performance Guideline.

KEEP GUTTERS CLEAN
AFTER THE LEAF DROP

Homeowner Responsibility: *Maintenance Alert! Gutters*, downspouts and valleys should be kept free of any leaves or other foreign debris. Any penetrations through the roof that exist should be carefully maintained with *caulking*, asphalt tar, roofing seals, etc. Any Homeowner add-ons such as antennas, satellite dishes, or solar collectors, may void the roof warranty and create a leak-prone penetration through the roofing or *flashing* material. The Homeowner should consult a qualified contractor or the Builder before making any changes or additions to the roof.

Condition #2: Shingles or Shakes Are Cupped or Curled

Potentially Impacting:

- Appearance
- *Useful life* of roof

Performance Guideline

Newly installed shakes or shingles should be flat within 1 inch of the surface plane.

Comments: Normal exposure to sunlight and rainfall results in loss of natural preservative oils from *wood shakes* and shingles, leading to some deformation of the wood. In addition, different rates of drying between the top and bottom surfaces of the shake or shingle can contribute to deformation of the wood. These events occur naturally and generally are not a significant problem, other than an appearance issue.

Builder Responsibility: The Builder should inspect shakes or shingles prior to installation on the roof and not use units that are significantly cupped or curled. Unacceptable installation should be corrected. Proper ventilation should be provided to the underside of the roof *sheathing*.

Homeowner Responsibility: ***Maintenance Alert!*** The Homeowner should provide periodic roof maintenance to extend the *useful life* of a wood roof. The Homeowner should schedule roof "tune-ups" by a qualified roofing contractor at a minimum of every five years. A "tune-up" can consist of replacing cupped or curled shakes and shingles, separating ridge caps, and blown off shingles. A "tune-up" is not expensive (compared to the cost of a new roof) and in most cases will substantially extend the life of the roof.

Condition #3: Shakes or Shingles Are Loose or Have Blown Off

Potentially Impacting:

- Integrity of the *underlayment* (*waterproofing*)
- Interior finishes
- Appearance
- Watertightness

Performance Guideline

Shakes and shingles should not blow off the roof under normal weather conditions for the geographic region. However, shakes and shingles may blow off as they age and erode. This is a normal part of the aging process of the Home. Hurricane or gale force winds in regions that do not normally experience these conditions may result in shakes or shingles being blown off the roof; this condition is not considered defective construction.

Comments: Every roof cover product that is installed needs to be carefully selected for that particular region. High wind areas require different fastening methods than those of moderate wind areas and low *slope* roofs require different and/or additional *flashing* assemblies.

Builder Responsibility: The Builder should perform repairs to ensure the roof is watertight. The Builder should follow the manufacturer's recommended nailing schedule. Visible fasteners are not acceptable, except at ridge caps. The Builder should replace any shingles or shakes blown off during normal weather events, unless damage is a result of improper maintenance by the Homeowner.

Homeowner Responsibility: ***Maintenance Alert!*** The Homeowner should remove leaves and other debris from *gutters*, downspouts and valleys. Older roofs that have not been maintained properly are more likely to experience blown off shakes and shingles.

Condition #4: Shingles Have Improper Exposure, Edge Lapping, or Spacing

Potentially Impacting:

- Integrity of structural framing members
- *Eave* performance
- Watertightness

Performance Guideline

Wood shake and shingle tolerances should not be less than that recommended by the roofing material manufacturer. In general, shingles should extend no less than 1½ inches and shakes should extend no more than 2 inches beyond the rake edge of the roof; and 1½ inches beyond the edge of an eave. If there are differences, the manufacturer's installation recommendations take precedence over this Guideline.

Comments: There is a variety of different shakes and shingles on the market. Each manufacturer has specific installation recommendations that need to be followed in order for the warranty to remain valid.

Builder Responsibility: The Builder should install all shake and shingle *exposures*, edge lapping and spacing in accordance with the manufacturer's recommendations.

Homeowner Responsibility: None.

Condition #5: Joints between Shingles in Successive Courses Are Not Adequately Offset

Potentially Impacting:

- Integrity of *underlayment*

Performance Guideline

The keyways (spaces between adjacent shingle or shakes) cannot be aligned vertically in any two successive rows of shakes or with three courses of wood shingles.

Comments: Running any two rows in a direct line exposes the *waterproofing* underlayment to the elements, which can lead to deterioration.

Builder Responsibility: The Builder should perform repairs necessary to conform to the Performance Guideline.

Homeowner Responsibility: None.

Condition #6: Shingles Have Improper Nail Fastening

Potentially Impacting:

- Safety issue related to falling objects
- *Underlayment* integrity
- Interior finishes
- Watertightness of structure

Performance Guideline

Each shake or shingle should be nailed with two approved nails or staples. Nails or staples should be galvanized or stainless steel. Fasteners should be long enough to penetrate the layers of roofing material and embed in the underlying plywood, OSB, or plank deck by at least ½ inch. Alternatively, nailing and fastening can conform to the manufacturer's installation recommendations. The entire roof system should be free of exposed nails and fasteners, except at ridges.

Builder Responsibility: The Builder should perform repairs necessary to conform to the Performance Guideline.

Homeowner Responsibility: None.

Condition #7: Roof Has an Accumulation of Organic Debris (Leaves, Moss, etc.)

Potentially Impacting:

- Performance and life span of the roof
- Appearance

Performance Guideline

This is a Homeowner maintenance item.

Builder Responsibility: None.

Homeowner Responsibility: ***Maintenance Alert!*** The accumulation of leaves, needles, sediment, and growth of moss or fungi on *wood shakes* or *shingles* can lead to premature degradation of wood. The Homeowner should retain a qualified roofing professional to perform a bi-annual (or annual in areas of high humidity and rainfall) roof cleaning which includes the removal of accumulated organic material.

Composite or Synthetic Roof System

General Subject Information: Numerous composite or synthetic materials are available for steep *slope*, water shedding roofs. The materials are engineered and manufactured to simulate the appearance of natural roofing materials, such as *wood shakes* or *shingles*, slate, or tile, while providing wind uplift and fire resistance. The manufactured products include fiber cement composites, formed metal panels, foil-laminate asphalt shingles, wood fiber based materials, fiberglass and polymer based products, and various recycled materials. These products and their respective installation methods are continually changing. The manufacturer's current design and installation recommendations should be consulted regarding proper design, installation, and maintenance of these products.

Condition #1: Roof Materials Are Cracked or Broken

Potentially Impacting:

- *Useful life* of the roof
- Interior finishes and furnishings
- Safety issues related to falling objects

Performance Guideline

Roof materials should be installed in whole or intentionally cut pieces, sized to fit.

Comments: Cracked or broken pieces may result from undetected flaws in the material which existed prior to installation, from damage occurring during shipping, or from action subsequent to installation, either related to construction of adjacent surfaces (for example, masonry or *stucco cladding* above roofs), or external impact (for example, hailstones or golf balls). New pieces with chipped or broken edges can usually be installed at *hips*, valleys, *rakes*, or other locations requiring cut pieces. These pieces should be identified and sorted during the loading process. Fiber cement or wood fiber based materials with pockets of poorly blended components can experience subsequent cracking or breakage.

Builder Responsibility: The Builder should inspect roof covering materials prior to installation, segregating pieces found to contain visible manufacturing or shipping related defects or damage that would adversely impact the function of the material installed. The Builder may retain those damaged sections for installation in locations that require cut pieces. Adequate protection should be provided for finished roof surfaces during subsequent work on adjacent surfaces. The Builder should correct unacceptable installations.

Homeowner Responsibility: the Homeowner should not walk on the roof, make any penetrations through, or fasten any item to the roof. Additionally, the Homeowner should retain a qualified roofing professional on a bi-annual or annual schedule to perform inspections of the roof, noting and replacing any cracked or broken materials.

Condition #2: Roof Materials Are Loose or Displaced

Potentially Impacting:

- *Useful life* of the roof
- Appearance
- Safety issues related to falling objects

Performance Guideline

Roof covering materials should be secured using approved materials and methods, and according to applicable codes and manufacturer's recommended fastening schedule. Properly secured materials should not be displaced by normally occurring wind conditions.

Comments: Unsecured pieces can be displaced and create damage by slipping further. Displaced pieces can also result in water intrusion into the structure. At locations where fastening of materials is difficult due to *flashing* or other impediments, an approved adhesive may be used to secure pieces to adjacent ones.

Builder Responsibility: The Builder should install materials using approved methods which conform to applicable codes and manufacturer recommendations. The Builder should correct unacceptable installations to conform to the Performance Guideline.

Homeowner Responsibility: The Homeowner should not walk on the roof, or make any penetrations through, or fasten any item to the roof. The Homeowner should retain a qualified roofing professional to perform annual inspections of the roof, noting and securing any materials found to be loose or displaced.

Condition #3: Roof Has Improper Exposure, Laps, and Spacing of Pieces

Potentially Impacting:
- *Useful life* of the roof
- Appearance
- Interior finishes and furnishings

Performance Guideline

Roofing materials should be installed, lapped, and spaced according to the manufacturer's published installation recommendations.

Comments: Improperly lapped or spaced materials can result in insufficient coverage of underlying or adjacent materials and roof *underlayment* material. This may result in intrusion into the structure by water runoff or wind-driven rain, and potential premature failure of the underlayment.

Builder Responsibility: The Builder should install materials lapped and spaced as recommended by the material manufacturer. The Builder should correct unacceptable installations to conform to the Performance Guideline.

Homeowner Responsibility: None.

Built-Up Roofing and Other Low Slope Roofs

General Subject Information: A *built-up roof* (BUR) system is simply layers of asphalt that serve as the *waterproofing* medium, sandwiched between various types of roofing *membranes* known as felts. In residential construction BUR systems are not as common as other roofing materials, but they can be found where low *slope* or flat roof conditions exist. From entry-level homes to *condominium* buildings to expensive desert and shore homes, built-up roofs often produce a particular look that the architect is trying to achieve. Three basic types of BUR systems are used: smooth surface, *aggregate* surface, and mineral surface. On lower sloped roof applications, the felt layers should be placed so that the flow of water is not against the sections where the *underlayment* felt laps over the next layer. This condition is called reverse lapping and can be an invitation to roof leaks.

Another type of low slope roof system is the single-ply roof. This system consists of a single membrane layer that is applied (usually with fasteners) over the underlayment (also called a *substrate*). The seams are sealed with a special sealant provided by the manufacturer.

A third type of low slope roof is the foam roof. Basically, a closed cell foam is sprayed over a wood deck to a level of thickness ranging from 1 to 3 inches. The finished surface should be smooth, and free from buckles and blisters. It is very important that the foam be protected by a coating to prevent ultraviolet degradation. Foam roofs provide excellent insulating values, particularly on roof designs where there is no *attic*.

It is important that the Builder conform to the roofing manufacturer's installation recommendations for the life of the roof and any manufacturer's warranty. The Homeowner should provide preventive maintenance to the roof as the life span may be greatly influenced by the presence or absence of proper roof maintenance.

Condition #1: Roof Has Standing Water (Ponding)

Potentially Impacting:

- Structural *frame*
- Interior finishes
- Interior furnishings

Performance Guideline

Minor ponding is acceptable provided that it does not exceed ½ inch in depth.

Comments: All roofs that are considered flat roofs should drain either over the edge of the roof or into an interior *roof drain* system with an *overflow drain*. Any ponding that exceeds the Guideline may cause premature deterioration to the roofing *membrane*.

Builder Responsibility: The Builder is responsible for providing drainage with a positive *slope* for the finished roof. A flat roof should have a minimum slope of ¼ inch of drop to the edge or drain for each 12 inches across the roof surface. The Builder should repair or replace any unacceptable condition that results from improper construction.

Homeowner Responsibility: ***Maintenance Alert!*** The Homeowner should perform bi-annual inspection and maintenance of the roof system. This should include clearing debris accumulated on the roof membrane, sealing cracks, tears or rips, and keeping drains, *gutters* and downspouts free of debris. Also, the Homeowner should adequately maintain the area where the roof turns up to a wall or skylight to prevent deterioration and leaks. If the roof has *parapet* walls, then the Homeowner must keep all overflow *scuppers* or primary and secondary drains free of leaves, gravel, and debris.

Condition #2: Roof Leaks

Potentially Impacting:

- Structural *frame*
- Interior finishes
- Interior furnishings

Performance Guideline

*All roof systems should be installed in a watertight fashion and should not allow water intrusion under normal inclement weather conditions; "normal" meaning what is typical for that particular geographic region. (Refer to expanded definition of "**Weather—Normal and Extreme**", page 4.)*

Comments: A roof should not leak during normal inclement weather. However, all roof systems may leak under extreme or abnormal weather conditions, which is acceptable.

Builder Responsibility: The Builder should install a watertight roof. If the roof leaks during normal weather, the Builder should perform repairs necessary to conform to the Performance Guideline (unless the leaks are determined to be the result of Homeowner negligence).

Homeowner Responsibility: ***Maintenance Alert!*** The Homeowner should not fasten after- market products such as deck boards, satellite dishes and solar panels to the roof system without consulting the original Builder or a qualified roofing contractor. The Homeowner should be aware that fastening a product to the roof system could cause the warranty to be voided. Walking on the roof should be kept to a minimum. If walking on the roof is necessary, such as to maintain roof top equipment, rubber walking pads should be placed on the roof.

Condition #3: Roof *Membrane* Has Bubbles or Blisters

Potentially Impacting:

- Integrity of the roof
- Structural integrity
- Interior finishes

Performance Guideline

Bubbles or blisters that exceed 12 inches in diameter are unacceptable. Small and unbroken bubbles/blisters that are less than 12 inches in diameter are considered acceptable. Bubbles or blisters that cover more than 20% of the roof are unacceptable.

Comments: Voids between two waterproof layers of roofing materials can cause bubbles or blisters. When moist air gets trapped between these two layers, an increase in temperature increases pressure. The pressure can cause the two layers to be pushed apart. Nearly all roofs can experience some bubbles and blisters. If the bubbles and blisters are unbroken and conform to the Performance Guideline, they should be left alone. Puncturing and attempting to repair the unbroken blisters can result in leaks where there were none previously.

Builder Responsibility: If bubbles/blisters do not conform to the Performance Guideline, the Builder should perform repairs to conform to the Guideline.

Homeowner Responsibility: ***Maintenance Alert!*** As the roof starts to age, the Homeowner should provide periodic maintenance to joints and separations. Areas that have received roofing tar or *caulking* materials will also require periodic maintenance due to age and structure movement. The Homeowner should pay particular attention to locations where dissimilar materials meet (for example, *plumbing vents* or metal *flashing*). The joining of dissimilar materials is a prime location for water intrusion, especially as tar and caulking become more brittle with weather exposure, age, and cracks.

Condition #4: Roof Membrane Has Splits or Tears

Potentially Impacting:
- Integrity of the roof
- Structural integrity
- Interior finishes

Performance Guideline

Splitting and tearing of the roof membrane is unacceptable.

Comments: There are several possible causes of splitting or tearing of a roof membrane. One cause may be stress from differential or seasonal movement of the *frame* of the Home. Residential buildings are usually constructed of wood and will likely expand and contract with changes in the weather. Excessive foot traffic on the roof is another possible cause of splitting and tearing. An invasive testing approach can be necessary to determine actual causes and their origin.

Builder Responsibility: The Builder should inspect the area in question. If the condition is not a result of Homeowner negligence, then the Builder should perform repairs necessary to conform to the Performance Guideline.

Homeowner Responsibility: The Homeowner should start a maintenance schedule as soon as the Home is occupied. As the roof ages, maintenance becomes increasingly important. Homeowner will need to provide maintenance to asphalt cements, joints and separations.

Maintenance Alert! The Homeowner should pay particular attention to where the roof meets dissimilar materials. The tie-in of dissimilar materials (materials that are not of the same kind, for example wood in contact with steel, *stucco* in contact with wood, etc.) are prime locations for water intrusion, especially over time, as roofing compounds like asphalt cement and *caulking* can become brittle, and can crack and separate.

Condition #5: Roof Has Bare Spots

Potentially Impacting:
- *Useful life* of roof
- Integrity of underlying felt
- Fire resistance of roof

Performance Guideline

An even layer of gravel or minerals should be firmly embedded into the top coat with no bare spots showing. Where the membrane turns up on vertical projections (such as parapet walls, skylights, and plumbing vents), flashing or granular surfacing suitable for exposure should be used to protect membranes.

Comments: Roofs with bare spots are more vulnerable to deterioration than those that are fully covered with gravel. Loose gravel under high wind conditions can also become a hazard. Since it is not possible to attain complete embedment of all *aggregate*, the Builder should use gravel with sufficient weight to resist wind *displacement*.

Builder Responsibility: If the roof is a surface gravel system, the Builder should furnish a roof that is fully coated or surfaced with gravel or mineral and roofing compounds. If at the time of installation, the roof does not conform to the Performance Guideline, the Builder should perform repairs necessary to conform to the Guideline. The Builder is not responsible if bare spots are created by extreme wind conditions or if the condition is caused by improper Homeowner use or lack of maintenance.

Homeowner Responsibility: ***Maintenance Alert!*** The Homeowner is responsible for keeping the roof, *roof drains*, *gutters* and downspouts free of debris. Gravel and mineral granules have a tendency to clog drains and fill gutters. The Homeowner should always check the roof prior to and after any prolonged inclement weather and/or winter rains and snow.

Condition #6: Roofing Material at the Roof-to-Wall Intersection Is Splitting

Potentially Impacting:

- Integrity of the roof
- Structural integrity
- Interior finishes and furnishings

Performance Guideline

Splits, tears or rips are not acceptable. A cant strip should be installed at all horizontal to vertical intersections to allow the 90-degree intersection to be reduced to two 45-degree angles.

Comments: A *common area* for water intrusion to occur is at a horizontal location that ties into a vertical surface. Many roof leaks occur at these *flashing* locations. Leaking that occurs at these locations is unacceptable and will require immediate attention.

Builder Responsibility: If roof leaks are a result of poor or inadequate flashing, *counter flashing* and/or the lack of adequate cant strips, and the leak is not the result of Homeowner negligence, the Builder should perform necessary repairs to conform to the Performance Guideline.

Homeowner Responsibility: ***Maintenance Alert!*** As a general rule, the Homeowner should avoid walking on the roof, especially locations where materials transition from the horizontal to the vertical. Resilient walking pads should be installed on roofs with mechanical equipment (such as air conditioners) that require maintenance.

Condition #7: Roof Membrane Has Unsealed Laps

Potentially Impacting:

- *Useful life* of the roof
- Interior finishes and furnishings
- Structural integrity

Performance Guideline

All laps of the roof membrane should be properly sealed.

Comments: Unsealed laps or "fishmouths" can occur as a result of poorly constructed overlaps in roof membrane systems. Unsealed laps can result in water migration into the roof system, which can reduce the performance and life span of the roof and installation components. In addition, if the open lap extends downward to a lower layer, water can find its way into the structure and cause further damage.

Builder Responsibility: The Builder should install the membrane roof system with all laps properly sealed.

Homeowner Responsibility: The Homeowner should retain a qualified roofing professional to perform an annual roof inspection.

Condition #8: Fasteners Back Out and Do Not Penetrate All Layers

Potentially Impacting:

- *Useful life* of the roof
- Interior finishes and furnishings
- Wind uplift resistance

Performance Guideline

All fasteners should be properly sized and installed per the manufacturer's instructions. In the absence of specific manufacturer's instructions, fasteners should penetrate all layers of the roof material and penetrate ¾ inch into the roof deck.

Comments: Fasteners of insufficient length or fasteners that are improperly installed can become loose from vibration, from fluttering of the *membrane* due to wind action, or from expansion and contraction due to temperature variations. Backed out fasteners can deform and puncture membranes and contribute to a reduction in wind uplift resistance of the roof system.

Builder Responsibility: The Builder should install the roof system with all fasteners properly sized and securely installed per manufacturer's specifications. The Builder should replace fasteners found to be backing out within the applicable warranty period.

Homeowner Responsibility: The Homeowner should retain a qualified roofing professional to perform annual inspections of the roof, noting and repairing any deficiencies that are found, such as backed out fasteners.

Condition #9: Roof Has an Accumulation of a Brown Residue from Asphalt Roofing Products

Potentially Impacting:

- Appearance

Performance Guideline

This is an acceptable and normal condition.

Comments: Formation of brown, "tobacco-juice" residue results from migration of surface oils from the asphalt based membrane during initial weathering. Once washed away by rainfall or rinsed with water, it is unlikely to recur. The only significant effect of this condition is a potential impediment to bonding of coatings applied to the roof surface. This possible impediment can be resolved by rinsing the roof surface prior to application of such coating.

Builder Responsibility: None.

Homeowner Responsibility: None.

Condition #10: Foam Has Separated from the Under-Deck

Potentially Impacting:
- Watertightness
- Appearance

Performance Guideline

Foam shall be properly adhered to the under-deck and shall not blister or separate.

Builder Responsibility: The Builder should perform repairs necessary to see that the foam does not blister and is adhered to the under-deck.

Homeowner Responsibility: None.

Condition #11: Foam Has Deteriorated from Ultraviolet Rays

Potentially Impacting:
- Watertightness
- Reduction of *useful life*

Performance Guideline

Foam shall not deteriorate from ultraviolet rays or crack within the warranty period. Foam shall be protected by an approved exterior coating.

Builder Responsibility: The Builder should perform necessary repairs to verify that the foam is properly protected from ultraviolet rays. The Builder should repair all cracks if this condition occurs within the warranty period.

Homeowner Responsibility: None.

Roof Ventilation

General Subject Information: Proper roof ventilation helps dissipate and reduce unwanted moisture in the *attic* during the winter and hot air during the summer. Vents that are located low on the roof system help bring in cooler air, while vents that are located closer to or on the *ridge* help remove warm or moist air. Louver style vents are often found on the *gable* ends of roofs. If a roof is not properly ventilated, condensation can develop and may cause mold and mildew growth, water staining at the interior, and deterioration of structural members. Improperly vented roofs will reduce the effectiveness of roof or attic *insulation*. This condition may cause roofing material warranties to be voided and may lead to roof *membrane* buckling. It should be noted that some manufacturers will not warranty their *shingles* if a closed spray foam insulation is used under the roof deck.

Condition #1: Attic Vent or Louver Leaks

Potentially Impacting:

- Structural *frame*
- Interior finishes
- Interior furnishings

Performance Guideline

*Vents and louvers should not leak under normal weather conditions for the geographic region. Some leakage during extreme weather conditions (out of the normal) may occur and is not considered indicative of defective construction. (Refer to expanded definition of "**Weather—Normal and Extreme**", page 4.)*

Comments: Construction is not considered defective if water penetrates through the vents or louver during extreme weather conditions for the geographical region. This is deemed to be outside the Builder's control. However, if water intrusion occurs between the vent and the exterior wall finish, the Builder should perform repairs to conform to the Performance Guideline. Also, if leakage occurs during the "normal" rainy or snow season, it is considered unacceptable.

Builder Responsibility: The Builder should perform repairs to eliminate any water intrusion during normal weather conditions. If water intrusion occurs between the vent and the wall finish and is a result of improper installation, the Builder should perform repairs to eliminate leaks.

Homeowner Responsibility: ***Maintenance Alert!*** The Homeowner should keep vents and louvers free from obstructions. The Homeowner should prevent birds and insects from nesting in vents.

Flashing

General Subject Information: Sheet metal *flashing* components provide a passive overlap that protects terminations or transitions of roofing materials from penetration by wind driven rain or runoff water (for example, at *plumbing vent* pipes, skylight curbs, roof edges, the base of walls, etc.). Rainwater is intended to pass across the flashing and down to the edge of the roof. Sheet metal flashings are also found at the inside and outside edges of coated decks. These flashings are designed to keep water from penetrating under the deck coating.

There are other applications for flashing in addition to roofs. Often, flashing is found at transitions of dissimilar materials, such as brick or stone transitioning to *stucco* or *siding*. This flashing serves as a water shedding component and prevents gaps from opening between two different materials. Another type of flashing called *counter flashing* is frequently installed where the shapes of materials require another piece of flashing to work as an additional component to keep water from entering the wall or roof cavity.

Flashing is also found at the perimeter of *exterior doors* and windows, but it is not generally visible. This flashing is often made of a flexible plastic or asphaltic material, is placed around the door or window openings and is covered with the finish stucco, brick, or siding. The purpose of door and window flashing is the same as roof and deck flashing: to keep water from entering the Home.

The painting and *caulking* of flashings by a qualified roofing contractor are routine maintenance items.

Condition #1: Sheet Metal Flashings Are Missing or Improperly Applied

Potentially Impacting:

- Watertightness
- Structural integrity
- Interior finishes

Performance Guideline

> *Flashing and other sheet metal should be furnished and installed per the current codes and the building designer's specifications. Roof flashing should not leak under normal conditions. The exceptions are that the Builder is not responsible for this condition when the causes of leaks are a result of ice build-up, snow, extreme wind-driven rain (as defined on page 4) or Homeowner negligence.*

Comments: Sheet metal flashing and *counter flashing* are integral parts of a properly designed and installed roof system. Flashings are installed at penetrations through the roof such as *plumbing vents*, flues, chimneys and skylights. Some other areas that have flashing are *roof valleys* and roof-to-wall intersections.

Builder Responsibility: To conform to the Performance Guideline, the Builder should repair any flashing leaks resulting from improper installation. In geographic areas where ice dams at eaves are known to occur, the Builder should install an electrical resistance device or waterproof *membrane* from the edge of the *eave* to 1 foot above the end of the eave.

Homeowner Responsibility: ***Maintenance Alert!*** The Homeowner is responsible for keeping all sheet metal valleys, *gutters* and downspouts free from ice build-up, snow, leaves and/or other debris. (Refer to "**Chapter Nine—Miscellaneous, Ice and Snow**", page 239.) This should be done safely from a ladder using a telescopic pole tool without walking on the roof or by a qualified roof maintenance service.

Condition #2: Flashing Has Rusted or Paint Has Peeled

Potentially Impacting:

- Watertightness of the structure
- Appearance

Performance Guideline

Sheet metal flashings, if properly maintained, should not rust. Painted flashings should not peel during the warranty period.

Comments: Nearly all sheet metal flashing is galvanized or bonderized (a metallic coating to prevent rust). Usually it is painted to match the roof or wall color. Sheet metal flashings should be prime coated before the final coat. The exception is lead and copper flashing, which is often not painted for aesthetic reasons.

Builder Responsibility: The Builder should repaint or replace the sheet metal flashings if they rust or peel within the warranty period.

Homeowner Responsibility: None during the warranty period. Afterwards, if sheet metal flashings show signs of rusting, the Homeowner should scrape off the rust and repaint.

Condition #3: Flashing Is Not Set Tight to the Shingles or Tile

Potentially Impacting:
- Watertightness of the structure
- Appearance

Performance Guideline

Sheet metal flashings should be no more than ¼ inch above the highest plane of the material that it is intended to cover.

Comments: A typical application of sheet metal flashing is where a roof and a wall intersect. The flashing should not be separated by more than ¼ inch above the thickest *shingle* or *tile* piece. The exception to this condition is flashing over tile known as "S" tile, Spanish tile or barrel tile, which is usually flashed with lead sheets. The lead is deformed and pressed over the round tile.

Builder Responsibility: The Builder should perform repairs to adjust the flashing and conform to the Performance Guideline.

Homeowner Responsibility: None. However, when repainting or re-roofing the Home, the Homeowner should take care not to bend the sheet metal or tear or puncture the lead flashings.

Condition #4: Flashings and Valleys Are Done Improperly or Are Missing

Potentially Impacting:
- Watertightness
- Interior finishes

Performance Guideline

Flashing and other sheet metal should be furnished and installed in compliance with the current code and in conformance with approved plans. Flashings should not leak.

Comments: Flashing is often the "weak link" in a roof system. Improperly designed or improperly installed flashing at roof penetrations (such as chimneys, skylights, *plumbing vents*, flues, or transitions from roof-to-wall) can result in insufficient coverage of the edges of shakes and *shingles*. Any exposed *underlayment* will quickly deteriorate in sunlight, and leaks are likely to follow.

Builder Responsibility: If it is determined that the cause of a roof leak is improperly installed or missing flashing, the Builder should perform repairs to conform to the Performance Guideline.

Homeowner Responsibility: ***Maintenance Alert!*** The Homeowner should conduct a yearly inspection to ensure that sheet metal *caulking*, sealant and asphalt have no cracks, voids or splits. The inspection, and any required maintenance, should be performed by a qualified and properly insured roofing contractor.

Condition #5: Kick Out Flashing Is Not Installed between the Wall and the Roof above the Gutter

Potentially Impacting:

- Watertightness of roof

Performance Guideline

If the roof meets the criteria described in the Comments above, kick out flashing should be installed as part of the roof assembly.

Comments: For composition *shingle* roofs, the code requires that kick out flashing be installed between the wall and the roof above the *gutter*.

Builder Responsibility: The Builder should install kick out flashing to conform to the Performance Guideline.

Homeowner Responsibility: None.

Condition #6: Crickets Are Missing

Potentially Impacting:

- Watertightness of roof

Performance Guideline

If the component meets the criteria described in the Comments above, a cricket should be installed. The cricket should have a slope at least two times the slope of the adjacent roof.

Comments: Where the plane of the roof is interrupted by another non-roofing component such as a wall or chimney and the flow of water is perpendicular to that component, a *cricket* should be installed if the component is wider than 30 inches. Crickets can be made from roofing materials or galvanized sheet metal or copper sheeting.

Builder Responsibility: If a cricket is missing, the Builder should perform a retrofit installation. Skylights with installation instructions from the manufacturer that do not require crickets are exempt.

Homeowner Responsibility: ***Maintenance Alert!*** The Homeowner should keep the roof *valleys* and the surrounding area free from leaves and other debris. This also applies to smaller areas where there is no cricket and sheet metal *flashing* is used.

Eaves

General Subject Information: The *eave* is a part of the roof that generally hangs out past the exterior walls. *Gutters* are often applied directly to the *fascia* board of the eaves. Eaves help protect the Home by preventing rain from coming directly down the face of the walls. Eaves also reduce direct sunlight into the residence that can damage interior finishes and furnishings. Ventilated eaves are generally not the cause of damage to interior finishes or furnishings. However, if there is water blockage (clogged gutters or valleys) and/or ice build-up (ice dams), there is the potential for water to be *drawn* back up the roof and migrate under the felt (*underlayment*) and cause interior damage. In areas where the average January temperature is 30 degrees or less, it is recommended that that an impervious *membrane* be installed under the roofing underlayment for 1 foot beyond the point where the Home wall and the roof intersect. If water backs up from melting ice dams, it will not be able to penetrate the impervious membrane. Another method to eliminate ice dams is to install electric heater cables beginning at the eaves and running about two feet up on the roof.

Condition #1: Leaks or Stains Appear at the Underside of the Eaves

Potentially Impacting:

- Watertightness
- Appearance
- Roof performance and structural integrity

Performance Guideline

*All roof systems should be installed in a watertight fashion and should not allow water intrusion under normal inclement weather conditions; "normal" meaning what is typical for that particular geographic region. (Refer to expanded definition of "**Weather—Normal and Extreme**", page 4.)*

Comments: Roof systems are designed for particular regions or geographic areas. For example, mountainous regions or valleys that have high and/or extreme wind conditions will require materials and fastening methods that are different than areas that typically have low or no wind conditions.

Builder Responsibility: If the roof *eave* leaks during normal regional weather and the leaks are a result of improper installation, the Builder should perform repairs to conform to the Performance Guideline.

Homeowner Responsibility: ***Maintenance Alert!*** The Homeowner is responsible for providing proper maintenance, including keeping *gutters* free from debris, clearing ice dams that may develop, and keeping all *flashing* from debris buildup.

Condition #2: Roof Sags or Bows at Eaves and Fascia

Potentially Impacting:

- Appearance
- Watertightness
- Interior finishes

Performance Guideline

Deviation from flatness (a horizontal line) at eaves or fascia board should be no greater than ½ inch in any 8 feet of length.

Comments: To understand what flatness is, imagine a perfectly straight line between two points. If the measurement is equal to or greater than ½ inch above or below that line, then it does not conform to the Performance Guideline. (Refer to Preface: "**How to Measure for Performance Guidelines**" if needed, page 12.)

Builder Responsibility: The Builder should correct the out of tolerance condition to conform to the Performance Guideline.

Homeowner Responsibility: ***Maintenance Alert!*** The Homeowner should maintain the roof eaves by providing adequate maintenance, for example painting, *caulking* and removal of any debris that might constrict the flow of water. This includes cleaning the *gutters* annually.

Chapter Five

EXTERIOR
COMPONENTS

includes:

Walkways and Driveways

Garage Doors

Decks and Patios

Windows and Patio Doors

French Doors and Other Exterior Doors

Chimneys and Flues

Gutters and Downspouts

Skylights

Paint and Stain

Brick and Masonry

References for this chapter:

- *Prescriptive Residential Wood Deck Construction Guide 2010,* American Forest and Paper Association, Inc.
- *Code Check Building 3rd ed.*, Taunton Press
- *International Building Code 2012,* International Code Council
- *International Residential Code 2012,* International Code Council
- *Handbook of Construction Tolerances*, by David Kent Ballast
- *Residential Construction Performance Guidelines*, NAHB 2011 ed.
- *South Carolina Residential Construction Standards 1997,* Residential Builders Commission of the South Carolina Department of Labor
- *California Building Code 2013*, California Building Standards Commission
- *Residential & Light Commercial Construction Standards*, by Don Reynolds
- *Workmanship Standards for Licensed Contractors 2009,* Arizona Registrar of Contractors
- *Homeowner Handbook 2003,* Greater Atlanta Home Builders Association
- *Technical Notes on Brick Construction,* Brick Industry Association
- *New Home Warranty Program 2010*, State of New Jersey Department of Community Affairs
- *NASCLA Residential Construction Standards 2009,* National Association of State Contracting Licensing Agencies

A comprehensive list of references by author and publisher is found in the Bibliography Section.

Chapter Five

Exterior Components

Walkways and Driveways

General Subject Information: When it comes to *concrete* there is one fact that all Homeowners, Builders, and tradespersons must realize: concrete will crack. Concrete *walkways* and *driveways* are constructed with *control joints* that create a weakened plane or thinner section of concrete. The purpose of control joints is to control and contain the cracking to specific areas, for example, the thinner section. Cracks in control joints are a normal occurrence and are considered acceptable. The degree to which concrete cracks or the deviation in vertical *displacement* is the determining criteria as to whether or not the cracking is unacceptable or within industry standards. There are many reasons that concrete products crack and most are not related to any structural problems. Similarly, driveways that are paved with asphaltic concrete will also crack.

Condition #1: Concrete Driveway Is Cracked

Potentially Impacting:

- Appearance
- Safety issues related to tripping hazard
- Structural integrity of the *driveway*

Performance Guideline

Any crack that exceeds ¼ inch in width or exceeds ¼ inch in vertical displacement is considered unacceptable. Minor cracking is normal. A crack that occurs along a joint that is cut into the driveway when it was poured is considered acceptable, provided the crack does not exceed ¾ inch in width. Further, this Guideline includes spacing control joints in the wet concrete at industry recommended intervals based upon the thickness of the slab. A nominal 4 inch thick slab should have control joints spaced 12 feet apart or less.

Comments: When trees are planted in the vicinity of any concrete work, there is the potential for the root system to eventually undermine the concrete and cause the concrete to crack, heave and/or settle. This holds true for *foundations* as well. If the driveway is used for large RV storage, it may crack due to the weight of the RV. RVs should be stored on a separate concrete *pad* that is reinforced with steel and is at least 6 inches thick. Moving vans should be parked on the street. Concrete trucks used by after-market contractors for pools and *patios* should be parked on the street, and their contents should be pumped to the desired location.

Builder Responsibility: If concrete cracking exceeds the Performance Guideline and is not a result of Homeowner misuse or negligence (this includes if the Homeowner overwaters the surrounding area causing the soil to expand), the Builder should perform repairs to conform to the Guideline. The Builder is also responsible for the replacement of landscape material damaged as a result of the repairs.

Homeowner Responsibility: ***Maintenance Alert!*** The Homeowner should maintain cracks that occur at control joints. This maintenance consists of filling the crack with a suitable concrete *caulk*. The Homeowner should also maintain the area around the driveway in a way that will not allow soils to be washed away from beneath the driveway. Tree roots are a primary cause for concrete to heave and/or crack in landscaped areas. When placing trees in the vicinity of any concrete product, it is important for the Homeowner to consider the potential growth of the root system. For example, palm trees have very small root balls, while the root system of a willow is extensive and will cause significant heaving of drives and walks. The Homeowner should seek the advice of a qualified landscape architect or contractor and install a root barrier system in these instances.

Condition #2: Walkway Is Cracked

Potentially Impacting:

- Appearance
- Safety issues related to tripping hazard
- Structural integrity of the sidewalk

Performance Guideline

Any crack that exceeds ¼ inch in width or exceeds ¼ inch in vertical displacement is unacceptable. Cracking that occurs at a control joint is acceptable unless the crack exceeds 1 inch in width and ¼ inch in vertical displacement. Minor cracking is considered normal.

Comments: Generally speaking, the further away from the foundation, the less compaction there is within the soils. *Concrete* sidewalks are much more susceptible to heaving or subsiding than a structural foundation. Not only is the soil potentially not as well compacted, but there may be a flow of irrigation water within the landscape. If the soils are expansive, water will cause the soils to expand; when the soils dry out they will contract. Both expansion and contraction apply an excessive amount of stress upon concrete.

Builder Responsibility: If concrete cracking exceeds the Guideline and the cracking is not a result of Homeowner negligence, the Builder should perform repairs to conform to the Performance Guideline. The Builder is also responsible for replacing landscape material damaged as a result of the repairs. The Builder is not responsible for repairs and replacing landscaping due to the Homeowner planting trees too close to sidewalks and *driveways*.

Homeowner Responsibility: ***Maintenance Alert!*** The Homeowner should maintain cracks that occur at control joints. The Homeowner should also maintain the area around the sidewalks in a way that will not allow soils to be washed away from beneath them. Tree roots generally pose the biggest threat to concrete sidewalks. When placing trees in the vicinity of any concrete product, the Homeowner should consider the potential for growth of the root system.

THIS TREE WAS PLANTED TOO CLOSE TO THE SIDEWALK. ITS ROOTS PUSHED UP THE CONCRETE.

Condition #3: Water Ponds on Sidewalk

Potentially Impacting:

- Safety issues related to slipping hazard

Performance Guideline

Any standing or ponding water that exceeds 3/8 inch in depth in a circle more than 1 foot in diameter is considered unacceptable. All water should drain off or evaporate within 24 hours of cessation of rain.

Comments: All sidewalks or any *concrete* subject to the outside elements should *slope* a minimum of ¼ inch vertically for every 1 foot horizontally. In other words, if the concrete sidewalk is 3 feet across, the sidewalk should slope in one direction ¾ inch from level and slope away from the foundation.

Builder Responsibility: The Builder should perform repairs necessary to conform to the Guideline provided the unacceptable condition was not caused by Homeowner actions. The Builder should replace landscape materials damaged as a result of the repairs.

Homeowner Responsibility: ***Maintenance Alert!*** The Homeowner should not permit irrigation to undermine the sidewalks. Erosion under the sidewalk will weaken it. Sidewalks need to have a very solid foundation in order to prevent unacceptable cracking or damage.

Condition #4: Concrete Driveway that Is Next to the Garage Is Higher than the Garage Slab

Potentially Impacting:

- Watertightness of garage
- Safety issues related to tripping hazard

Performance Guideline

A concrete driveway should never be higher than the interior portion of the adjacent garage slab. A deviation in two adjoining sections of concrete should not be greater than ½ inch between the two adjoining surfaces.

Comments: The driveway portion of the concrete should not exceed the height of the garage slab. This can cause a buildup of water at the *garage door* entry and may present a tripping hazard. A good practice is to pour the driveway slab up to ½ inch lower than the garage slab. This allows for future movement of the driveway slab. Garage floors typically have a 3% *slope* from front to back to allow water to drain.

Builder Responsibility: The Builder should perform repairs necessary to conform to the Guideline unless the condition results from Homeowner misuse or negligence.

Homeowner Responsibility: None provided that the Homeowner has done nothing to alter the lot drainage, which could cause the driveway to heave above the garage slab.

Condition #5: Driveway Approach Is Too Steep Causing Vehicles to Scrape or to Bottom Out

Potentially Impacting:
- Vehicle integrity and appearance
- Appearance of the *driveway* approach

Performance Guideline

The driveway approach should meet the standards of the local municipality or state at the time of construction.

Comments: During design and engineering of the site, the streets and lots are calculated to provide positive water drainage away from streets and residences. These designs are fairly standard and they take into consideration wheelbase and clearance of most vehicles. However, vehicles with exceptionally long wheelbases or vehicles that have been lowered may scrape or bottom out.

Builder Responsibility: If the driveway approach does not meet the local municipal standard, the Builder should perform repairs necessary to conform to the Performance Guideline. The Builder is not responsible for making the driveway approaches suitable for all vehicles.

Homeowner Responsibility: None.

Condition #6: Concrete Driveway Is Spalling, Scaling, or Chipping

Potentially Impacting:
- *Driveway* structural integrity
- Appearance

Performance Guideline

The surface of the concrete should not disintegrate to the point that the aggregate is showing in more than 10% of the driveway surface area.

Comments: The Builder is not responsible if the Homeowner spills chemicals, oils, salts, etc. on concrete that can cause premature breakdown. This includes the use of rock salt to remove snow and ice. If the soils contain minerals that cause concrete degradation over time, the Builder is not responsible. In geographic areas with continuous freeze and thaw conditions, concrete *spalling* can be expected to occur.

Builder Responsibility: The Builder should perform repairs to conform to the Performance Guideline unless the condition results from Homeowner misuse, negligence, or uncontrollable acts of nature.

Homeowner Responsibility: The Homeowner should not spill acidic products or create excessive landscape moisture that may cause damage to the concrete surface. If the Homeowner uses rock salt as an ice-removing agent, the Homeowner assumes the risk of damage to the concrete and surrounding landscape.

Condition #7: Concrete Stoop Is Pulling Away From the Foundation

Potentially Impacting:
- Appearance
- Safety issues related to tripping hazard

Performance Guideline

Concrete stoops that join to the foundation should not separate from the foundation by more than ½ inch.

Comments: When the foundation of the Home and steps/stoops are poured at separate times, there is a possibility that they will move at different rates. This may result in minor heaving, settling and/or separation. The above Performance Guideline also applies in situations where *expansion joints* separate concrete.

Builder Responsibility: If the steps or stoops are separated from ½ inch to 1 inch, the Builder may fill the separation or replace the stoop. The Builder should replace stoops that are separated by gaps in excess of 1 inch.

Homeowner Responsibility: The Homeowner is responsible for maintaining separations up to ½ inch. Concrete *caulk* may be used to fill the gap.

Condition #8: Driveway or Walkway Is Not a Uniform Color

Refer to the "**Decks and Patios**" section of this chapter, Condition #8, page 101.

Garage Doors

Condition #1: Garage Door Leaks Water/Snow at Top, Jambs, or Threshold

Potentially Impacting:
- Contents of garage
- Intended use of garage

Performance Guideline

Garage doors should be installed according to the recommendations of the manufacturer. Some water or snow can be expected to enter around the door under high wind conditions. This is acceptable. The garage slab should slope toward the door at 3 inches per 20 feet. The driveway surface at the garage door should be sloped to inhibit the entrance of water. There should also be a vertical drop of up to ½ inch between the driveway slab and the garage slab to act as a weather break. If the garage is located at the bottom of a down sloped driveway with more than a 2% slope, the 2 feet of driveway closest to the garage slab should be sloped away from the garage slab at the rate of ¼ inch per foot. A drain that runs parallel to the garage door(s) is also acceptable.

Builder Responsibility: The Builder should make adjustments to conform to the Performance Guideline. The Builder should adjust the door in the event that excessive water enters at the *jambs* and head. Garage door *weather stripping* can be an effective way to conform to the Performance Guideline.

Homeowner Responsibility: *Maintenance Alert!* The Homeowner is responsible for adequate maintenance and protection of the garage door including damage to the door, frame, and/or guides. Proper lubrication of the door tracks and operating mechanism is discussed in the "**Homeowner Maintenance Summary, Garage Doors**", page 256. If a slot drain has been installed in the driveway in front of the garage, it is subject to clogging. The Homeowner should clean the drain more frequently than a conventional drain.

Condition #2: Garage Door Fails to Operate Properly or Gets Jammed

Potentially Impacting:

- Intended use of *door*

Performance Guideline

Barring damage caused by Homeowner misuse, garage doors should operate smoothly and completely as intended by the manufacturer.

Builder Responsibility: Unless the Homeowner has been negligent or abusive in the use of garage doors, the Builder should make adjustments to malfunctioning doors in accordance with the manufacturer's specifications.

Homeowner Responsibility: The Homeowner should maintain the garage doors in accordance with the manufacturer's recommendations and avoid abusive or negligent use of doors that could result in damage. One piece garage doors may sag with age. It is the Homeowner's responsibility to keep the metal rods that span the top and bottom of the door in tight condition and proper alignment.

Condition #3: Garage Door Does Not Fit at Bottom or Sides

Potentially Impacting:

- Intrusion of precipitation, heat and cold air

Performance Guideline

Assuming that the garage door is weather stripped, it should fit flush with the garage slab and tight on all sides.

Builder Responsibility: The Builder should make adjustments to the *weather stripping*. This includes making adjustments if the frame (rough opening) is out of square. If the garage door has been hit or damaged in any way by the Homeowner, the Builder has no responsibility.

Homeowner Responsibility: None.

Condition #4: Garage Door Has Shrunk and Shows Unpainted Wood around the Edges

Potentially Impacting:

- Appearance

Performance Guideline

Depending upon climatic conditions, it is normal for wooden panels to shrink. This is not a defective condition.

Builder Responsibility: None.

Homeowner Responsibility: If the condition is objectionable, the Homeowner should paint the panels as part of routine maintenance.

Condition #5: Garage Door Opens "Mysteriously"

Potentially Impacting:

- Security of garage, Home, and contents

Performance Guideline

Garage door openers should operate only on their own assigned frequencies. Random external signals should not cause the door to open or close.

Comments: The condition of mysterious opening and closing of garage doors sometimes occurs when the door is equipped with an automatic opener. The transmitter may share a radio frequency with other devices, such as another garage transmitter in the neighborhood or an airplane flying overhead. Signals from these transmitters activate the automatic door opener. Most openers have programmable code switches that can be changed if the above condition occurs. Newer openers have rolling codes that change automatically and cannot be readily copied.

Builder Responsibility: If the Homeowner reports a problem of random openings or closings of the automatic door opener, the Builder should instruct the Homeowner on the procedure to change the opener code or to program the transmitter to the receiver.

Homeowner Responsibility: The Homeowner should read the instruction manual furnished with the automatic door opener.

Decks and Patios

General Subject Information: Decks and *patios* are accessory structures used to enhance the architecture and livability of the Home. Most decks and patios are not installed by the Builder, except as part of a planned community such as a *condominium* or patio Home project. Because decks are exposed continually to weather, they require more maintenance and have a shorter *useful life* than other exterior components. Lumber used for decking that is exposed to the weather should be rot resistant such as cedar, redwood and *pressure treated* fir, or preferably, a composite material that will need minimal maintenance in order to avoid premature aging and deterioration. Apart from original construction, the useful life of a deck and patio will depend upon the degree of Homeowner maintenance, the annual precipitation in the area, local weather conditions, and which direction the deck or patio faces.

Condition #1: Water Ponds on Decks and Patios

Potentially Impacting:

- *Useful life* of deck
- Safety issues related to slipping hazard

Performance Guideline

There should be no more than 3/8 inch of water standing in a ponded area 24 hours after cessation of rain (assuming that deck drains, if installed, are maintained in a free flowing condition by the Homeowner).

Comments: Decks and *patios* should be constructed with a minimum *slope* of ¼ inch of drop for every one foot of length away from the Home. That is to say, the deck or patio should be 1 inch lower 4 feet away from the Home than at the edge of the Home. Some enclosed decks that are not designed to drain over the outer edge have drains located in the deck surface. Decks constructed in this manner should also have *overflow drains*. The deck surface should be sloped to these drains so that the deck drains freely within 24 hours after cessation of rain. A spaced board surface deck (including composite boards made to look like wood) should drain directly through the deck to the ground below.

Builder Responsibility: If the condition is a result of original construction, the Builder should repair the surface of the deck or patio to create the proper slope, for example ¼ inch to the foot, so that the deck surface conforms to the Performance Guideline. This Guideline does not apply to spaced board decks.

Homeowner Responsibility: ***Maintenance Alert!*** The Homeowner should keep decks clean and free of dirt and debris so that they will not become slippery or clog the deck drains during storms. If deck drains are installed, the Homeowner should flush the drains with a garden hose after the fall leaf drop and in the spring season. Overflow drains should be inspected to ensure that they are not clogged with leaves or other debris. Potted plants should not be placed directly on the deck surface. They should be placed on stands or spacers to allow air to circulate underneath. The Homeowner should not apply snow melting chemicals to wood or composite decks.

DEBRIS SHOULD COME OUT
THE OTHER END OF THE PIPE.

FLUSH YARD AND DRIVEWAY DRAINS ANNUALLY

Condition #2: Deck Posts, Beams, or Joists Are Rotting

Potentially Impacting:

- Structural integrity
- Appearance
- *Useful life* of deck

Performance Guideline

Exposed deck structural members such as posts, beams, and joists should be pressure treated wood or code-approved wood that is naturally resistant to decay.

Builder Responsibility: The Builder should construct deck structural members using pressure treated lumber or code approved wood that is naturally resistant to decay. If pressure treated lumber is cut on-site, the cut ends should be treated with an approved wood preservative. Treated lumber, fir, cedar, redwood, and some decay resistant tropical hardwoods such as "Panlope" may be used as deck top boards. Man-made composite material may be used as top boards also.

Homeowner Responsibility: ***Maintenance Alert!*** The Homeowner should perform an annual inspection of the deck and re-nail loose boards and raised nails or other fasteners. Top boards should be recoated with a good quality deck sealer every one or two years, depending upon the amount of exposure. The underside of the deck should be kept free of debris and storage materials so air can circulate underneath. The bottom of posts should be maintained 6 inches away from the soil. Landscape shrubs should not be allowed to grow around posts as moisture may rot the posts.

Condition #3: Deck Is Not Flashed at Home/Deck Connection

Potentially Impacting:

- Structural integrity of the Home
- Structural safety of the deck

Performance Guideline

Decks attached to a Home or other habitable structure should be flashed with an approved flashing material between the Home and deck connection. Flashing should cover the top of the ledger completely and be sloped away from the Home to prevent water from running between the back of the ledger and the exterior surface of the Home. Building paper is not an acceptable flashing material.

Builder Responsibility: The Builder should install deck ledgers with an approved flashing material that runs behind the water-resistant *membrane*, behind the exterior surface of the Home, and over the top edge of the ledger.

Homeowner Responsibility: None.

Condition #4: Deck Ledger Is Not Connected to the Framing Members of the Home

Potentially Impacting:

- Structural integrity of the deck
- Safety issues related to deck collapse

Performance Guideline

All deck ledgers should be connected to the frame members (of nominal 2 inch thickness) of the Home by using lag screws or through-bolts. The size of the screws or bolts and the spacing is found in the literature of manufacturers who make deck connection hardware. Nailing or screwing the ledger to the siding or stucco is not acceptable. This condition will inevitably result in the deck pulling away from the Home.

Builder Responsibility: The Builder should construct the deck so the ledger is properly lag screwed or through-bolted to the frame of the Home.

Homeowner Responsibility: None, but if a separation occurs between the ledger and the Home, the Homeowner should stop using the deck until repairs are made.

Condition #5: Nail Heads or Screws Protrude Above the Surface of the Deck Boards

Potentially Impacting:

- Appearance
- Safety issues related to tripping hazard

Performance Guideline

At the time of the walkthrough, nail heads, screws, or other fasteners that protrude above the deck board surface by more than 1/16 inch are considered unacceptable.

Builder Responsibility: The Builder should re-nail or screw fasteners to conform to the Performance Guideline.

Homeowner Responsibility: After the walkthrough, the Homeowner is responsible for re-nailing or tightening screws of deck boards. Deck boards shrink as they dry out and they also move up and down with seasonal temperature changes. ***Maintenance Alert!*** If the deck has wooden railings, the Homeowner should tighten the rail *post* bolts every six months during the first two years of occupancy as a safety precaution.

Condition #6: Deck Boards Are Split, Bowed, Warped, or Cupped (Applies to Wood and Composite Decks)

Potentially Impacting:

- Appearance
- Reduced *useful life* of the deck

Performance Guideline

At the time of installation and during any warranty period that may be offered, splits shall not exceed 1/8 inch; warps or bows shall not exceed 3/8 inch in 8 feet of length; cups shall not exceed ¼ inch in 5 ½ inches of width.

Builder Responsibility: The Builder should replace defective material to conform to the Guideline.

Homeowner Responsibility: The Homeowner should not place heavy objects on the deck. Fasteners should be tightened annually, and if the deck is made of wood, stain or sealer applied as needed (usually annually). The Homeowner should not set potted plants directly on a wood deck surface. Ceramic spacers should be used to allow air to flow underneath the pot.

Condition #7: Concrete Patio Surface Is Cracked and Separated

Potentially Impacting:

- Appearance
- Life of *patio* surface materials
- Safety issues related to tripping hazard

Performance Guideline

*Patios and decks should be constructed on soils and sub-surfaces that are properly drained and compacted sufficiently to prevent excessive movement. Decks and patios should be constructed to slope away from the Home with a slope of ¼ inch to the foot. Cracks in hard surfaces (such as concrete) exceeding ¼ inch in width, or ¼ inch in vertical displacement, are unacceptable. Modular pavers are subject to individual differential settlement, but should not have surfaces that are vertically offset by more than ¼ inch from one paver to the adjoining one (Refer to the "**Walkways and Driveways**" section of this chapter, Condition #1, page 95.)*

Builder Responsibility: The Builder should construct patios to conform to the Performance Guideline. If modular pavers are used, the Builder should conform to the manufacturer's installation recommendations.

Homeowner Responsibility: The Homeowner should maintain all drainage courses and catch basins so they are free of dirt, leaves and other debris.

Condition #8: Finished Concrete Surface Has Blotchy/Mottled Color

Potentially Impacting:

- Appearance

Performance Guideline

Assuming that each batch of concrete has been prepared with the same amount of color additive, non-uniform surface color on concrete is considered acceptable.

Comments: Concrete, whether natural in color or colored by adding agents to the mix, is not likely to dry (*cure*) in a uniform manner. Many factors influence the surface appearance of concrete that is less than a year old. Factors include the amount of moisture in the underlying soil and the humidity during the first 30 days after the installation. The more moisture in the soil and air, the greater the chances for non-uniform surface color. Over time (usually within two years) the non-uniform color is likely to gradually become uniform as the surface of the concrete reacts to the air.

Builder Responsibility: None.

Homeowner Responsibility: None.

Windows and Patio Doors

General Subject Information: Windows come in many different types such as side vent, single hung, double hung, and fixed. Patio doors are, for industry purposes, considered a large window. Both window and patio door frames can be made of metal (usually aluminum), wood, plastic (PVC), fiberglass, or a combination of these materials. The installation methods and operation of windows and patio doors are similar. It is not the purpose of this section to provide extensive information on the various types of windows and patio doors, but simply to cover several conditions that may occur with windows and patio doors.

Condition #1: Glass Is Scratched or Broken

Potentially Impacting:

- Visibility
- Appearance
- Occupant comfort

Performance Guideline

At the time of the walkthrough, glass that is visibly scratched from a distance of 11 feet under daylight conditions (but not direct sunlight) is unacceptable. Damage to glass after the Homeowner takes delivery of the Home is not the Builder's responsibility. The same Performance Guideline applies to damaged screens.

Builder Responsibility: The Builder should replace broken or scratched glass and any damaged screens if noted at walkthrough.

Homeowner Responsibility: The Homeowner should inspect all windows and patio doors prior to delivery of the Home, especially on Homes that have a stucco exterior finish. Sand from the stucco may find its way onto the glass and window washers can accidentally make small scratches in the glass when they are trying to clean it. Never use an abrasive cleaner on glass.

Condition #2: Glass Has Imperfections

Potentially Impacting:

- Appearance
- Visibility

Performance Guideline

Imperfections that are part of the manufacturing process (as opposed to scratches), such as waviness and "cat's eye", which are visible from a distance of 6 feet under normal lighting conditions, are considered unacceptable.

Builder Responsibility: The Builder should replace glass that does not conform to the Performance Guideline.

Homeowner Responsibility: None.

Condition #3: Windows and Patio Doors Are Difficult to Open and Close

Potentially Impacting:

- Occupant comfort

Performance Guideline

All windows and patio doors should open and close freely ("freely" is defined as without having to exert undue pressure or force by an adult of average strength). All latches and locks should operate in a similar manner.

Builder Responsibility: The Builder should adjust and/or otherwise correct malfunctioning mechanisms to conform to the Performance Guideline. The Builder is responsible for window and patio door problems caused by foundation or *frame* problems. The Builder is not responsible for damage caused by Homeowner misuse or lack of proper maintenance.

Homeowner Responsibility: ***Maintenance Alert!*** Windows and patio doors installed in Homes today require little maintenance. Doors and windows have a tendency to "stick" during the winter months because the wood frame of the Home takes on moisture, thereby expanding slightly; this is acceptable. The Homeowner should routinely lubricate the rollers and slides with an approved window lubricant (available at any hardware store) and adjust the rollers on the patio doors. In addition, the Homeowner should routinely brush and vacuum the patio door tracks and window tracks.

Condition #4: Window Is Fogged between Panes of Glass

Potentially Impacting:

- Visibility
- *Insulation* value

Performance Guideline

Dual glazed or triple glazed window and patio door seals should not rupture during the manufacturer's warranty period, provided there is no misuse by the Homeowner.

Comments: Most windows and patio doors installed in new or remodeled Homes are *dual pane* glass consisting of two panes of glass made into a "sandwich" with a dead air space in the middle. In colder climates or areas where sound transmission is a factor, such as near an airport or railroad, three panes of glass are often used. The glass sandwich is sealed so that air cannot enter or leave the space. This dead air space provides an insulating and noise reduction quality that windows with single pane glass do not have. However, when the seal is broken, moisture enters between the panes and the window becomes foggy. Seal materials have greatly improved in recent years, allowing manufacturers to extend their warranties. The warranty on dual glazed or triple glazed windows is likely to be a manufacturer's warranty.

Builder Responsibility: Within the warranty period, the Builder should assist the Homeowner in dealing with the manufacturer to replace windows and patio doors whose seals have failed. This excludes failures caused by Homeowner negligence or misuse (see below).

WEATHER STRIPPING SAVES MONEY ON UTILITY BILLS

Homeowner Responsibility: None, however, the Homeowner may unknowingly cause window seal failure by tinting the inside pane. This causes excessive heat buildup between the panes of glass and the seals are likely to rupture. Window damage caused by tinting is not the responsibility of the Builder. (Refer to Preface: "**Ten Most Common Mistakes Made by New Homeowners**", page 20.)

Green Tip! When daylight is visible at the edges of windows and the bottom of *doors*, it is time to replace the *weather stripping*.

Condition #5: Window Grids Disintegrate

Potentially Impacting:

- Appearance

Performance Guideline

Window grids should not disintegrate or drop down inside the panes.

Comments: *Dual pane* windows are often manufactured with a grid of plastic or aluminum inside the panes to give an impression of individual panes of glass. It is unacceptable if these grids fail because they were not properly secured or because of disintegration from ultraviolet rays.

Builder Responsibility: The Builder should replace windows whose grids have failed. Exception: if the Homeowner has tinted the inside of the windows or otherwise caused the condition, the Builder is not responsible for failed grids.

Homeowner Responsibility: None. However, the Homeowner should not tint the inside pane of dual or triple pane windows.

Condition #6: Patio Door Leaks at Sill (Bottom), Window Leaks at Head (Top) or Sill (Bottom)

Potentially Impacting:
- Occupant comfort
- Structural integrity

Performance Guideline

*Windows should not leak at any point regardless of the location of the leak. (See extreme weather exception at **Condition #7** below.)*

Comments: A window or patio door that leaks should not be allowed to go unrepaired. A window that leaks at the top may not be flashed properly at the head or an opening higher up on the wall (such as an attic vent) that is not properly flashed. A window that leaks at the bottom may be leaking because 1) the sides and sill are not properly flashed, 2) the lower corners of the window frame itself are not properly sealed, or 3) the weep holes are plugged. A patio door that leaks at the bottom may be leaking because of improper sill flashing or because the outside patio or deck is too high.

FIRST, CLEAN JOINT...
THEN APPLY CAULKING
INSPECT AND CAULK
TRIM ANNUALLY

Builder Responsibility: The Builder should diagnose the cause of the leak. If the condition is a result of improper construction, the Builder should perform repairs.

Homeowner Responsibility: *Maintenance Alert!* The Homeowner should annually inspect and clean debris from all windows and patio door weep holes and caulk all outside corners of the sill. This maintenance is especially important in areas that have trees with small leaves and areas that experience dust storms.

Condition #7: Windows Leak When the Wind Blows Hard

Potentially Impacting:
- Occupant comfort and health
- Interior damage

Performance Guideline

The Performance Guideline for rain and wind intrusion is use residential windows and doors that are labeled with the appropriate American Architectural Manufacturer's Association (AAMA) "R"-rating for the geographical area of the Home. For example, an oceanfront Home should usually have windows and doors with a higher "R" rating than a Home in a wooded valley.

Comments: Wind-driven rain can sometimes penetrate window weather seals and joints. Wind-driven rain can also blow back through the *weep holes* into the interior of the Home. Windows should be selected in accordance with the AAMA "R"-ratings that match window systems with weather conditions found in the geographic location of the Home. Exception: even a properly selected window may leak if exposed to extreme wind or rain. During a storm it is not unusual to find that the *sill* track of the window is filled with water; this condition is acceptable. At the conclusion of the inclement weather (wind and rain), the water will drain out of the track through the weep holes. Weather extremes are defined on page 4.

Builder Responsibility: The Builder should install windows and *patio doors* that meet the appropriate AAMA standards for the geographic area of the Home. If this standard is met, the intrusion of wind-driven rain during extreme weather conditions is acceptable.

Homeowner Responsibility: In order to mitigate the intrusion of water at the sills the Homeowner should keep the sills free of debris and the weep holes open.

Condition #8: Screens Are Damaged or Missing

Potentially Impacting:

- Home ventilation

Performance Guideline

All window and door screens shall be in place in an undamaged condition at the time of the walkthrough. After the walkthrough, missing or damaged screens become the Homeowner's responsibility.

Builder Responsibility: The Builder should install all window and door screens in an undamaged condition prior to the walkthrough.

Homeowner Responsibility: None.

French Doors and Other Exterior Doors

General Subject Information: *French doors* have become a popular *door* style in homes today. Other *exterior doors* include the front door, rear door and the garage pedestrian door. Sliding *patio doors*, actually considered a specialty window, are covered in the "**Windows and Patio Doors**" section of this chapter, page 106. Generally, if doors open, or swing, into the Home, they offer a better degree of weather protection. Many manufacturers will not warrant their doors if they are installed with an outward swing.

Condition #1: Water Enters Walls and Interiors through the Head (Top), Jambs (Sides) and Threshold (Sill)

Potentially Impacting:

- Wall components
- Interior finishes
- Structural integrity

Performance Guideline

Water entering through the top, sides, bottom, or under the door is considered unacceptable unless the water is a result of excessive wind-driven rain. Pedestrian doors in garages are not covered by this Guideline and are often installed without a threshold.

Comments: Proper *flashing* of head, jambs and *sills* of doors is essential in preventing water intrusion. All flashing should be installed in the proper sequence, "fish-scale" style with each successive layer partially overlapping the one below it, and integrated with the Home wrap, *building paper*, or *rain screen* so that water is directed to exterior surfaces. Manufacturers of *exterior doors* generally provide specific installation and maintenance recommendations. These recommendations should be adhered to strictly.

Builder Responsibility: The Builder should repair any exterior door that leaks as a result of improper original installation.

Homeowner Responsibility: ***Maintenance Alert!*** The Homeowner should keep threshold weeps and other drainage paths clean and free of obstructions and debris. If exterior door *trim* and joints between the doorframe and the exterior wall surface are *caulked*, inspect caulking annually and re-caulk (including the threshold) as necessary to maintain a weather-tight seal. Keep doors closed during wet weather. Depending upon geographic location and exposure, the *weather stripping* at the doors will need to be replaced every three to five years. Many doors have adjustable weather stripping at the bottom. If daylight is visible while looking outside under the door bottom, adjust the weather stripping by loosening the four or five screws on the bottom weather strip metal bar, and gently push the bar down so the strip under the door meets the threshold. Retighten the screws.

Condition #2: Doors Are Warped, Out-of-Level, Hung Crooked or Not Plumb

Potentially Impacting:

- *Door* performance
- Weather tightness

Performance Guideline

The vertical and horizontal planes of the door should not vary from a true plane by more than ¼ inch. Doors should not be installed out of true level and plumb by more than 1/8 inch. The individual leaves of a paired set of doors should be installed in alignment with each other. Doors should remain in any position in which they are placed without closing or opening by themselves. If doors move on their own, it is an indication that they are out of plumb. All exterior doors should be hung so the distance between the door and any part of the doorjamb is not more than 3/16 inch.

Comments: Initial door installations should be made in secure, plumb, level and square rough openings of the size specified by the manufacturer. Doors should be set in place within the Performance Guideline specified above. Any *interior door* manufactured in wood should be painted with a prime coat and a *finish coat*. Any exterior door manufactured in wood should be painted with a prime coat plus two finish coats. All six sides of a door should be painted promptly after installation to prevent moisture from entering the wood fibers. This will particularly affect the door head, where end *grain* may be exposed. Sufficient clearance should be left at the door head to prevent any *header* deflection from transferring a load to the doorframe that may cause the door(s) to bind. The door frame jambs should be securely attached to the rough frame in order to prevent door sag. With some types of doors it is advisable to attach hinges using long hinge screws that will penetrate rough jambs by at least 1¼ inch. Doors that are significantly out-of-plumb will swing open (or closed) by themselves. This is an annoyance and is not acceptable workmanship. External forces, such as settlement, can also cause out-of-level and out-of-plumb conditions described above. Look for cracks in *drywall* radiating outward from the upper corners of door openings (usually at approximately 45 degrees). This is a fairly reliable indicator of movement in the structural *frame* of the Home, but is not necessarily unacceptable. The acceptability is governed by the width and length of the drywall or *plaster* crack (Refer to "**Chapter Six—Interior Components, Plaster and Drywall**", page 158.)

Builder Responsibility: The Builder should install doors to conform to the Performance Guideline and the door manufacturer's installation requirements. The Builder should ensure that door components subject to moisture exposure are completely and effectively protected as soon as possible after the initial installation. The Builder is responsible for correcting any material, workmanship or inadequate design that results in improper door performance.

Homeowner Responsibility: The Homeowner should not place any load on door leaves (such as hanging heavy clothing or allowing children to swing on the doors), as they are not designed for this purpose and may sag over time. Keep door leaves and frames in good condition by repainting and re-*caulking* on a periodic basis. Adhere to the manufacturer's recommendations. Sometimes it is necessary to correct the fit of wood doors either because of minor swelling or because surrounding finishes were replaced with materials of different thickness (for example, floor coverings). Any such corrections should be done professionally and any bare wood should be immediately and completely sealed. If the bottom of a door is cut due to a change in flooring material, the fresh cut should be sealed.

Condition #3: Exterior Hardware Is Corroded or Stained

Potentially Impacting:

- Appearance
- *Door* performance

<u>Performance Guideline</u>

Hardware exposed to exterior atmospheric conditions should be corrosion-resistant. Hardware exposed to salt air in a marine environment or air containing corrosives from pollutants should be made of materials suitable for use in such environments (for example, stainless steel or admiralty brass).

Comments: Hardware exposed to outdoor conditions requires special attention, both in selection and maintenance. The fact that an item of hardware is corrosion-resistant does not mean that it will not become discolored. For example, bright brass hardware, which is commonly used in exterior applications, has a factory-applied lacquer coating. Consumers are often not aware of this and when the lacquer finish eventually breaks down (as it almost certainly will) dark spots will appear. The consumer may then conclude that the product is unacceptable; this is not the case. Proper maintenance at this time will restore the finish, but more frequent care will be required in the future. It is advisable to wait for two days after applying varnish, paint, or stain to a door before installing brass hardware to avoid chemical reactions between the brass and the curing finish that could cause staining. Hardware with a dark bronze finish requires the least maintenance.

Builder Responsibility: The Builder should install appropriate hardware for the specific environmental exposure of the Home.

Homeowner Responsibility: ***Maintenance Alert!*** The Homeowner should read the manufacturer's maintenance and care recommendations. Keep hardware clean and bright by polishing on a regular basis with a clean, soft cloth. Do not allow dust and other harmful materials to accumulate. To preserve the factory-applied coating, avoid any abrasive products such as cleaners or polishing pads. While good care will extend the life of brass coatings, they will eventually break down and dark spots may appear. When tarnish reaches an undesirable level, the hardware should be removed from the door and the remaining lacquer coating completely removed. The coating removal should be done in accordance with the manufacturer's recommendations.

Chimneys and Flues

General Subject Information: The vast majority of fireplaces and *flues* that are installed in new homes are metal factory-built assemblies. The traditional masonry fireplace and chimney is being phased out, and gas log type fireplaces are gaining popularity. Factory-built assemblies will provide good service if properly used and maintained. (See "**Chapter Six—Interior Components, Fireplaces**" for further information, page 133.)

Condition #1: Chimney Cap Does Not Drain

Potentially Impacting:

- Water-resistance of cap
- Life of cap

Performance Guideline

Chimney caps should be built so that tops have sufficient slope to avoid ponding of water.

Builder Responsibility: The Builder should correct any improperly fabricated or installed caps.

Homeowner Responsibility: The Homeowner should include an inspection of the chimney cap and flue termination whenever the chimney flue is maintained by a professional cleaning service. Promptly notify Builder of any problem identified. If the original installation secured the chimney cap through the horizontal surface of the *chase* cover, the Homeowner must periodically check the *caulking* of the attachment screws to avoid water penetration. The chimney cap is not designed to carry a person's weight, and standing upon the cap may cause it to collapse.

Condition #2: Flue Enclosure Is Open for Entire Height (through Floors and Ceilings)

Potentially Impacting:

- Fire resistance of chimney assembly

Performance Guideline

Flue enclosures should be blocked with sheet metal fitted to the opening and the flue where passing through each floor and ceiling assembly. These sheet metal assemblies are called fire blocking.

Builder Responsibility: The Builder should retrofit any fire blocking missing from original construction.

Homeowner Responsibility: Flues may pass through an unfinished *attic*. If missing fire blocking is discovered, the Homeowner should notify the Builder.

Condition #3: Within the Chimney, Water Runs Down the Outside of the Flue

Potentially Impacting:
- Chimney framing
- Interior finishes

Performance Guideline

Where the flue exits through the chimney cap, a storm collar should be installed to deflect water away from the penetration. Water should not run down the outside of the flue. During periods of high wind driven rain, some leakage is to be expected and is acceptable.

Builder Responsibility: If a storm collar is missing or leaks, the Builder should make the necessary corrections to conform to the Performance Guideline.

Homeowner Responsibility: The Homeowner should promptly inform the Builder of any leaks; except leaks during periods of high wind driven rain.

Condition #4: Fireplace Does Not Draw Properly

Potentially Impacting:
- Occupant comfort and safety
- Interior air quality
- Ability to keep a fire going

Performance Guideline

Fireplace and chimney assemblies should be sized and installed in a manner that permits smoke and other products of combustion to exit freely through the flue without putting smoke into the room.

Builder Responsibility: If the condition is a result of improper installation, the Builder should make corrections to achieve proper airflow in the flue. It is advisable to consult the fireplace manufacturer for their recommendations regarding flue diameter, permissible flue offsets, the shape and size of flue terminations, etc. as these factors may vary according to the type of system installed.

Homeowner Responsibility: The Homeowner should reference "**Chapter Six—Interior Components, Fireplaces**" for recommendations regarding cleaning the flue, page 133. Dirty flues can cause poorly drawing fireplaces. Also, overloading the fireplace with too much fuel may cause both smoke and fire to enter the room. The Homeowner should never burn newspapers or gift wrap in a fireplace. If glass fireplace *doors* are installed as part of the fireplace, they must be closed during the burning operation. Fireplaces that do not have glass doors should not have them added unless specifically approved by the manufacturer.

Gutters and Downspouts

General Subject Information: Geographic areas of the country experience rainfall or snow that varies from minimal (Southwest) to extreme (Pacific Northwest, Florida and Hawaii). Throughout the rest of the country, year-round precipitation is common, so it is important to plan for rainwater management. Control of rainwater from *roofs* is important for the long-term satisfactory performance of Homes. Significant amounts of water can flow over the edge of a *sloped* roof during a strong rainstorm. If uncontrolled, this water will flow down wall surfaces and increase the likelihood of leaks at windows, *doors* and through wall surface coverings. When water from the roof hits the ground next to a Home, water and soil can splash onto the lower surfaces of the structure. This may produce unsightly and potentially damaging conditions. Although they are usually not required by code, *gutters* are the best way to control water flow from eaves. *Downspouts* direct water from the gutters to the ground in a controlled manner. In semi-arid areas of the country with little rainfall, it is a frequent practice for Builders not to include gutter and downspout systems with their homes. (See "**Chapter Eight—Grounds, Drainage**" for additional information, page 227.) If installed, downspouts and gutters should be sized according to the Sheet Metal and Air Conditioning Contractors' National Association (SMACNA) guidelines or with International Plumbing Code design criteria.

FAILURE TO KEEP GUTTERS CLEAN CAN RESULT IN RUSTING AND LEAKING!

Condition #1: Gutters Contain Standing Water after Rainfall

Potentially Impacting:

- *Gutter* life
- Water-borne insects
- Gutter performance

Performance Guideline

Gutters, if installed, should be installed with a downward slope (1/16 inch per 3 lineal feet) in the direction of the nearest downspout, if the frame of the Home permits such installation. Alternatively, gutters may be installed level with downspouts. Gutters and downspouts should be installed in a manner that permits water to drain or evaporate completely from gutters within a period less than 24 hours after the cessation of rainfall in summer and 36 hours in winter. This time period shall be extended if weather conditions such as heavy winter fog or snow persist in the region. No part of a gutter should be installed with a back-slope (sloping away from the nearest downspout).

Builder Responsibility: The Builder should either correct the slope of the gutter or add more downspouts to conform to the Performance Guideline.

Homeowner Responsibility: ***Maintenance Alert!*** The Homeowner should keep gutters free of leaves, toys, or other debris. Accumulated debris can negatively affect the slope of a level gutter. Further, the acid produced by decaying leaves and bird feces will degrade a metal gutter. Gutters should be cleaned annually and more frequently if mature trees are adjacent to the Home.

Condition #2: Gutter or Downspout Joints Leak

Potentially Impacting:

- *Gutter* and *downspout* life
- Adjacent *trim*, walls and ground surface below
- Gutter coating (paint, etc.)

Performance Guideline

Gutter and downspout joints should be assembled so that they do not leak.

Builder Responsibility: The Builder should perform repairs so the seams at gutters and downspouts do not leak.

Homeowner Responsibility: None.

Condition #3: Gutter Ends Are Embedded in Wall Surface Material

Potentially Impacting:

- Moisture resistance of wall

Performance Guideline

Gutters should not be embedded into stucco or other cladding materials and should terminate no closer than 1 inch from the surface of intersecting walls.

Comments: Gutters are sometimes installed before the application of surface materials, such as stucco, panel *siding*, or lap siding. If insufficient space is provided between framing and gutter terminations, it may be impossible to obtain complete stucco or siding coverage, resulting in potential wall leaks.

Builder Responsibility: If gutter ends are embedded or are too tight to wall surface materials, the Builder should perform repairs to conform to the Performance Guideline.

Homeowner Responsibility: None.

Condition #4: Gutters Overflow

Potentially Impacting:

- Home components below the overflow
- Utility of areas below the overflow

Performance Guideline

The Builder should size gutters so that they do not overflow under normal rainfall conditions. The frequency and cross-sectional area of gutters should be adequate to serve the computed maximum flow of storm water as defined by the rainfall tables in plumbing codes. The shapes of gutters should be selected so that water flowing off the roof is intercepted by the gutter and does not wash over the front edge of the gutter. Water falling from upper roofs without gutters directly onto lower roofs is acceptable.

Comments: Design criteria for gutter size and type are sometimes determined by the architect. Usually, it is determined by the Builder's specialty contractor according to published data including roof area, roof *slope*, and *roof cover* material (shake, *tile*, *shingles* etc.).

Builder Responsibility: If overflow is a result of improper or inadequate installation and not from the inadequate Homeowner maintenance, the Builder should make adjustments to the rainwater collection system so gutters do not overflow during periods of heavy rainfall (as opposed to extreme, for example not normal, conditions for the area).

Homeowner Responsibility: ***Maintenance Alert!*** Annual maintenance of gutters and downspouts is important to avoid leaks and prolong the life of the system. The Homeowner should thoroughly clean the gutters. If the Home is in an area with mature trees, it is a good idea to place gutter screens along the gutter length and in the top opening of each downspout to help minimize obstructions by leaf debris.

If a gutter or downspout leaks, the Homeowner should have it repaired at the first opportunity. If gutters are made of galvanized sheet metal (as opposed to aluminum or plastic), their *useful life* will be greatly reduced if the Homeowner allows acidic bird droppings, tree leaves or pine needles to accumulate in the gutter.

Condition #5: Gutters Do Not Extend Fully to the *Gable* Ends of the Roof

Potentially Impacting:

- Home components below the overflow

Performance Guideline

Gutters should provide complete coverage along the roof eave. However, the Builder may elect to install gutters only on a portion of the Home, such as over an exterior doorway or patio. The Builder is not required by code to install gutters unless it is required by local ordinance.

Builder Responsibility: Unless the architectural design of the Home shows otherwise, the Builder should install gutters to run completely along the eave. An exception to this is the use of a *dutch gutter*, or diverter, at certain locations to divert rainwater to less vulnerable areas (for example, over an entryway).

Homeowner Responsibility: None.

Condition #6: Storm Flow from Downspout Discharges at Home Foundation

Potentially Impacting:

- *Foundations*
- Sidewalks and *patios*
- Landscaping

Performance Guideline

At a minimum, storm water should be discharged on splash blocks and channeled away from the Home foundation at least 5 feet to a drainage swale or approved storm drain.

Builder Responsibility: The Builder should construct the Home so as to direct rainwater away from the foundation. This can be accomplished by grading, use of splash blocks, *downspout* extensions, or with an underground piping system.

Homeowner Responsibility: ***Maintenance Alert!*** The Homeowner should not alter the finished *grades* around the Home that were provided by the Builder unless it is done according to code, and as directed by a landscape architect or civil engineer. Keep all drainage swales free of debris. Flush out the underground pipe system (if the Home has one) with a garden hose prior to the start of the winter and after trees have dropped their leaves.

Condition #7: Downspout Makes "Pinging" Noise during Rain Storms

Potentially Impacting:

- Occupant annoyance

Performance Guideline

Due to many factors beyond the control of the Builder, such as architectural design, rainwater collection requirements, and widely varying degrees of sensitivity of noise threshold by the occupants, the Builder is not responsible for downspout noise.

Builder Responsibility: None.

Homeowner Responsibility: If downspout noise exists to the extent and/or in a location that adversely affects the quality of habitability (such as outside a bedroom window) the following suggestions can mitigate the noise:

- If the bottom of the downspout is "kicked out" from the wall and is not inserted into a collection pipe, the Homeowner can glue a piece of carpet padding into the kicked out portion. The Homeowner should make sure the metal is clean and dry before applying watertight glue. The Homeowner should inspect the downspout during rainy periods and make sure it is clear of leaves or debris.
- If the downspout has several twists and turns or the bottom is not accessible, the Homeowner can hang a galvanized steel or plastic chain with one inch wide links into the top 3 to 5 feet of the downspout. The top link should be hung from a copper or brass rod that is at least 12 inches long. It is important that the chain and the rod be made of a material that does not rust. Inspect

the chain frequently during periods of rain and clean as necessary. The chain should decrease the downspout noise.

Skylights

General Subject Information: Skylights are simply windows in the roof. Like windows, skylights can either be inoperable (fixed) or operable (capable of being opened). The most commonly used skylights are made of acrylic plastics or glass often shaped in the form of a dome and set in an aluminum frame. Some skylights have flat plate glass in them. Another type of skylight is a tube design that directs light through the *attic* into a light diffuser at ceiling level.

Condition #1: Skylight Leaks

Potentially Impacting:

- Interior finishes
- Roof framing integrity

Performance Guideline

Skylights should be installed so they do not leak. Skylights may leak as a result of failures in the frame or glazing or more commonly because of incorrect installation.

Builder Responsibility: The Builder should reset and properly waterproof improperly installed skylights. The Builder is responsible for administering any manufacturer's warranty work in the event of a failure of the skylight assembly.

Homeowner Responsibility: None, except as identified in "**Chapter Four—Roofs**".

Condition #2: Moisture Condenses on Interior Surfaces of the Skylight

Potentially Impacting:

- Interior finishes

Performance Guideline

Moisture condensation on the interior surface of skylight glazing is considered acceptable. However, condensation moisture that is excessive and finds its way into surrounding finishes and cavities is unacceptable.

Builder Responsibility: The Builder should install skylights to conform to the Performance Guideline. The Builder should reconstruct improperly detailed skylight perimeters so condensation is adequately trapped and allowed to evaporate.

Homeowner Responsibility: The Homeowner is responsible for the amount of humidity created in kitchens, baths, laundry rooms and other areas that produce water vapor. The Homeowner should always turn on the ventilation fans when using these rooms.

Condition #3: Moisture Appears between the Panes of a Dual Pane Skylight

Potentially Impacting:

- Skylight *insulation* value
- Appearance

Performance Guideline

Moisture trapped between the panes of a dual pane skylight indicates a broken seal. This is unacceptable.

Builder Responsibility: If the broken seal occurs within the manufacturer's warranty period, the Builder should replace the skylight glazing.

Homeowner Responsibility: None. However, the Homeowner should not tint the inside surface of a dual pane skylight, as that may void the warranty.

Condition #4: Skylight Admits Too Much Heat

Potentially Impacting:

- Occupant comfort

Performance Guideline

A Home with skylights must conform to international or state energy conservation standards. Assuming energy calculations have been done correctly, heat gain through a skylight is considered acceptable.

Builder Responsibility: The Builder should install skylights to comply with state and local energy requirements, and the energy calculations for the Home.

Homeowner Responsibility: The Homeowner should install heat reflecting or absorbing systems according to their own taste and in accordance with the manufacturer's recommendations. If a particular skylight warms the room too much and the Homeowner feels uncomfortable with its performance, there are several screening and shading techniques and products available to provide additional protection.

Paint and Stain

General Subject Information: Simply defined, stains are liquids that penetrate into the surface (usually wood) to allow the *grain* to be visible, while paints cover the surface of the material thus making the grain not visible. There are two exceptions to this: solid body stains cover the wood grain and certain paint *primers* penetrate the wood grain. Correct preparation of surfaces to receive paints and stains and the selection of an appropriate product for the use intended are essential in achieving a satisfactory finish. It is equally important that the Homeowner performs adequate maintenance and refinishing at suitable intervals. The durability of painted and stained surfaces is also directly related to the exposure to which it is subjected. Surfaces that receive direct sun or the full force of storms can be expected to require more frequent refinishing. The first coat of paint, the one applied during construction, is the coat that will last the shortest time, as the material beneath the paint absorbs a much greater percentage of the first coat of paint than successive coats.

Condition #1: Stains from Underlying Surfaces Bleed Through

Potentially Impacting:
- Appearance

Performance Guideline

Colors, markings, wood sap, tannins, etc., which are on the surface of or are within the composition of underlying materials should not bleed through to the surface of paint coatings.

Builder Responsibility: The Builder should properly prepare and clean paint and stain surfaces. If components of an underlying material have an inherent tendency to bleed through, the Builder should apply stain-blocking coatings or *primers* before proceeding with painting or staining.

Homeowner Responsibility: None.

Condition #2: Paint Is Chalky or Faded

Potentially Impacting:
- Paint life
- Appearance
- Water-resistance of surfaces

Performance Guideline

Paint should not chalk (become powdery and white) or fade during the manufacturer's warranted life of the product.

Comments: Some types and colors of paints are more susceptible to fading and chalking when exposed to direct sunlight than other types and colors. For example, dark colors are more prone to fading than lighter colors. Manufacturers can provide useful guidance for selection of paints that will perform effectively under particular climatic conditions.

Builder Responsibility: The Builder should select paints and stains that are suitable for the exposure and climate zone of the Home.

Homeowner Responsibility: ***Maintenance Alert!*** It is important that the Homeowner observe the condition of painted surfaces on a periodic basis. An annual inspection is recommended. Paints first begin to show signs of wear in limited areas. Maintenance and touch up should be undertaken before paint degradation proceeds too far. This can significantly extend the life of the overall paint job.

Green Tip! Always use low VOC (Volatile Organic Compounds) paints and *caulks* when repainting.

LOW VOC PAINTS REDUCE AIR POLLUTION
LOW VOC

Condition #3: Paint Flakes or Peels

Potentially Impacting:

- Moisture resistance of surfaces
- Appearance

Performance Guideline

Paint should not flake or peel during the manufacturer's warranted life of the product.

Comments: Paints that flake or peel prematurely tend do so because the surfaces to which they were applied were not adequately prepared. Sometimes *primers* are omitted or surfaces may be too damp or dirty. Paints sometimes flake off metal surfaces because they are very smooth and non-absorbent. Surface preparation with dilute acids or chemical bonding agents is usually required. Factory prime coats often need to be supplemented with a coat of primer applied at the construction site.

Builder Responsibility: The Builder should make appropriate paint selections and properly prepare surfaces to receive paints. In the case of premature flaking or peeling, the Builder should take action to remediate the unacceptable condition, up to and including stripping and repainting affected surfaces, as may be required to provide a durable finish.

Homeowner Responsibility: The Homeowner should maintain paint surfaces in a clean and well-ventilated condition. Inspect painted surfaces periodically and touch up any initial onset of premature aging or deterioration that is observed.

Condition #4: Paint Is Applied Too Thin, Too Thick, or In a Spotty Manner

Potentially Impacting:

- Paint life
- Appearance
- Water-resistance of surfaces

Performance Guideline

All surfaces to receive paint should be uniformly coated without any unpainted or too lightly painted spots (called holidays in the painting trade). Paint coatings should be applied to at least the minimum thickness recommended by the manufacturer. Paint should not be applied too thick, which usually results in spots that are more reflective than surrounding surfaces (painters call these spots "shiners"). Paint should be applied smoothly and evenly, without any runs or drips.

Builder Responsibility: The Builder should apply paint to conform to the Performance Guideline. Any areas that are not painted in conformance to the Guideline should be repainted properly.

Homeowner Responsibility: None.

Condition #5: Paint or Stain Is Over-Sprayed on Adjacent Surfaces

Potentially Impacting:

- ♦ Appearance

Performance Guideline

Visible over-spray of paints or stains on surfaces that are not intended to receive paint or stain coatings is not acceptable. Over-spray clearly visible at a distance of 5 feet under normal natural lighting conditions is unacceptable.

Builder Responsibility: The Builder should protect surfaces that are not to be painted and which may be subject to over-spray damage. If over-spray occurs despite protective measures, the Builder should clean the affected areas in a manner that does not damage the affected surfaces.

Homeowner Responsibility: None.

Condition #6: Paint Is Stained or Has Mildew/Fungi Growth

Potentially Impacting:

- ♦ Appearance
- ♦ Paint life

Performance Guideline

Mildew and fungi that affect exterior surfaces may be difficult or impossible to avoid in some particularly moist and cool locations and are not considered a failure to comply with the Performance Guideline. Molds and mildews that appear on interior surfaces as a result of leaks are considered unacceptable. Interior surfaces similarly affected by condensation may be considered either acceptable or a Homeowner maintenance item, depending upon circumstances.

Comments: Mold and mildew on exterior painted surfaces generally have different causes and effects than those on interior painted surfaces. Growths and stains on exterior surfaces are generally the result of constant exposure to cool, damp and shady conditions, whereas interior manifestations are often the result of leaks or condensation. (Refer to "**Chapter Nine—Miscellaneous, Mold and Mildew**" for more information, page 241.)

Builder Responsibility: The Builder is responsible for selecting paints that are reasonably resistant to the establishment and spread of mildews and fungi on exterior walls. Paints are now formulated with mildewcide and fungicide additives that inhibit the growth of mildew and fungi. The Builder should use these types of products on exterior walls when the orientation and climate at the home site indicates their use is necessary. At interior walls, if mildews and molds become established as a consequence of leaks in the exterior walls, roof above, or any other building component, it should be the Builder's responsibility to correct the leaks and to clean and restore affected areas (if leaks are a result of improper construction).

Homeowner Responsibility: ***Maintenance Alert!*** The Homeowner should periodically inspect exterior surfaces to determine if mildew or fungus growth is occurring. Growth of any of these organisms should be addressed by the proper cleaning and application of products that will kill the organisms and retard their return. This should be done promptly upon observation of mildews or fungi, because once established, these organisms are progressively more difficult to control and eradicate. At interior locations, the Homeowner should always use the mechanical ventilation in bathrooms, laundry rooms, and kitchens while these rooms are in use, and regularly air out rooms that have windows. If the Homeowner observes significant condensation on interior surfaces (usually at windows and cool exterior walls), an effort should be made to find the right balance of natural and mechanical ventilation to minimize the problem.

Condition #7: Lacquer or Varnish Peels and Flakes

Potentially Impacting:

- Appearance

Performance Guideline

Clear exterior lacquer and varnish coatings are not recommended for use on exterior surfaces, even if it is marine grade varnish. These coatings usually deteriorate within the first year and require substantial maintenance in the future. Deteriorated exterior varnished and lacquered surfaces are not considered acceptable. Interior varnished and lacquered surfaces may be appropriate, provided they are not applied in locations subject to extensive direct sunlight or excessive moisture.

Builder Responsibility: The Builder should replace peeling or flaking exterior and interior lacquers and varnishes that have not been subjected to Homeowner abuse.

Homeowner Responsibility: The Homeowner should keep all varnished and lacquered surfaces reasonably free of excessive moisture, heat, dust and from other damaging conditions. Relatively frequent maintenance and recoating with a high quality marine grade or spar varnish should be anticipated and performed by the Homeowner.

Condition #8: Stained Exterior Surface Is Blotchy or Has Uneven Color

Potentially Impacting:

- Appearance

Performance Guideline

Stains are absorbed by wood to different degrees, depending on the prevalence of sapwood, knots, and the character of the tree from which the wood product was made. Stains on synthetic surfaces may be more regular, but some variation is still inevitable. Stained surfaces, however, should not be excessively blotchy, or vary markedly in color.

Builder Responsibility: The Builder should prepare surfaces and apply appropriately selected stains in strict accordance with the manufacturer's directions and recommendations, and in a manner that minimizes extreme variations in color or blotchiness. Surfaces that do not comply with the Performance Guideline should be cleaned and re-coated in a manner that achieves a reasonable degree of regularity.

Homeowner Responsibility: The Homeowner is responsible for keeping stained surfaces clean and free of debris. Adequate ventilation of exposed surfaces should be provided. Shrubs should not grow against the side of the House. The Homeowner should recoat stained surfaces at intervals recommended by the manufacturer.

Condition #9: Painted Stucco Does Not Permit Moisture to Escape

Potentially Impacting:

- Structural integrity / framing
- Interior humidity

Performance Guideline

Stucco surfaces that are designed to receive paint should be coated with products that allow water vapor to pass from the inner surface to the outer surface. The use of impermeable membrane paints on exterior surfaces is not considered acceptable for this application.

Comments: Some *elastomeric* paints used to coat exterior surfaces of stucco are completely waterproof. When such paints are used, there is a risk of trapping moisture within wall cavities. This can result in lumber deterioration and the onset of molds because water from minor leaks or condensation moisture cannot readily dry out. For this reason, it is important to use *cement plaster*-compatible paints on stucco. Fortunately, this condition has become well known, and paint manufacturers are very conscious of the need to specify the correct type of paint for use on cement plaster (stucco) surfaces.

Builder Responsibility: The Builder should apply only breathable surface coatings to stucco exteriors according to the methods and thickness recommended by the manufacturer.

Homeowner Responsibility: None.

Condition #10: Paint Brush or Lap Marks Show

Potentially Impacting:

- Appearance

Performance Guideline

When viewed in normal daylight at a distance of 6 feet, brush marks or lap marks should not be visible. Artificial light is not acceptable as a light source when evaluating paint or coatings according to this Guideline.

Comments: Many paints manufactured today are difficult to apply without leaving brush or lap marks. Consequently, most paint applicators prefer to use an airless sprayer to achieve a uniform application. Problems arise when trying to touch up with a brush.

Builder Responsibility: The Builder should take corrective measures to conform to the Guideline.

Homeowner Responsibility: None.

Brick and Masonry

General Subject Information: This section includes structural and non-structural brickwork, stonework and *concrete* block walls (also known as concrete masonry units or "CMU's"). A structural application may be a foundation wall or chimney. A non-structural application may be brick *veneer* that is applied over a structural wall to enhance its appearance. Fireplace faces and surrounds made of faux stone are another example of a non-structural application. Faux stone, which is made from polyurethane, is lightweight with a hard exterior so it can withstand extreme weather elements. These would also fall under the category of stonework, although the material is not real stone.

Condition #1: Chimney Is Cracked

Potentially Impacting:

- Appearance
- Structural integrity
- Watertightness

Performance Guideline

Cracks in mortar joints in excess of 1/8 inch are not acceptable. Cracks that run through brick or stone (as opposed to mortar joints) in excess of 1/8 inch are not acceptable. Cracks that run through both the mortar joints and the brick or stone in excess of 1/8 inch are not acceptable; they may be a telltale sign of an underlying structural deficiency.

Builder Responsibility: The Builder should perform repairs by *repointing* masonry cracks. Bricks or stone that are cracked in excess of 1/8 inch shall be replaced. Any cracks that are greater than 3/8 inch shall be investigated by a structural engineer or architect, and the Builder should perform the recommended repairs.

Homeowner Responsibility: None.

Condition #2: Masonry Wall or Masonry Veneer Is Cracked

Potentially Impacting:

- Appearance
- Watertightness

Performance Guideline

Cracks in excess of 1/8 inch are considered unacceptable.

Builder Responsibility: For all unacceptable conditions, the Builder should replace brick, stone or CMU's if they are cracked in excess of 1/8 inch.

Homeowner Responsibility: The Homeowner should not alter the finish *grade* around any masonry wall. The Homeowner should ensure that rainwater flows away from the wall.

Condition #3: Cut Bricks below Openings in Masonry Walls Are of Different Thickness

Potentially Impacting:

- Appearance

Performance Guideline

Cut bricks used in the course directly below an opening in a masonry wall shall be uniform in size to a tolerance of ¼ inch. In addition, there shall be no brick pieces or "chips" that are smaller than 1 inch in any direction.

Builder Responsibility: The Builder should replace bricks that do not conform to the Performance Guideline.

Homeowner Responsibility: None.

Condition #4: Brick or CMU Courses Are Not Straight and Mortar Joints Vary in Thickness

Performance Guideline

Using a line of sight along a mortar joint, the mortar joint must be within ½ inch of the same elevation from beginning to end. Additionally, the mortar joint may not vary in thickness by more than ¼ inch in 10 feet of length.

Builder Responsibility: The Builder should correct unacceptable walls to conform to the Performance Guideline.

Homeowner Responsibility: None.

Condition #5: Brick Is Disintegrating (Spalling)

Potentially Impacting:

- Appearance
- Structural integrity

Performance Guideline

New brick that spalls or disintegrates is unacceptable. This Guideline includes manufactured used brick. Actual used brick may exhibit some superficial spalling and as long as at least 90% of the volume of the brick remains intact, it is considered acceptable.

Builder Responsibility: The Builder should replace bricks that do not conform to the Performance Guideline.

Homeowner Responsibility: The Homeowner should brush and wash off the white powdery substance (*efflorescence*) that sometimes appears on brick surfaces during wet weather.

Condition #6: Attached Masonry Veneers Do Not Have Weep Holes at the Base

Potentially Impacting:

- Watertightness
- Structural integrity

Performance Guideline

Accent stone or brick, known as veneer stone, needs to be installed with an approved vapor barrier or rain screen behind it and weep holes every 33 inches maximum at the bottom.

Comments: Stone and brick veneer is a popular wall *cladding* and is not a structural component of the Home. Typically, they are applied over a vapor barrier and wire mesh *lath*. Because there is a possibility that water can enter behind the veneer, weep holes need to be inserted as part of the installation process. The omission of weep holes and *flashing* is one of the most common construction defects nationally.

Builder Responsibility: If weep holes have not been installed, the Builder should replace the stone or brick cladding.

Homeowner Responsibility: None. However, the Homeowner should look for any moisture or areas with mold around windows *sills* and baseboards. This could be a sign that the *drainage plane* behind the cladding is not performing in an acceptable manner.

Condition #7: Masonry Columns Are Not Plumb and/or In Line

Potentially Impacting:

- Appearance

Performance Guideline

Masonry columns should be in line within ¼ inch and plumb within ¼ inch, in 8 feet of height and length.

Comments: Masonry columns, whether stone, brick, or cast should be properly plumbed and lined. In addition, masonry clad columns that have a wood or metal *post* inside should be vented at both the top and bottom to allow air circulation and to prevent rot or rust.

Builder Responsibility: The Builder should perform repairs to conform to the Performance Guideline.

Homeowner Responsibility: None.

Condition #8: Mortar Joints Have Color Variations

Potentially Impacting:
- Appearance

Performance Guideline

Color variations in mortar joints are not considered an acceptable condition unless there is a distinct variation when viewed at a distance of 10 feet under normal daylight conditions.

Builder Responsibility: If there is a distinct variation that does not meet the Performance Guideline, the Builder shall achieve a more uniform coloration using a mortar coloring agent.

Homeowner Responsibility: None.

Chapter Six

INTERIOR COMPONENTS

includes:

Fireplaces

Insulation

Interior Doors and Door Hardware

Closets

Finish Flooring

Plaster and Drywall

Countertops

Appliances

Cabinets and Vanities

Stairs and Railings

Moldings and Trim

Mirrors, Shower and Tub Enclosures

References for this chapter:

- *The Complete Idiot's Guide to Trouble Free Home Repair*, by David Tenenbaum
- *Problems, Causes, and Cures*, National Wood Flooring Association
- *Residential Construction Performance Standards*, NAHB 2001 ed.
- *Residential & Light Commercial Construction Standards*, by Don Reynolds
- *Indiana Quality Assurance Builder Standards 2009,* Indiana Builders Association.
- *Workmanship Standards for Licensed Contractors 2009,* Arizona Registrar of Contractors
- *Homeowner Handbook 2003,* Greater Atlanta Home Builders Association
- *California Building Code 2013,* California Building Standards Commission
- *Installation Recommendations,* Mirror Division of the Glass Association of North America
- *NASCLA Residential Construction Standards 2009,* National Association of State Contracting Licensing Agencies
- *New Home Warranty Program 2010,* State of New Jersey Department of Community Affairs
- *International Residential Code 2012,* International Code Council
- *South Carolina Residential Construction Standards 1997,* Residential Builders Commission of the South Carolina Department of Labor

A comprehensive list of references by author and publisher is found in the Bibliography section.

Chapter Six

Interior Components

Fireplaces

General Subject Information: Fireplaces that are installed in Homes today function more as decorative items than as sources of heat. Many fireplaces are considered gas appliances and are not equipped to burn anything other than the gas supplied to them. A wood burning fireplace operating without its glass *doors* closed is likely to *draw* more heat from the room than the heat it radiates into the room. Wood burning fireplaces are illegal in most states. (Refer to "**Chapter Five—Exterior Components, Chimneys and Flues**" for additional information, page 113.)

Condition #1: Water Drips into Fireplace during Rainstorm

Potentially Impacting:

- Ability to keep the fire going
- Fireplace performance
- Interior finishes and furnishings

Performance Guideline

Water should not drip into the fireplace during normal rainstorms. However, rainwater may pass down the chimney into the fireplace during extreme wind driven storms.

Comments: A typical chimney built today should be capped with a code-approved *spark arrester*, usually underneath a metal bonnet. A few fireplaces are still constructed with a masonry *flue*. Such chimneys will have a spark arrester, but they may not have a metal, *stucco* or *concrete* cap. Because all chimneys must be open to the outside in order to perform, they may admit some rainwater during periods of extreme wind-driven rain.

Builder Responsibility: If water drips into the fireplace during normal or light rainstorms, it is most likely due to a seam leak at the *chase* cover or the rain cap. The Builder should repair the leak.

Homeowner Responsibility: The Homeowner should keep the *damper* closed when the fireplace is not in use. Note: If the fireplace is used for burning wood, be certain there are no live coals or embers before closing the damper. Otherwise, poisonous gases could enter the room. ***Maintenance Alert!*** The flue must be cleaned (swept) periodically from the top, going downward, in accordance with the manufacturer's instructions and according to the amount of use of the fireplace. This is a dirty job that is best left to professional chimney sweeps. Failure to keep the chimney clean can result in dangerous flue fires high up in the chimney. Special chimney cleaning logs are available and their manufacturer claims they accomplish the same task as a chimney sweep.

Condition #2: Fireplace Won't Draw (Room Becomes Smoky)

Potentially Impacting:

- Occupant health and safety related to air quality

Performance Guideline

Fireplaces should be constructed so that all gases from combustion exhaust through the chimney flue.

Builder Responsibility: The Builder should construct the fireplace assembly, including *firebox*, flue, external combustion air *vents*, chimney, and termination cap in accordance with the code and the fireplace manufacturer's installation instructions.

Homeowner Responsibility: The Homeowner should always open the damper before starting a fire. Do not overload the firebox with too much fuel or improper fuel (such as holiday gift wrap). Use only the fuel that is approved by the manufacturer (a gas log fireplace is not suited to burn wood or paper). If installed, the Homeowner should close glass *doors* during fireplace operation. The Homeowner should not block the combustion air vent on the outside wall.

Condition #3: Refractory Panel Is Cracked

Potentially Impacting:

- Fireplace safety
- Appearance

Performance Guideline

*Refractory panels that crack more than 1/16 inch or crack to the extent that the panel breaks into pieces during the warranty period are considered unacceptable. (**Important!** Refer to **Homeowner Responsibility** below.)*

Builder Responsibility: The Builder should replace cracked refractory panels if damage is not a result of Homeowner misuse.

Homeowner Responsibility: ***Maintenance Alert!*** The Homeowner should "*cure*" new refractory panels by building a series of small, low-heat fires before fully using the entire fireplace. It is important that the Homeowner reads the owner's instruction manual and avoids creating high heat fires with items such as wrapping paper, composition logs, or lumber. Always place logs into the *firebox* using metal tongs; logs thrown into the firebox may hit the refractory and crack it. Avoid burning any composite wood material such as particleboard or *pressure treated* lumber scraps. Burning such material can give off toxic fumes.

DO NOT BURN WRAPPING PAPER!

USE THE CORRECT FUEL FOR THE FIREPLACE IN YOUR HOUSE

Condition #4: Damper Is Rusty

Potentially Impacting:

- Fireplace operation

Performance Guideline

The damper should be free of rust and operate smoothly at the time of the walkthrough.

Builder Responsibility: The Builder should perform repairs to conform to the Performance Guideline.

Homeowner Responsibility: ***Maintenance Alert!*** Dampers will rust because water vapor is formed when any type of fuel is burned. It is normal to expect some rust on the damper and its hinges. If the damper becomes difficult to operate, the Homeowner should spray the hinges with a rust removing lubricant. Do not spray when a fire or hot coals are present. Caution: The spray may be flammable.

Condition #5: Glass Doors Do Not Operate Freely

Potentially Impacting:

- Fireplace operation

Performance Guideline

At the time of the walkthrough, glass fireplace doors should open and close freely without sticking and should close with a gap of no more than ¼ inch.

Builder Responsibility: The Builder should perform repairs or adjustments so the glass door operation conforms to the Guideline.

Homeowner Responsibility: None. However, the Homeowner should keep the glass doors closed during fireplace operation.

Insulation

General Subject Information: *Insulation* is important for Home comfort and decreased dependency on energy consumption. In a new Home, insulation is likely to require compliance with state or local energy codes. In most states that have building permit requirements, the building department that issues the building permit requires the Builder to submit a series of calculations showing the Home will comply with the minimum requirements of the energy code. Because the energy code deals with energy consumption, it is important to note that insulation is just one of the components of proper energy conservation. Other components include efficient *furnaces*, water heaters, window glazing, Energy Star™ appliances, compact fluorescent lights, LED lighting, air conditioning and *weather stripping*. It is possible to balance a less efficient furnace with increased insulation provided that the energy value calculation of the entire Home meets the code. Code requirements can vary depending upon designated climate zones in each state. A Home in the mountains that looks identical to one at sea level may have a significantly different insulation package.

Typically, insulation comes in three forms: 1) batts, which are often fiberglass, pink or yellow in color, and 15 or 23 inches wide by 8 or 10 feet long; 2) loose fill, which looks like packing material, and is generally blown through a large hose into the *attic* space; and 3) spray on foam or rigid foam for wall cavities and roof *rafters* or *trusses*. Rigid foam insulation is also used to insulate foundation walls. Because insulation is only one component in the total energy saving package, it can be very difficult for a Homeowner to determine if the insulation package is acceptable or not, but the following are some common examples of insulation problems.

Condition #1: There Is No Insulation in the Attic

Potentially Impacting:

- ♦ Occupant comfort
- ♦ Energy consumption

Performance Guideline

Some insulation should be present in every attic built over habitable space unless an alternative approved by the building department exists. Occasionally, on desert style homes with flat roofs and no attic, part of the roof assembly is made of insulating foam, and this qualifies as ceiling/roof insulation.

Builder Responsibility: The Builder should install insulation that meets the *R-Values* specified in the compliance section of the building permit.

Homeowner Responsibility: None.

Condition #2: Attic Insulation Is Not Uniformly Thick

Potentially Impacting:

- ♦ Energy consumption

Performance Guideline

Attic insulation does not have to be uniformly thick as long as the entire attic meets code required R-Values.

Comments: Sometimes wind will blow through *attic vents* and move the insulation.

Builder Responsibility: None, if the overall insulation meets the R-Values specified in the compliance section of the building permit.

Homeowner Responsibility: None. However, if the wind has moved the insulation significantly, leaving spots of bare ceiling *drywall*, the Homeowner should go into the attic and rake it back.

Condition #3: Insulation Is Placed against the Eave Vents, the Foundation Vents, or the Chimney

Potentially Impacting:

- *Attic* and *crawl space* ventilation
- Occupant comfort

Performance Guideline

Insulation should not be placed against the eave (attic) or foundation vents. Good installation practice requires that at least 1 inch of open space should be left between the end of the insulation and the vent screen to allow for proper air circulation. Where it may contact a chimney flue, loose fill insulation shall be separated from the flue by an insulation shield approved by the fireplace manufacturer.

Builder Responsibility: The Builder should remove any originally installed insulation that blocks the airflow of eave and foundation vents. The Builder should install insulation to meet the above Performance Guideline.

Homeowner Responsibility: None.

Condition #4: Home Is Too Hot in Summer, Too Cold in Winter

Potentially Impacting:

- Occupant comfort
- Energy consumption

Performance Guideline

Each new Home should be built in compliance with applicable state or local energy code. However, there is no guarantee that an individual level of comfort will be met.

Builder Responsibility: None, provided the Builder built the Home to conform to the state or local energy code, or in the absence of a state or local code, the custom and practice of builders in that geographic area.

Homeowner Responsibility: Much of the comfort a Home provides depends on the lifestyle of the occupants. For example, it is unrealistic to expect that an air conditioner turned on at 5 p.m. on a hot summer day could effectively and entirely cool the Home by bedtime. (Refer to "**Chapter Seven—Utility Systems, Cooling**", page 199.) In wintertime, *furnaces* should be programmed to come on in the morning at least 30 minutes before the time occupants wake up. Constant adjustments to the thermostat will result in uneven temperatures and periods of discomfort. Also, installation of insulating drapes and shades is an effective way to increase Home comfort and decrease energy consumption.

Condition #5: Insulation Batts Do Not Fit Tight to Framing Members

Potentially Impacting:

- ♦ Heating and cooling comfort
- ♦ Energy consumption

Performance Guideline

In order to achieve maximum insulation performance, batts must be installed tight to the framing members, without gaps. There should also be a tight fit around plumbing lines and electrical boxes.

Builder Responsibility: If loose fitting insulation is present, the Builder should make adjustments to close gaps in insulation.

Homeowner Responsibility: None.

Green Tip! Adding insulation to an *attic* is the most economical way to save on energy bills. Note that in southern and northwestern states with high humidity, the *vapor barrier* is omitted.

A GOOD INSULATION PACKAGE IS THE LEAST EXPENSIVE WAY TO SAVE ON HEATING AND COOLING COSTS

Additional Information

- Insulation is probably the least expensive way to provide year-round comfort in a Home. If a Homeowner wants to decrease energy consumption, adding insulation to the attic is most effective. If additional insulation is installed, care should be taken not to block *eave* vents or allow insulation material to touch vents from gas-fired appliances. (Refer to **Condition #3** above, page 137.)
- Do all new homes require *dual pane* windows and under-floor insulation? No. As stated under "**General Subject Information**", the Builder is entitled to make substitutions, such as a more efficient *furnace* and air conditioner, as long as the entire Home complies with the requirements of the energy code (if applicable).

Interior Doors

Condition #1: Door Is Warped

Potentially Impacting:

- ♦ *Door* operation
- ♦ Appearance

Performance Guideline

Interior doors that are warped more than 1/4 inch in a 6 foot 8 inch height or 3/8 inch in an 8 foot height are considered unacceptable.

Builder Responsibility: The Builder should replace doors that do not conform to the Performance Guideline.

Homeowner Responsibility: None.

Condition #2: Door Panels Have Split

Potentially Impacting:
- Appearance
- Privacy

Performance Guideline

Door panels that have split entirely through and allow light to pass through are considered unacceptable (this Performance Guideline applies to exterior doors also).

Builder Responsibility: The Builder should perform repairs to conform to the Performance Guideline.

Homeowner Responsibility: None.

Condition #3: Door Hangs Crooked in Jamb

Potentially Impacting:
- *Door* performance
- Appearance

Performance Guideline

Doors that vary more than ¼ inch in measurement from the closest distance to the jamb to the furthest distance to the jamb or head are considered unacceptable.

Builder Responsibility: If the condition is a result of improper or inadequate installation, the Builder should make adjustments to doors and jambs to conform to the Performance Guideline.

Homeowner Responsibility: The Homeowner should not hang anything heavy on a door or doorknob. This can pull the top hinges out of adjustment and negatively affect the door swing.

Condition #4: Door Latch Does Not Engage in the Strike

Potentially Impacting:
- *Door* operation
- Privacy

Performance Guideline

Door latches should engage firmly in the strike.

Builder Responsibility: If the condition is a result of improper or inadequate installation, the Builder should make adjustments to conform to the Performance Guideline.

Homeowner Responsibility: The Homeowner should not hang anything heavy on a door or doorknob. This can pull the top hinges out of adjustment and negatively affect the proper engagement of the latch.

Condition #5: Door Opens or Closes by Itself

Potentially Impacting:

- *Door* performance

Performance Guideline

Doors should stay open when opened and stay closed when closed. "Phantom" openings and closings are considered unacceptable. Seasonable humidity changes that result in impaired door swing performance is acceptable.

Builder Responsibility: If the condition is a result of improper or inadequate installation, the Builder should make adjustments to conform to the Performance Guideline.

Homeowner Responsibility: The Homeowner should not hang anything heavy on a door or doorknob. This can pull the top hinges out of adjustment and negatively affect the door swing.

Condition #6: Bottom Edge of Door Is Cut Too High or Too Low

Potentially Impacting:

- Appearance
- Privacy
- *Door* performance

Performance Guideline

A door that swings over carpeted areas should not drag on the carpet. Doors should be cut to leave a gap no larger than 1 inch above the uppermost tufts of the carpet. A door that swings over a non-carpeted surface should be cut to leave a gap no larger than ½ inch above the floor surface. Exception: Doors opening to utility areas, such as laundry rooms and pantries, may have a gap up to 1-3/8 inches from the finish floor. This condition arises often when vinyl flooring is glued to a concrete slab, and it is considered acceptable (see comments below).

Comments: With the exception of a small number of custom homes, most doors are manufactured as completed assemblies, consisting of a door hung with hinges in a *jamb*. Manufacturers of "pre-hung" doors routinely hold the bottom of the door up to 1-3/8 inches from the bottom of the jamb.

This allows clearance for a variety of finish floor coverings of different thickness, such as wood, carpet, tile and vinyl.

Builder Responsibility: If the condition is a result of improper or inadequate installation, the Builder should perform repairs to conform to the Performance Guideline.

Homeowner Responsibility: If the Homeowner changes the type or texture of finish flooring or provides his or her own finish flooring, the Builder is not responsible.

Condition #7: Pocket Door Binds between the Pockets

Potentially Impacting:

- *Door* performance

Performance Guideline

Doors should not rub and/or bind in their pockets during normal operation.

Comments: *Pocket doors* should not be warped to the point that they rub on the sides of the pockets.

Builder Responsibility: The Builder should furnish and install pocket doors to conform to the Performance Guideline. If a door does not operate within the Guideline, the Builder should perform appropriate repairs and refinish any existing work damaged by such repairs.

Homeowner Responsibility: The Homeowner should operate the doors in a normal fashion and avoid slamming doors back and forth. Also, adjustment of door guide may be required.

Door Hardware

Condition #1: Doorknob Mechanism Operates Stiffly

Potentially Impacting:

- *Door latch* performance

Performance Guideline

Doorknob mechanisms should operate smoothly without requiring a great deal of effort to disengage the strike or deadbolt.

Builder Responsibility: The Builder should repair or replace unacceptable door latch mechanisms if their performance is not a result Homeowner misuse or neglect.

Homeowner Responsibility: ***Maintenance Alert!*** The Homeowner should lubricate door latch mechanisms annually with a dry lubricant made for door latch mechanisms.

Condition #2: Doorknob Is Tarnished

Potentially Impacting:
- Appearance

Performance Guideline

Doorknobs may tarnish over time. This is a Homeowner maintenance item.

Comments: The life of doorknobs and levers depends on finish type, location, and amount of use. Bright brass finishes are most susceptible to tarnishing. Scratching from finger rings, oil from hands and air pollution will contribute to the tarnishing process.

Builder Responsibility: The Builder should replace only doorknobs that are tarnished at the time of the *walkthrough*.

Homeowner Responsibility: The Homeowner should learn about the proper care of metal finishes, especially bright brass, and conduct appropriate maintenance for the particular metal finish. If the Home is located in a marine environment, expect pitting and tarnishing of the hardware finishes unless the hardware is labeled "lifetime finished". In all cases, the Homeowner should refer to the manufacturer's warranty and maintenance requirements.

Closets

Condition #1: Closet Pole Falls or Pulls Out of Wall Rosettes

Potentially Impacting:
- Function of closet

Performance Guideline

Closet poles should fit firmly into rosettes, and should not be held away from the inside end of the rosettes by more than 1/8 inch. Poles should have an intermediate support for every 4 feet of length.

Builder Responsibility: The Builder should perform repairs to conform to the Performance Guideline.

Homeowner Responsibility: The Homeowner should not overload closet poles with heavy clothing or too much clothing. This will cause the pole to deflect and pull out of the rosette.

Finish Flooring

General Subject Information: *Subfloors* for each of the flooring types (hardwood, ceramic tile, granite, marble, *resilient flooring*, and carpet) must be level, well supported, securely fastened and stiff enough to prevent unacceptable deflection (bending). (Refer to "**Chapter Two—Wood**

Subfloors and Ceilings" for more information, page 39.) The following typical conditions can affect all types of floors.

Condition #1: Floor Is Not Level, Squeaks, Has Excessive Deflection (Sagging) or Excessive Flexibility (Bounce)

Potentially Impacting:

- Occupant comfort

Performance Guideline

Finish floors should not deviate more than ¼ inch from true level in a horizontal distance of 8 feet. No point in the surface of a floor should be more than 1/8 inch above or below the plane of the floor. Squeaks are usually the result of separate parts of the floor moving relative to each other and rubbing against nails. Floors should be designed to accommodate building code required live loads. Squeaks should be located and corrected before finish flooring is installed.

Builder Responsibility: The Builder should perform repairs or replace finish flooring that deviates from the Performance Guideline, if the condition is a result of improper or inadequate installation and not a result of Homeowner misuse.

Homeowner Responsibility: The Homeowner should maintain flooring using products and methods approved by the manufacturer and/or trade association whose products have been installed. The Homeowner should avoid overloading floors and consult with the Builder or a qualified engineer prior to placing exceptionally heavy objects on a floor to ensure the floor load capacity will not be exceeded. If the Homeowner installs a finish floor, the Homeowner assumes complete responsibility for the condition of the *subfloor* or *slab* from the point of installation.

Hardwood Flooring

Condition #1: Floorboards Cup or Crown

Potentially Impacting:

- Appearance
- Life of finish floor
- Safety issue related to tripping hazard

Performance Guideline

Hardwood flooring should be installed in a manner that will prevent cupping and crowning. This includes, among other measures, proper acclimatization of floor material prior to installation and the use of suitable moisture barriers under the flooring. Cupping or crowning should not exceed 1/16 inch in a 3 inch span as measured across the individual board.

Builder Responsibility: If cupping or crowning exceeds the Guideline, the Builder should replace or repair the floor to conform to the Guideline. The Builder should provide the Homeowner with written information on hardwood floor care at the time of the *walkthrough*.

Homeowner Responsibility: The Homeowner should maintain hardwood floors in accordance with the manufacturer's recommendations. Spills should be removed immediately. The Homeowner should avoid detergents and use only the cleaning products recommended by the manufacturer or installer. Some minor random cupping or crowning can be expected over time due to changes in humidity; this condition is acceptable.

Condition #2: Floor Has Scalloped or Abraded Surface

Potentially Impacting:

- Appearance

Performance Guideline

Wood floors should be finished without gouges, abrasions or scalloping. Some unevenness can be expected because portions of the grain of wood are softer than others.

Builder Responsibility: The Builder should repair or replace unacceptable boards noticed at the *walkthrough*. The Builder should give the Homeowner written information from the flooring manufacturer on hardwood floor care at the time of the walkthrough.

Homeowner Responsibility: The Homeowner should bring any surface gouges and abrasions to the attention of the Builder at the walkthrough and prior to the move-in. The Builder is not responsible for gouges and abrasions noticed after the walkthrough. The Homeowner should maintain hardwood floors according to the manufacturer's recommendations. The Homeowner should not clean floors with detergents and use only the cleaning products recommended by the manufacturer or installer.

Condition #3: Floor Has Gaps between Adjacent Floorboards

Potentially Impacting:

- Appearance
- Life of finish floor
- Ease of cleaning

Performance Guideline

Manufactured (pre-finished) floors should be installed in strict accordance with the manufacturer's instructions and should perform in accordance with the manufacturer's warranty. Regarding floors finished in the field, floor joints should be tight and without gaps at the time of installation. Gaps between boards are the result of shrinkage. Although wood flooring materials are dried by the manufacturer, they still contain moisture. New wood floors should not be subjected to extreme variations in temperature or humidity. Gaps should not occur in more than 5% of the total length of joints in a floor, and no gap should exceed 1/32 inch in width for boards that are 2¼ inches or wider.

Builder Responsibility: If gaps between boards exceed the Performance Guideline, the Builder should replace or repair the floor as necessary to conform to the Guideline. The Builder should give the Homeowner written information on hardwood floor care at the time of the *walkthrough*.

Homeowner Responsibility: The Homeowner should maintain hardwood floors in accordance with the manufacturer's recommendations and prevent spills or liquids from remaining on floors. The Homeowner should avoid detergents and use only cleaning products recommended by the manufacturer or installer. In future years, it may be necessary to fill gaps between boards with wood filler in a matching color.

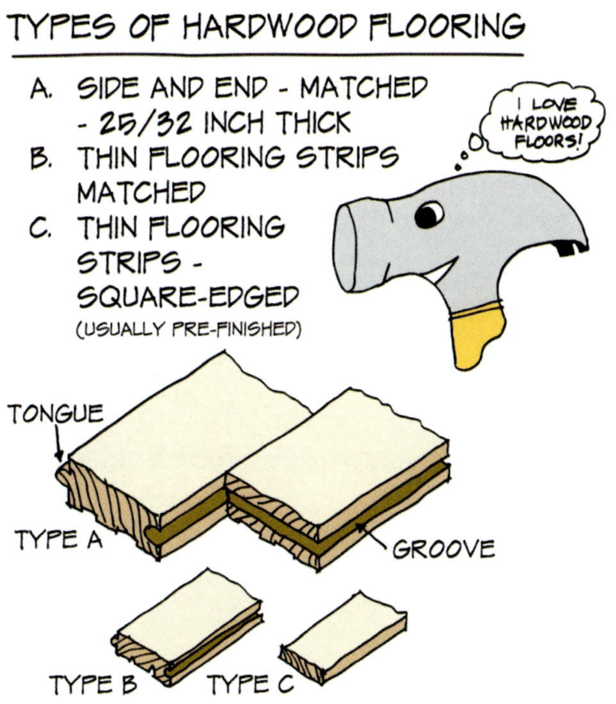

TYPES OF HARDWOOD FLOORING
A. SIDE AND END - MATCHED - 25/32 INCH THICK
B. THIN FLOORING STRIPS MATCHED
C. THIN FLOORING STRIPS - SQUARE-EDGED (USUALLY PRE-FINISHED)
I LOVE HARDWOOD FLOORS!
TONGUE
TYPE A
GROOVE
TYPE B
TYPE C

Condition #4: Floorboards Have Color Variations

Potentially Impacting:

- Appearance

Performance Guideline

Wood floors naturally have color variation. The same species of wood may come in many different colors and floorboards may vary accordingly.

Builder Responsibility: None.

Homeowner Responsibility: If uniformity of color is important to the Homeowner, advance arrangements should be made with the Builder at the time the flooring selection is completed, so that the Homeowner is present when the floor is being installed. The Homeowner should be aware that direct sunlight could cause wood floors to become lighter; the Builder is not responsible for this condition. The floor under area rugs and large pieces of furniture will remain as the original wood or stain color (usually darker). Removal of the rug or relocation of the furniture will allow the floor to reach a uniform color.

Condition #5: Floorboards on Pre-Finished Floors Are Not Level with One Another at Sides or Ends

Potentially Impacting:

- Appearance
- Life of finish floor
- Safety issue related to tripping hazard

Performance Guideline

Finish floorboards should not be higher or lower than the immediately adjoining board by more than .012 inch measured with a feeler gauge.

Builder Responsibility: The Builder should perform repairs to conform to the Performance Guideline unless the condition results from Homeowner misuse or improper maintenance.

Homeowner Responsibility: The Homeowner should be aware of appropriate floor care. If liquid is spilled on the floor or if areas of high humidity exist in poorly vented rooms, the floorboards may swell and become uneven. The Builder is not responsible for this condition.

Condition #6: Hardwood Floor Buckles Up From Subfloor

Potentially Impacting:
- Appearance
- Life of finish floor

Performance Guideline

Finish floorboards should not separate or buckle from the underlying subfloor.

Builder Responsibility: The Builder should investigate the cause of the problem, for example, installation issue, subfloor moisture, and perform repairs to conform to the Performance Guideline, unless the condition results from Homeowner misuse or improper maintenance.

Homeowner Responsibility: The Homeowner should be aware of appropriate floor care. If liquid is spilled on the floor or if areas of high humidity exist in poorly vented rooms, the floorboards may swell and buckle up from the subfloor. The Builder is not responsible for this condition.

Condition #7: Floorboard Edges Have Splinters or Chips after Installation

Potentially Impacting:
- Appearance
- Safety issue related to splinters

Performance Guideline

Whether the floor is pre-finished or sanded and finished in place, there should be no splinters or chips remaining after installation is complete.

Builder Responsibility: The Builder should repair or replace boards that do not conform to the Performance Guideline.

Homeowner Responsibility: The Homeowner should be aware of appropriate floor care and maintain hardwood floors in accordance with the manufacturer's recommendations. The Homeowner should avoid detergents and not allow spills or liquids to remain on floors. Use only the cleaning products recommended by the manufacturer or installer.

Condition #8: Dark Lines in Wood Appear Perpendicular to the Floorboard

Potentially Impacting:

- Appearance

Performance Guideline

Dark lines, known as sticker lines, across floorboards that cannot be removed during the sanding process are considered unacceptable. Dark lines clearly visible at a distance of 6 feet under normal daylight conditions are considered unacceptable.

Comments: Wood floorboards that are to be sanded and finished in place are shipped in bundles. The boards in the bundle are separated by small rectangular pieces of wood called "stickers". Under moist conditions, the stickers will "bleed" into the floorboards and impart a dark color across the board. If the bleed is not severe, it can be removed when the rough floor is being sanded.

Builder Responsibility: The Builder should replace or re-sand floorboards that do not conform to the Performance Guideline.

Homeowner Responsibility: The Homeowner should maintain hardwood floors in accordance with the manufacturer's recommendations. The Homeowner should avoid detergents and not allow spills or liquids to remain on floors. Use only the cleaning products recommended by the manufacturer or installer.

Condition #9: Floorboards Are Discolored or Rotting, Particularly under Area Rugs

Potentially Impacting:

- Appearance
- Air quality

Performance Guideline

Floorboards should not discolor (turn very dark) and rot or become brittle and crumble.

Comments: This condition can occur when pre-finished flooring is applied over a *concrete slab*. This condition worsens when the Homeowner places a rubber pad or rubber backed area rug over the floor. Although the concrete slab is likely to have a plastic *vapor barrier* under it, water vapor can pass through the slab in small amounts into the living area. Pre-finished floorboards are sealed very tightly at the factory and water vapor from the slab has difficulty passing through the wood. The addition of a rubber backed rug or tightly woven rug traps the moisture even more. While it is possible to successfully install pre-finished hardwood flooring over a concrete slab, it should be performed only by a specialty contractor who is very experienced at this trade. There are several manufacturers of pre-finished hardwood floors, and each manufacturer has its own set of installation instructions that should be strictly adhered to.

Builder Responsibility: The Builder should perform repairs to conform to the Performance Guideline unless the damage results from Homeowner misuse or negligence.

Homeowner Responsibility: If the Homeowner covers a pre-finished hardwood floor with an area rug, he or she is responsible for monitoring the condition of the wood at reasonable intervals such as every three months. Alternatively, the Homeowner can obtain a separate warranty from the manufacturer of the floor or place the area rug on the concrete slab and install the wood floor around it. The Homeowner should also be aware that direct sunlight will cause wood floors to become lighter. The Builder is not responsible for this condition.

Green Tip! **Bamboo Flooring and Cabinets:** Bamboo has become quite popular for flooring and cabinets in recent years. Bamboo is considered "green" because it is sustainable and renewable. Bamboo, which is actually a form of grass, is replenished fairly quickly after it has been harvested. This contrasts with hardwood flooring tree species that take decades to replenish. However, bamboo flooring has additional maintenance and care procedures that should be followed to keep the appearance attractive and prolong the life of the floor. Unless it is rare old growth bamboo, today's bamboo is soft and is easily dented and scratched. Extra care must be taken to keep bamboo floors free from dirt, grit, and hard traffic use.

Ceramic and Clay Tile Flooring

Condition #1: Tiles Are Cracked and/or Loose

Potentially Impacting:

- Appearance
- Safety issue related to tripping hazard
- Life of finished floor

Performance Guideline

Tiles with cracks visible at a distance of 4 feet and any loose tiles that can be moved by hand are not acceptable.

Builder Responsibility: The Builder should replace cracked tiles and reset loose tiles that do not conform to the Performance Guideline.

Homeowner Responsibility: The Homeowner should be aware that ceramic and clay tiles are brittle and they can be cracked, chipped or broken by placing or dropping heavy objects on them. The Builder is not responsible for the resulting damage.

Condition #2: Grout Is Cracked

Potentially Impacting:

- Appearance
- Floor deflection

Performance Guideline

*Hairline cracks can occur in grout and are considered acceptable. Cracks larger than 1/32 inch should be re-grouted by the Builder. If continual cracking occurs, the underlying floor may be deflecting. If this condition persists, it should be repaired as set forth in "**Chapter Two—Wood Subfloors and Ceilings**", Condition #3, page 40.*

Builder Responsibility: The Builder should repair or replace the unacceptable condition to conform to the Performance Guideline.

Homeowner Responsibility: The Homeowner should become familiar with the proper procedures for cleaning and caring for tile floors. Grout is very porous. If the Builder has not sealed the grout as part of the tile installation process, the Homeowner should seal the grout within 30 days of occupancy.

Condition #3: Tiles Are Out of Plane

Potentially Impacting:

- Appearance

Performance Guideline

This Guideline will vary depending upon the type of tile installed. Tiles can vary from flat ceramic, to raised pattern, to uneven terra cotta and slate. For tile that is flat, adjoining tiles should be no more than 1/16 inch higher or lower than the surrounding tiles. For tile that is handmade with uneven surfaces, the butts at the grout joints should not exceed ¼ inch in elevation from surrounding tiles.

Builder Responsibility: The Builder should repair or replace the unacceptable condition to conform to the Performance Guideline.

Homeowner Responsibility: The Homeowner should become familiar with the proper procedures for cleaning and caring for tile floors.

Granite, Marble, and Other Stone Flooring

General Subject Information: Granite, marble, and other stone flooring are natural products. There are many other stone products available today such as limestone, slate and travertine. Because these are natural products, the color and veining of these flooring materials varies and are never exactly alike. The Homeowner should expect variations from installations in other similar homes.

Condition #1: Flooring Is Cracked

Potentially Impacting:

- Appearance
- Life of finish floor

Performance Guideline

Granite, marble, and other stone are rigid and susceptible to hairline cracking. This is a normal condition. Cracks in excess of 3/64 inch are unacceptable.

Comments: Granite, marble, and other stone flooring are vulnerable to deflection and impact damage (dropping heavy items on their surfaces). Floors should be designed to a very high level of stiffness. Unusually heavy items should not be placed onto a stone floor. It would be wise for the Homeowner intending to place a very heavy item (such as a piano) onto a stone tile floor to advise the Builder of this fact. The Builder may elect to add extra support at those locations.

Builder Responsibility: The Builder should repair or replace the unacceptable condition to conform to the Performance Guideline.

Homeowner Responsibility: The Homeowner should examine floors carefully at the time of the *walkthrough*. The Homeowner should not place unusually heavy items on stone flooring unless the Builder was notified and has provided appropriate support. (Refer to "**Additional Information about Stone Flooring**" below.)

Condition #2: Flooring Is Stained

Potentially Impacting:
- Appearance

Performance Guideline

The Builder should deliver a marble, granite, or other stone flooring free of stains with a consistent surface sheen or texture. The Homeowner should carefully examine the surface of the marble, granite, or other stone floor prior to taking delivery of the Home. The Builder will not accept responsibility for stained conditions if they are not noted at the time of the walkthrough. Many times, what appear to be stains are actually natural variations in the color and veining of the stone.

Builder Responsibility: The Builder should repair or replace the unacceptable condition noted at the time of walkthrough.

Homeowner Responsibility: The Homeowner should carefully examine the floor during the walkthrough. (Refer to "**Additional Information about Stone Flooring**" below.)

Condition #3: Flooring Shows Scratches and Abrasions

Potentially Impacting:
- Appearance

Performance Guideline

The Homeowner should note any scratches and abrasions during the walkthrough. The Builder should deliver a marble, granite, or other stone floor free of scratches and abrasions with a consistent surface sheen or texture.

Comments: Marble, granite, and tumbled stone will naturally have numerous pits and voids. Small pits are considered part of the "achieved look" of the surface and should not be deemed as unacceptable. The manufacturer or installer usually fills voids in excess of 3/8 inch in diameter.

Builder Responsibility: The Builder should repair or replace the unacceptable condition noted at the time of the walkthrough.

Homeowner Responsibility: The Homeowner should carefully examine the floor during the walkthrough. (Refer to "**Additional Information about Stone Flooring**" below.)

Additional Information about Stone Flooring

- Granite and particularly marble are susceptible to staining and etching by ordinary household products and fluids. Take caution with items such as vinegar, tomato paste, toilet-bowl cleaner, and cleaners containing ammonia, as they can easily stain and etch marble and granite. Pet urine will stain and etch stone flooring.
- While marble and particularly granite appear to be smooth and hard, the surfaces can actually contain small pits. The surface can appropriately be filled by the manufacturer with clear epoxy filler or colored filler.

Vinyl or Resilient Flooring

Condition #1: Flooring Has Wide Seams or Joints

Potentially Impacting:

- Appearance

Performance Guideline

Sheet and vinyl tile resilient floors should be laid with tight joints or seams. Any separation in excess of 1/32 inch is unacceptable.

Builder Responsibility: The Builder should perform necessary repairs and replacements to conform to the Performance Guideline.

Homeowner Responsibility: The Homeowner should follow the flooring manufacturer's cleaning and care instructions for vinyl flooring.

Condition #2: Flooring Shows Delamination

Potentially Impacting:

- Appearance
- Life of finish floor

Performance Guideline

Occasionally, resilient floors will separate from the underlayment, particularly at edges. Such delamination is unacceptable and should be corrected by re-gluing.

Builder Responsibility: The Builder should perform the necessary repairs or replacements to conform to the Performance Guideline.

Homeowner Responsibility: The Homeowner should follow the flooring manufacturer's cleaning and care instructions for vinyl flooring. To extend the life of vinyl flooring, the Homeowner should use area rugs or mats at workstations, use dirt-trapping mats at *exterior doors*, and immediately remove any spilled liquids. Vinyl flooring is water-resistant, but not totally waterproof.

Condition #3: Flooring Is Discolored

Potentially Impacting:

- Appearance
- Life of finish floor

Performance Guideline

Floors should not become discolored as a result of moisture underneath the finish floor. If discoloration is a result of chemical or natural products with staining properties being allowed to remain on the surface of the resilient material without prompt cleaning, the Builder is not responsible.

Builder Responsibility: The Builder should perform repairs or replacements to conform to the Performance Guideline if the condition results from moisture underneath the finish floor and not if the damage results from Homeowner misuse or negligence.

Homeowner Responsibility: The Homeowner should not allow chemical or natural products with staining properties to remain on the finish floor. The Homeowner should follow the flooring manufacturer's cleaning and care instructions for vinyl flooring and immediately remove spilled liquids.

Condition #4: Adhesive Appears on the Flooring Surface

Potentially Impacting:

- Appearance

Performance Guideline

Adhesives should not appear through the surface around joints or seams.

Comments: Adhesives are used to attach *resilient floors* to the *underlayment*. Sometimes the adhesives do not set up properly and under the pressure of foot traffic, they may be forced up through the seams of the resilient floor.

Builder Responsibility: The Builder should perform repairs or replacements to conform to the Performance Guideline. If after thoroughly cleaning with a manufacturer-approved cleaning agent the unacceptable condition recurs, the Builder should remove the flooring along with the existing adhesive and re-lay the flooring.

Homeowner Responsibility: The Homeowner should follow the flooring manufacturer's cleaning and care instructions for vinyl flooring.

Condition #5: *Telegraphing* Shows Irregular Surface beneath Flooring

Potentially Impacting:

- Appearance

Performance Guideline

Various types of irregularities such as cracks in concrete subfloors, unevenness in subfloors or trapped debris may show through resilient flooring appearing as unsightly bumps and lines. When observed from a distance of 6 feet under normal lighting conditions these conditions are unacceptable.

Comments: Some vinyl (or resilient) flooring is not recommended for use over a concrete subfloor. The Homeowner who chooses a non-recommended flooring product assumes responsibility for the performance of that flooring.

Builder Responsibility: The Builder should perform repairs or replacements to conform to the Performance Guideline. The Builder should advise the Homeowner on which flooring products are not recommended for installation over a concrete subfloor.

Homeowner Responsibility: The Homeowner should be aware that if the flooring they have chosen is not recommended for installation over a concrete subfloor, visible bumps and lines may result that are not the Builder's responsibility. The Homeowner should follow the flooring manufacturer's cleaning and care instructions for vinyl flooring.

Condition #6: Subfloor Nail or Screw Heads Are Visible

Potentially Impacting:

- Appearance

Performance Guideline

Nail or screw heads or other covered debris that are visible from a distance of 3 feet under normal lighting conditions are unacceptable and do not conform to the Guideline.

Builder Responsibility: The Builder should perform repairs or replacements to conform to the Performance Guideline. The Builder should properly clean the *subfloor* before installation of the flooring to prevent debris from showing through the finished floor.

Homeowner Responsibility: None.

Condition #7: Bubbles Appear in Flooring

Potentially Impacting:

- Appearance

Performance Guideline

Bubbles in excess of 1/8 inch high are not acceptable.

Comments: Bubbles that appear in vinyl or *resilient flooring* within one week of installation are a sign of air trapped underneath or excess flooring adhesive.

Builder Responsibility: The Builder should perform repairs or replacements to conform to the Performance Guideline.

Homeowner Responsibility: None.

Condition #8: Flooring Pattern Does Not Match or Align

Potentially Impacting:

- Appearance

Performance Guideline

Patterns should match or align within 1/8 inch in a 6 foot length of flooring.

Builder Responsibility: The Builder should perform repairs or replacements to conform to the Performance Guideline unless the damage results from Homeowner misuse or negligence.
Homeowner Responsibility: The Homeowner should follow the flooring manufacturer's cleaning and care instructions for vinyl flooring.

Condition #9: Cuts, Tears, or Scratches Appear on the Surface

Potentially Impacting:

- Appearance

Performance Guideline

At the time of the walkthrough there should be no cuts, tears or scratches on the flooring surface that are visible from a distance of 6 feet under normal lighting conditions.

Builder Responsibility: The Builder should perform repairs or replacements to conform to the Performance Guideline unless the damage results from Homeowner misuse or negligence.

Homeowner Responsibility: None. The Homeowner should be aware that the actions of moving into a Home can scratch or otherwise damage floor surfaces.

Carpet Flooring

Condition #1: Carpet Seams Are Visible

Potentially Impacting:

- Appearance

Performance Guideline

Visibility of carpet seams is acceptable unless the seam is not butted tightly and the seaming tape shows.

Comments: The visibility of seams depends on the type of carpet installed and more importantly, on the height of the pile. Carpets with short nap, or pile, or with Berber type weaves will show seams. Higher pile carpets, including plush and shag carpeting, can be installed so that seams tend not to show. Carpet is a textile product that is manufactured in 12 foot widths. If the room is wider than 12 feet, it will have a seam.

Builder Responsibility: The Builder should perform necessary repairs to conform to the Performance Guideline.

Homeowner Responsibility: The Homeowner should follow the carpeting manufacturer's cleaning and care instructions.

Condition #2: Carpet Is Loose

Potentially Impacting:

- Appearance

Performance Guideline

Carpets should be stretched tightly with no loose areas. If the carpet is loose, the Builder should have it re-stretched.

Builder Responsibility: The Builder should perform repairs to conform to the Performance Guideline.

Homeowner Responsibility: The Homeowner should follow the carpeting manufacturer's cleaning and care instructions.

Condition #3: Carpet Pile Is Crushed

Potentially Impacting:

- Appearance

Performance Guideline

Carpets, especially those with long fibers like a plush or shag, are wound tightly on rolls as part of the manufacturing process. Over time, pile crushes should return to their intended level of resilience. This condition is not a defect.

Builder Responsibility: None.

Homeowner Responsibility: The Homeowner should vacuum frequently during the first two weeks after the *walkthrough* in order to help raise the pile.

Condition #4: Carpet Fibers Separate from Backing

Potentially Impacting:

- Appearance

Performance Guideline

Carpet fibers usually do not separate from backing unless the carpet has been cleaned with improper products or has been allowed to remain wet for an extended period of time. Proper carpet maintenance is a Homeowner responsibility.

Builder Responsibility: The Builder should ensure that the carpeted floor conforms to the Performance Guideline.

Homeowner Responsibility: The Homeowner should not allow the carpet to remain wet for extended periods of time and should promptly clean any spills in accordance with the material manufacturer's recommendations.

Condition #5: Carpet Is Faded or Discolored

Potentially Impacting:

- Appearance

Performance Guideline

Proper carpet maintenance is a Homeowner responsibility. Some fading is unavoidable in areas that are exposed to sunlight. Spots are usually the result of spills or pet accidents. The Homeowner should promptly neutralize and remove any spills in a manner consistent with the manufacturer's recommendations.

Builder Responsibility: The Builder should repair or replace any carpet fading or discoloration noted at the time of the *walkthrough*.

Homeowner Responsibility: The Homeowner should choose carpet colors and types that will provide the longest life in locations with sun exposure. Carpet continuously exposed to sunlight may fade. The Homeowner should promptly clean spills in accordance with the material manufacturer's recommendations.

Condition #6: Pad Is Missing under Portions of the Carpet

Potentially Impacting:
- Occupant comfort

Performance Guideline

Carpet padding that is missing is unacceptable and should be added by the Builder. Some Builders choose, however, to eliminate padding from closets that are not walk-in closets. This condition is acceptable in those areas.

Builder Responsibility: The Builder should perform the repairs to conform to the Performance Guideline.

Homeowner Responsibility: None. However, Homeowners should follow the manufacturer's care and cleaning instructions.

Condition #7: Carpet Texture Does Not Align at Seams

Potentially Impacting:
- Appearance

Performance Guideline

Texture at seams should run in the same direction. "Quarter turns" (joining the carpet at 90 degrees to the texture run of the other piece) are not acceptable.

Builder Responsibility: The Builder should perform the repairs to conform to the Performance Guideline.

Homeowner Responsibility: None. However, Homeowners should follow the manufacturer's care and cleaning instructions.

Condition #8: Carpets Have Dark Soil Line at Stair and Baseboard Edges

Potentially Impacting:
- Appearance

Performance Guideline

Soil staining of carpets due to air infiltration can be reduced, but not entirely eliminated, at stair and baseboard edges. The Builder should seal the plate behind the baseboard and stair edges with foam, caulk, or by making the joints tight.

Builder Responsibility: The Builder should ensure that that there are no soil lines visible at the time of the *walkthrough*.

Homeowner Responsibility: The Homeowner can expect some soiling to occur at baseboard and stair edges even if the Builder has made a good faith effort to seal the edges. The Homeowner should consider this when selecting carpet colors. Light colors can show edge marks in a short period of time.

Condition #9: Carpet Has a Bump at the Transition between Carpet and Hard Surface Flooring

Potentially Impacting:

- Appearance
- Safety issue related to tripping hazard

Performance Guideline

There should be no more than a ¼ inch vertical displacement between different finish flooring surfaces. Ramping or floating the subfloor is an acceptable method to conform to the Performance Guideline. Ramps should extend under the carpet at the rate of 1 foot horizontal for every ¼ inch vertical. Specifically designed transition strips made of metal or wood may be placed at the transition threshold.

Builder Responsibility: The Builder should perform repairs to conform to the Performance Guideline.

Homeowner Responsibility: None.

Plaster and Drywall

General Subject Information: *Plaster* and *drywall* are materials used to cover most of the interior walls of a Home. Drywall, also known as *Sheetrock®*, *gypsum board*, or wallboard, is the predominant interior wall covering. Plaster, while used exclusively until about 50 years ago, is used primarily in custom applications today. Both products have the same basic ingredients: gypsum and bonding or strengthening agents. While plaster is mixed and applied on the job-site, drywall is made in a factory in sheets that are typically 4 feet x 8 feet x ½ or 5/8 inch thick. Drywall is nailed or screwed to the wall *studs*, and the joints are covered with a paper tape and a gypsum based compound. Special corner pieces, known as *beads*, are screwed, nailed, or adhesively attached to wall corners. When the walls are smooth, they are textured with more gypsum compound. The texturing process may be accomplished by hand troweling or by spraying with a machine. Spray texturing, which is the method of choice today, can be made with a number of different patterns such as knock down, eggshell, fog and dash. Some patterns are intentionally rough and irregular while others are supposed to be uniform throughout. Smooth finished drywall surfaces are typically found only in custom homes.

Condition #1: Drywall/Plaster Is Cracked

Potentially Impacting:

- Appearance

Performance Guideline

Cracks in excess of 3/32 inch in width are considered unacceptable.

Comments: As the wood *frame* of the Home dries, cracks can be expected to appear in the *plaster* or *drywall*. Common places for cracks to appear are at the heads of windows and where walls and ceiling planes intersect. By and large, drywall and plaster cracks that meet the Guideline are a Homeowner maintenance item.

Builder Responsibility: Unless frame or foundation movement is causing significant cracking, the Builder should perform repairs to conform to the Performance Guideline. If frame or foundation movement is causing the cracking, the Builder must first remedy this condition before attempting drywall or plaster repairs.

Homeowner Responsibility: The Homeowner is responsible for maintaining drywall and plaster cracks less than 3/32 inch. The Homeowner should patch cracks with spackle or *caulk*.

Condition #2: Drywall Has Nail Pops

Potentially Impacting:

- Appearance

Performance Guideline

Nail pops that are visible from a distance of 6 feet under normal light conditions are unacceptable. Nail pops that have cracked the surface or with exposed heads are unacceptable. This Performance Guideline also applies to drywall screws.

Builder Responsibility: The Builder should perform repairs to conform to the Performance Guideline.

Homeowner Responsibility: None.

Condition #3: Corner Bead or Tape Seam Pops

Potentially Impacting:

- Appearance

Performance Guideline

Corner beads that are cracked or pulled away from walls or tape seams that have pulled away and are visible from any angle at a distance of 6 feet under normal lighting conditions are considered unacceptable.

Builder Responsibility: The Builder should perform repairs to conform to the Performance Guideline.

Homeowner Responsibility: None.

Condition #4: Drywall Crowns in Ceiling, Drywall Bows on Walls

Potentially Impacting:

- Appearance

Performance Guideline

Drywall crowns in ceilings should not exceed ¼ inch in a 32 inch distance across. Drywall bows in walls should not exceed 3/16 inches in a 32 inch distance across.

Builder Responsibility: The Builder should repair drywall crowns or bows in excess of the Performance Guideline. Floating and retexturing is considered an acceptable repair method.

Homeowner Responsibility: None. If the Homeowner performs measurements to determine compliance with the Guideline, it should be made with a level or true straight edge tool no less than 6 feet in length.

Condition #5: Surface Texture Is Uneven or Irregular

Potentially Impacting:

- Appearance

Performance Guideline

Textured surfaces should be consistent with the applicator's intent; texture that is designed to be knocked down should be reasonably uniform, and texture that is designed to be sprayed on without further treatment should be reasonably uniform throughout, when viewed from a distance of 6 feet under normal lighting conditions. This Performance Guideline for texture workmanship does not apply to garages and other utility areas which may also be drywalled and textured. No more than 10% of the wall surface should contain dimples, blotches, tool marks, or other irregularities visible from a distance of 6 feet under normal lighting conditions.

Comments: Surface texture is more art than science, and determining unacceptable texture is quite subjective. Hand textured walls and ceilings clearly bear the "signature" of the applicator, can be irregular, and may be very difficult to match by another applicator. Spray textured walls that are knocked down may have patches of texture that run together when compared to other areas. Unless these patches dominate the appearance of the wall, this would be considered normal application. Areas that are not knocked down or areas that contain numerous tool marks are not acceptable. Texture that is fogged (light coating) and texture that is egg-shell (medium coating) is intended to have a uniform, but bumpy appearance. The best measure of texture evaluation is consistency from wall-to-wall and from room-to-room.

Builder Responsibility: If more than 10% of the wall surface contains dimples, blotches, tool marks or other irregularities that are visible when viewed at a distance of 6 feet under normal lighting conditions, the Builder should perform repairs to meet the Performance Guideline.

Homeowner Responsibility: The Homeowner should realize that wall and ceiling texturing is an art and not a precise science. Irregularities should be expected. These irregularities are often more prominent at night when single light sources, such as light fixtures, cast shadows. Determining wall texture performance by feeling it is not an acceptable measure.

Countertops (General)

General Subject Information: The following types of countertop materials are commonly used in residential construction: ceramic tile, granite, marble, plastic laminate, solid surface, *concrete*, and cultured marble. These specific types of countertops are discussed individually in following sections. The Performance Guidelines below are for countertops in general.

Condition #1: Countertop Is Not Level

Potentially Impacting:

- Appearance
- Functional

Performance Guideline

Countertops should not exceed ¼ inch of rise or drop in any 8 foot direction. Exception: certain tiles are made with an intentionally irregular, lumpy surface and these irregularities are acceptable (see below Ceramic Tile Countertops, Condition # 1: Uneven Surface).

Builder Responsibility: The Builder should take corrective measures to level the countertop, including leveling the cabinets, if necessary.

Homeowner Responsibility: None.

Condition #2: Backsplash Is Loose

Potentially Impacting:

- Function
- Appearance

Performance Guideline

Countertop backsplashes should be tightly adhered to the wall.

Builder Responsibility: The Builder should perform the corrections to repair the loose backsplash.

Homeowner Responsibility: The Homeowner should be aware that cabinets expand and shrink with room moisture. Cracks will occur between the top and the splash. The Homeowner should patch cracks with *caulk* or *grout*.

Ceramic Tile Countertops

Condition #1: Countertop Surface Is Uneven

Potentially Impacting:

- Appearance

Performance Guideline

Since there are a number of different types of ceramic tile, ranging from rough handmade varieties to precisely manufactured types, it is impractical to apply any one standard to all ceramic tiles. The general Performance Guideline for an entire countertop is no more than 1/8 inch of uneven surface (as measured between highest and lowest points) in any direction in 8 feet horizontally. For handmade tiles, the condition is established by using a long straightedge that rests on multiple high points along the countertop length. For very regular manufactured tiles, in addition to the level Guideline, no point should occur more than 1/16 inch above or below a line parallel to the surface, and adjacent tiles should not be more than 1/32 inch out of level with each other. Countertops can be totally level but should never slope away from drainage points such as sinks or basins.

Builder Responsibility: The Builder should perform repairs to conform to the Performance Guideline for the specific ceramic tile.

Homeowner Responsibility: None. However, the Homeowner should follow the manufacturer's care and cleaning recommendations for the specific ceramic tile.

Condition #2: Countertop Grout Joints Are Uneven

Potentially Impacting:

- Appearance

Performance Guideline

Different types of tiles call for grout joints of different widths. However, within any one area of tile (for precise and manufactured tiles), joints should not vary more than 1/16 inch from the widest to the narrowest.

Builder Responsibility: The Builder should perform repairs to conform to the Performance Guideline for the specific ceramic tile.

Homeowner Responsibility: None. However, the Homeowner should follow the manufacturer's care and cleaning recommendations for the specific ceramic tile.

Condition #3: Countertop Grout Joint Is Cracked

Potentially Impacting:

- Appearance

Performance Guideline

Hairline cracks may appear in grout joints where there are changes in the plane of the tile surface and where tile abuts a dissimilar material, such as at a backsplash, sink or wall. Excluding joints at changes in plane, cracks exceeding 5% of the total length of grout joint in any one-tile installation are considered unacceptable.

Builder Responsibility: The Builder should perform repairs to conform to the Performance Guideline unless the condition is a result of inadequate Homeowner maintenance or misuse.

Homeowner Responsibility: ***Maintenance Alert!*** The Homeowner should maintain *caulking* and repair incidental grout cracking, especially at backsplash and sink openings.

Condition #4: Countertop Has a Cracked Tile

Potentially Impacting:

- Appearance

Performance Guideline

Where cracks align across a number of consecutive tiles, the usual cause is movement of underlying building components. Isolated cracks in individual tiles may indicate Homeowner abuse of the countertop. Cracks should not exceed 1/32 inch in width.

Builder Responsibility: If an underlying problem is identified after investigation, the Builder should perform repairs to conform to the Performance Guideline.

Homeowner Responsibility: The Homeowner should not place unusually heavy objects on tile surfaces and should avoid dropping things on the tiles. The Homeowner should follow the manufacturer's care and cleaning recommendations for the specific ceramic tile.

Condition #5: Countertop Color and Texture Varies

Potentially Impacting:

- Appearance

Performance Guideline

Tile used in any one area should be from the same batch, or lot, providing consistent appearance throughout. This does not apply to certain types of handmade tile in which variations are a desirable characteristic. Obvious changes in color and texture within a field of tile are not acceptable where the tile is intended to be of consistent appearance.*

*For the purpose of this Manual, "unacceptable color variation" is defined as an obvious difference in color in the opinion of one or more independent observers who are qualified experts in the subject of tile manufacturing and/or installation. A similar general definition applies to "unacceptable texture variation."

Comments: The Homeowner should note that *trim* tiles (the tile that caps the top or edge of a wall or countertop) are not manufactured in the same batch as the flat, or field, tiles. Consequently, there may be variations in color between trim and field tiles.

Builder Responsibility: The Builder should perform repairs to conform to the Performance Guideline.

Homeowner Responsibility: None. However, the Homeowner should follow the manufacturer's care and cleaning recommendations for the specific ceramic tile.

Condition #6: Countertop Has Loose Tiles

Potentially Impacting:

- Appearance

Performance Guideline

Generally, tile should not come loose from the underlying surface to which it is applied. More specifically, tile can come loose as a result of improper original application of mortar; excessive deflection of the underlying material to which tile is applied or because of impact from heavy objects.

Builder Responsibility: If the condition is a result of improper installation or construction and not a result of Homeowner misuse, the Builder should perform repairs to conform to the Performance Guideline for the specific ceramic tile.

Homeowner Responsibility: None. The Homeowner should avoid dropping heavy objects on the tile surfaces. The Homeowner should follow the manufacturer's care and cleaning recommendations for the specific ceramic tile.

Condition #7: Water Penetrates Through Countertop

Potentially Impacting:

- Appearance
- Integrity of underlying surfaces

Performance Guideline

Properly installed, countertops intended for use that involve exposure to significant amounts of water (food preparation areas, countertops adjacent to sinks and basins, etc.) should include a water resisting system adequate to prevent leaks through the countertop assembly.

Builder Responsibility: The Builder should perform repairs to conform to the Performance Guideline for the specific ceramic tile.

Homeowner Responsibility: None. However, the Homeowner should follow the manufacturer's care and cleaning recommendations for the specific ceramic tile.

Granite, Marble, Stone and Concrete Countertops

Also refer to the "**Granite, Marble, and Other Stone Flooring**" section of this chapter, page 149.

General Subject Information: Granite, marble and other stone countertops are natural products. *Concrete* contains natural products that are mixed together. There are many other stone products available such as limestone, slate and travertine. Because these are natural products, their color and veining are never exactly alike. The Homeowner should expect variations from installations in other similar homes. Granite, marble, and other stone surfaces are vulnerable to impact damage (dropping heavy items on their surfaces). Concrete is more resistant.

Condition #1: Countertop Is Cracked

Potentially Impacting:

- Appearance
- Life of countertop

Performance Guideline

Cracks in excess of 1/32 inch are considered unacceptable. Cracks may be related to improper or inadequate installation, or a result of inadequate support. Improper use may also be a cause (see ***Homeowner Responsibility*** *below).*

Builder Responsibility: After investigation, the Builder should repair or replace unacceptable countertops unless the damage results from Homeowner improper use. Specialists in stone restoration should repair cracked marble. Before undertaking such repairs, the Builder should correct any underlying causes.

Homeowner Responsibility: The Homeowner should maintain countertops in accordance with the recommendations of the material manufacturer and supplier. Maintain *caulking* and repair incidental *grout* cracking, especially at *backsplash* and sink openings. Do not drop heavy objects on countertops. Do not stand on countertops without a protective separation such as a rubber-backed floor mat.

Condition #2: Countertop Color and Texture Varies

Potentially Impacting:

- Appearance

Performance Guideline

Countertops made up of multiple pieces should be assembled with reasonably well matched colors. Severe variations in surface texture and color are unacceptable. (Refer to the unacceptable color variation definition described above, Condition #5, page 163.)

Builder Responsibility: The Builder should ensure that the countertop conforms to the Performance Guideline at the time of *walkthrough*.

Homeowner Responsibility: While individual perceptions of both texture and color are truly subjective in nature, a good rule of thumb is if the Homeowner buys the Home before the finish surfaces are set, the Homeowner should approve their placement. If the Homeowner buys the Home after the finish surfaces are installed, the Homeowner accepts the finishes as installed.

Condition #3: Countertop Is Stained

Potentially Impacting:

- Appearance

Performance Guideline

Granite, marble, and stone can be stained by a variety of products and natural materials, juices, etc. Protection of the surface is a Homeowner Responsibility. Any preexisting stains should be noted at the time of the Homeowner walkthrough.

Builder Responsibility: The Builder should correct any preexisting stains noted at the walkthrough. If preexisting stains cannot be corrected, the Builder should replace the countertop.

Homeowner Responsibility: The Homeowner should examine countertops carefully at the walkthrough. The Builder cannot be held responsible for this type of damage unless it is identified and disclosed at the time of the walkthrough. The Homeowner should maintain countertops in accordance with the recommendations of the material manufacturer and supplier. The Homeowner should use only cleaning products approved by the manufacturer or the applicable trade association for the material (for instance, the Marble Institute of America for granite and marble countertops). Do not use abrasives to clean any type of countertop. Avoid placing hot pots, pans, etc., in direct contact with the countertop.

Condition #4: Countertop Has Chips

Potentially Impacting:

- Appearance
- Maintenance

Performance Guideline

Granite, marble, and stone countertops should not be delivered to the Homeowner scratched or chipped. Repairs of chips and scratches prior to the walkthrough are acceptable provided the repair cannot be distinguished at a distance of 6 feet under normal lighting conditions. Chips on a countertop of any material should not penetrate more than 1/16 inch from the edge of the seam or grout joint unless the manufacturing process (as with tumbled stone) intentionally created edge chips.

Builder Responsibility: The Builder should repair or replace countertops to conform to the Performance Guideline unless the damage results from Homeowner misuse or negligence.

Homeowner Responsibility: The Homeowner should examine countertops carefully at the walkthrough. The Homeowner should maintain countertops in accordance with the recommendations of the material manufacturer and supplier. Do not drop heavy objects on the countertop.

Condition #5: Countertop Seams Are Visible

Potentially Impacting:

- Appearance
- Maintenance

Performance Guideline

Granite, marble, and stone countertops are natural products, and it is not always possible to join pieces without seams showing. This is particularly true for plain or simple patterns (grains). Tight seams that are visible are not a defect.

Builder Responsibility: None.

Homeowner Responsibility: The Homeowner should examine countertops carefully at the *walkthrough*. The Homeowner should maintain countertops in accordance with recommendations of the material manufacturer and supplier. If the Homeowner has a concern about visible seams, it should be discussed at the walkthrough.

Condition #6: Countertop Has Excessive Lippage

Potentially Impacting:

- Appearance
- Maintenance

Performance Guideline

Lippage greater than 1/64 inch is considered unacceptable.

Builder Responsibility: The Builder should adjust the portions of the countertop to conform to the Performance Guideline.

Homeowner Responsibility: None.

Plastic Laminate Countertops

Condition #1: Countertop Has Open Joints

Potentially Impacting:

- Appearance
- Watertightness

Performance Guideline

A properly assembled plastic laminate countertop should have tight hairline joints without any openings where adjoining pieces meet. Joints that are separated by more than 1/32 inch are considered unacceptable.

Builder Responsibility: The Builder should repair or replace countertops to conform to the Performance Guideline unless the condition results from Homeowner misuse or negligence.

Homeowner Responsibility: The Homeowner should examine countertops carefully at the *walkthrough*. The Homeowner should maintain countertops in accordance with recommendations of the material manufacturer and supplier. Do not put hot pans directly on laminate countertops.

Condition #2: Countertop Shows Delamination

Potentially Impacting:

- Appearance
- Life of countertop

Performance Guideline

Delamination occurs when the plastic laminate does not adhere to the underlayment. This is usually an adhesive application or curing problem. Edge strips are most commonly affected by this type of problem. Delamination is unacceptable and should be corrected by the Builder unless there is evidence of abusive use by the Homeowner.

Builder Responsibility: The Builder should repair or replace countertops to conform to the Performance Guideline unless the condition results from Homeowner misuse or negligence.

Homeowner Responsibility: The Homeowner should maintain countertops in accordance with recommendations of the material manufacturer and supplier. The Homeowner is responsible for maintaining *caulking*, especially at *backsplash* and sink openings.

Condition #3: Countertop Is Bowed

Potentially Impacting:

- Appearance
- Usefulness of countertop

Performance Guideline

Laminate tops should not bow or warp more than 1/16 inch in each foot of length.

Builder Responsibility: The Builder should repair or replace countertops to conform to the Performance Guideline.

Homeowner Responsibility: The Homeowner should maintain countertops in accordance with recommendations of the material manufacturer and supplier. The Homeowner is responsible for maintaining caulking, especially at *backsplash* and sink openings. The Homeowner should avoid allowing water to stand on the countertop and putting hot objects on the countertop.

Condition #4: Countertop Edges Are Irregular

Potentially Impacting:

- Appearance

Performance Guideline

Unacceptable trimming can include edges that are not straight and edges that are burned because of overheating of trimming cutters. Trimmed edges should be very straight and neat. The edge exposure area should be of a constant width throughout the countertop.

Builder Responsibility: The Builder should repair or replace countertops to conform to the Performance Guideline.

Homeowner Responsibility: None. However, the Homeowner should maintain countertops in accordance with recommendations of the material manufacturer and supplier.

Condition #5: Countertop Has Stains and Burns

Potentially Impacting:

- Appearance

Performance Guideline

The countertop should be delivered to the Homeowner without stains, scratches or burns.

Builder Responsibility: The Builder should repair or replace any unacceptable conditions noted at the time of the *walkthrough*.

Homeowner Responsibility: The Homeowner should examine countertops carefully at the walkthrough. The Builder cannot be held responsible for this type of damage unless it is identified and disclosed at the time of the walkthrough. The Homeowner should maintain countertops in accordance with the recommendations of the material manufacturer and supplier. The Homeowner should use only cleaning products approved by the material manufacturer and never use abrasive cleaners. The Homeowner should avoid placing hot objects on countertops.

Condition #6: Countertop Does Not Fit Properly

Potentially Impacting:

- Appearance
- Watertightness

Performance Guideline

The top and backsplash pieces should fit together without gaps. The installer is likely to caulk these joints with a compatible caulk. If there is a gap between the backsplash and the wall, this gap should also be caulked so that it is not visible. No gap should be more than 1/8 inch wide, whether caulked or not.

Builder Responsibility: The Builder should make corrections so the countertops conform to the Performance Guideline.

Homeowner Responsibility: The Homeowner should promptly remove spills on the countertop. Liquids can penetrate the seams and cause the *underlayment* to swell.

Solid Surface Countertops

"Solid surface countertops" refers to the class of plastics called acrylic or polyester, or to blends of plastics and fiberglass. This includes products with names such as Avonite™, Cerata™, Corian™, Corinthian™, Fountainhead™, Gibralter™, Hi-macs™, Staron™, Surrell™, Swanstone™ Zodiac™, and many other synthetic surfaces.

Condition #1: Countertop Has Open Seams

Potentially Impacting:

- Appearance
- Watertightness

Performance Guideline

Depending on the selected color and veining, there should be no conspicuous seams in the finished countertop. Proficient solid surface countertop installers are able to bond adjacent pieces so that the joint is virtually invisible. Some solid surface pieces may be "softseamed" with a flexible silicone (such as the narrow solid surface strip behind slide-in ranges).

Builder Responsibility: The Builder should repair or replace countertops to conform to the Performance Guideline.

Homeowner Responsibility: The Homeowner should examine countertops carefully at the *walkthrough*. The Homeowner should maintain countertops in accordance with the recommendations of the material manufacturer and supplier.

Condition #2: Countertop Has a Rough Surface

Potentially Impacting:

- Appearance
- Cleanliness

Performance Guideline

To finish solid surface countertops it is often necessary to sand the surface. The resulting final surface should be smooth and consistent throughout. Surface texture variations that are clearly rough to the touch are considered unacceptable.

Builder Responsibility: The Builder should repair or replace any unacceptable conditions noted at the time of the *walkthrough*.

Homeowner Responsibility: The Homeowner should examine countertops carefully at the walkthrough. The Homeowner should maintain countertops in accordance with the recommendations of the material manufacturer and supplier.

Condition #3: Countertop Has Stains and Burns

Potentially Impacting:
- Appearance

Performance Guideline

There should be no stains or burns on any portion of the countertop at the time of the Homeowner walkthrough.

Builder Responsibility: The Builder should repair or replace any unacceptable conditions noted at the time of the walkthrough.

Homeowner Responsibility: None. However, the Homeowner should examine countertops carefully at the walkthrough. The Homeowner should maintain countertops in accordance with the recommendations of the material manufacturer and supplier. The Builder cannot be held responsible for this type of damage unless it is identified and disclosed at the time of the walkthrough.

Condition #4: Countertop Has Blemishes and Scratches

Potentially Impacting:
- Appearance

Performance Guideline

A solid surface countertop is a product that is manufactured under closely controlled conditions. The countertop should be delivered to the Homeowner free of blemishes and scratches.

Builder Responsibility: The Builder should repair or replace countertops to conform to the Performance Guideline.

Homeowner Responsibility: None. However, the Homeowner should examine countertops carefully at the *walkthrough*. The Homeowner should maintain countertops in accordance with the recommendations of the material manufacturer and supplier. The Builder cannot be held responsible for this type of damage unless it is identified and disclosed at the time of the walkthrough.

Cultured Marble Countertops

General Subject Information: Cultured marble countertops are synthetic products. Unlike other solid surface countertops discussed in previous sections (which are considered the "new generation" of solid surface countertops), cultured marble has been around for at least 60 years. The Performance Guidelines for cultured marble are less rigorous than for the new solid surface products. There is an upgraded version of cultured marble known as "onyx". Onyx has a smoother top and more uniform color spread than basic cultured marble. Performance Guidelines for cultured marble countertops also apply to onyx countertops.

Condition #1: Countertop Does Not Fit Properly

Potentially Impacting:

- Appearance
- Watertightness

Performance Guideline

Top and backsplash pieces should fit together without gaps. The installer is likely to caulk these joints with a compatible caulk. If there is a gap between the backsplash and the wall, it should also be caulked so that no gap is visible. No gap should be more than 1/8 inch wide whether caulked or not.

Builder Responsibility: The Builder should repair or replace countertops to conform to the Performance Guideline.

Homeowner Responsibility: None. However, the Homeowner should examine countertops carefully at the *walkthrough*. The Homeowner should maintain countertops in accordance with the recommendations of the material manufacturer and supplier.

Condition #2: Countertop Has Blemishes and Inconsistent Color

Potentially Impacting:

- Appearance

Performance Guideline

Color swirls can vary significantly in cultured marble. In general, the color swirls should be consistent throughout the top and should not be concentrated in any one spot. The same Performance Guideline applies to metal sparkles, if added to the mix.

Builder Responsibility: The Builder should repair or replace countertops to conform to the Performance Guideline.

Homeowner Responsibility: None. However, the Homeowner should examine countertops carefully at the *walkthrough*. The Homeowner should maintain countertops in accordance with the recommendations of the material manufacturer and supplier.

Condition #3: Countertop Has Voids in the Surface

Potentially Impacting:

- Appearance

Performance Guideline

There should be no voids (depressions) in the surface more than 1/32 inch in depth or larger than 1 inch in diameter. Even if this Guideline is compliant there should be no more than 4 such voids on the surfaces in 8 square feet of surface.

Builder Responsibility: The Builder should repair or replace countertops to conform to the Performance Guideline unless damage results from Homeowner misuse or negligence.

Homeowner Responsibility: The Homeowner should examine countertops carefully at the *walkthrough*. The Homeowner should maintain countertops in accordance with the recommendations of the material manufacturer and supplier and avoid dropping heavy objects on the countertop.

Condition #4: Countertop Leaks at Joints and Fittings

Potentially Impacting:

- Appearance
- Cabinet contents / integrity

Performance Guideline

All penetrations at the faucets, sink rims and backsplashes should be watertight. Cultured marble countertops with integrated bowls should not have any cracks that are visible from a distance of 3 feet and can withstand water temperatures of 130 degrees Fahrenheit without cracking.

Builder Responsibility: The Builder should repair unacceptable conditions to conform to the Performance Guideline.

Homeowner Responsibility: The Homeowner should maintain countertops in accordance with the recommendations of the material manufacturer and supplier. If at any time the Homeowner discovers product or installation problems, the Homeowner should promptly notify the Builder.

Appliances

General Subject Information: There are two broad categories of appliances in a Home: 1) kitchen and laundry type appliances such as dishwasher, oven, range, dryer, etc.; and 2) system appliances such as *furnace*, air conditioner, water heater, and gas burning fireplace. Smoke and carbon monoxide alarms are often considered appliances. With respect to warranty responsibility, the Builder may treat each category differently. It is important that Homeowners understand their responsibility in dealing with appliance warranty claims.

Generally, it is the custom and practice of the Builder to exclude the kitchen appliances from the Home warranty. Kitchen appliances are warranted by their manufacturer and have online warranty registration cards for the Homeowner to complete. If the appliance is not performing as intended, a service technician from the appliance manufacturer is the provider for repair services. Manufacturers have a specific product warranty that is not necessarily linked to the Builder's warranty. For system appliance claims, the sub-contractor who made the original installation may also perform repairs. A third party repair service that has contracted with the manufacturer may perform the repairs.

ENERGY STAR
ENERGY STAR® APPLIANCES
SAVE SIGNIFICANT ENERGY

Green Tip! Always use appliances that are Energy Star® rated.

Condition #1: Appliances Do Not Perform as Intended

Performance Guideline

All appliances should function in the manner that the manufacturer intended.

Comments:

- When does an unacceptable appliance become a Builder Responsibility as opposed to a manufacturer's responsibility? The rule of thumb is as follows: if the problem is contained within the appliance itself, it is the appliance manufacturer's responsibility. If the problem is outside the appliance, it is the Builder's Responsibility. For example, if the dishwasher does not operate properly because the *door latch* won't close, it is the manufacturer's responsibility. However, if a water supply hose to the dishwasher is leaking, it is the Builder's Responsibility.

- What if it is not easy to tell who is responsible for the unacceptable condition? For example, if the *furnace* does not come on, is it a faulty thermostat or is the furnace not performing as intended? If the air conditioner does not start (after remaining idle all winter) is it a faulty *compressor* or a blown fuse? Depending upon the warranty, the Builder might contact the appliance manufacturer for the Homeowner or the Builder may expect the Homeowner to make the contact directly. Assuming the Homeowner has not abused the appliance and the unacceptable condition occurs within the manufacturer's warranty period, the manufacturer is the likely source of repair.
- Homeowner registration of appliances with the manufacturer within the first 10 days of taking delivery of the Home is essential.

Manufacturer's Responsibility: Repair the appliance in a prompt manner in accordance with the manufacturer's warranty.

Builder Responsibility: The Builder should install appliances in strict accordance with installation instructions furnished by the manufacturer and repair any faulty installation.

Homeowner Responsibility: The Homeowner should register all appliances with the manufacturer. The Homeowner should read and follow the manufacturer's operating instructions and before making a service call, follow the Trouble Shooting Guide found at the back of most appliance owner's manuals.

Cabinets and Vanities

General Subject Information: There are two conditions common to cabinets or vanities: 1) the finish is wearing prematurely; or 2) the drawer slide brackets fail. Cabinet finishes tend to age more in hot, humid rooms and in areas that surround sinks due to water that is splashed on the finish. Other typical problems include gaps that appear between cabinet cases or *doors* and drawer panels that sag or that do not align.

Condition #1: Cabinets Designed to Set Flush with the Ceiling Have a Visible Gap, Space, or Separation

Potentially Impacting:

- Appearance

Performance Guideline

Any unintended space or gap along the top or sides of cabinet frames that exceeds 1/8 inch is considered unacceptable.

Comments: As the new Home acclimates to its setting, the structure will have a tendency to contract as the rough lumber dries out. This has the potential to affect interior finishes and is considered normal. However, if the condition worsens, this may indicate a lack of fastening or the lack of adequate backing for proper cabinet support.

Builder Responsibility: All cabinets should have the proper backing in the wall to support whatever product is being applied to that particular wall. If the cabinet or vanity does not conform to the Performance Guideline and is not the result of Homeowner negligence, then the Builder should repair as necessary to conform to the Performance Guideline.

Homeowner Responsibility: The Homeowner should use caution not to overload upper cabinets. Heavy plates and dishes and canned goods do not belong in upper cabinets. (Refer to Preface: "**Ten Most Common Mistakes Made by New Homeowners**", page 19.)

Condition #2: Cabinets Are Not Set Flush with One Another

Potentially Impacting:

- Appearance

Performance Guideline

The face (front) of a cabinet should not be more than 1/8 inch out of line with connecting portions of other cabinet pieces. Corners should not be out of line more than 3/16 inches.

Builder Responsibility: If cabinets do not meet the Performance Guideline, the Builder should perform repairs or replace unacceptable cabinetry. When finishing or refinishing, the Builder should attempt to match the material, color and sheen of the original cabinetry.

Homeowner Responsibility: The Homeowner should properly maintain all cabinets, particularly cabinetry located in areas subject to moisture, for example kitchens, bathrooms or laundry rooms. Water should not be allowed to remain on any wood products whether sealed or not. If it is determined that the damage results from improper or lack of maintenance by the Homeowner, the Builder is not responsible.

Condition #3: Cabinet Frame Is Out of Square

Potentially Impacting:

- Appearance

Performance Guideline

Cabinet frames shall not be out of square by more than ¼ inch when measured diagonally.

Builder Responsibility: If the cabinets do not conform to the Performance Guideline, the Builder should repair or replace unacceptable cabinetry.

Homeowner Responsibility: None.

Condition #4: Cabinet Door Is Warped

Potentially Impacting:
- Appearance
- Function / performance

Performance Guideline

Cabinet doors should not warp more than 3/16 inch from the face of the frame. If the door is flat, but the frame is warped, the same Performance Guideline applies.

Comments: Cabinets in contact with water and the lack of proper maintenance are major contributing factors to warping. Cabinetry in the proximity of water, for example, in front of a sink, may need refinishing more often than other cabinets in the Home.

Builder Responsibility: If the condition does not result from Homeowner negligence, the Builder should replace, either in part or in whole, cabinet or cabinetry, including doors and drawer fronts, that do not conform to the Performance Guideline. When finishing or refinishing, the Builder should attempt to match the material, color and sheen of the original cabinetry.

Homeowner Responsibility: The Homeowner should periodically inspect cabinets, drawer fronts and doors for excessive wear, warping, and deterioration of the finish.

Condition #5: Cabinet Drawer Guide Is Broken

Potentially Impacting:
- Operation

Performance Guideline

At the time of the walkthrough, all doors and drawers should function smoothly and properly for their intended purpose.

Comments: Drawer guides that support the drawer opening commonly fail. Drawer guides are often made of plastic and may break over time. This is an inexpensive replacement item that can be purchased at a hardware store.

Builder Responsibility: If a drawer or door does not conform to the Performance Guideline, the Builder should perform the necessary repairs or replacement.

Homeowner Responsibility: Homeowners should be careful not to overload drawers. This puts additional stress on the guides, which could cause them to fail prematurely.

Condition #6: Cabinet Drawer Is Binding during Opening

Potentially Impacting:
- Operation

Performance Guideline

Cabinet doors and drawers should open and close smoothly without tugging or pulling.

Comments: Drawers should not be overloaded and should operate smoothly. Both doors and drawers should operate with reasonable ease and effort.

Builder Responsibility: If a drawer or door does not conform to the Performance Guideline, the Builder should repair or replace the drawer or door.

Homeowner Responsibility: The Homeowner should operate doors and drawers smoothly and easily. Do not overload the drawers. ***Maintenance Alert!*** Metal drawer guides should be lubricated with light lubricating oil every two years.

Condition #7: Cabinet Door Swings Open and/or Will Not Stay Closed

Potentially Impacting:

- Appearance
- Function/performance

Performance Guideline

All door hinge mechanisms and catches should operate and function as intended. Whether closing or opening, the door should operate smoothly with reasonable ease or effort. Cabinets should be installed level and plumb to ensure proper operation.

Comments: Cabinet hinges can become loose and occasionally may need to be retightened or adjusted, a relatively simple Homeowner maintenance item.

Builder Responsibility: If the door or door hardware does not conform to the Performance Guideline, the Builder should repair or replace door hinges or catches as necessary.

Homeowner Responsibility: Doors can go out of adjustment, depending upon the care and use that they have been put through. The Homeowner should not slam, hang objects from, or pull on the door as this will cause hinge mechanisms to weaken at their fastening points and within the mechanisms themselves. Periodically inspect hinges and retighten if necessary.

Condition #8: Cabinet Doors or Drawers Have Cracks in the Panels and/or Panels Are Loose and Rattle

Potentially Impacting:

- Appearance

Performance Guideline

Panel inserts in drawers and doors should not crack. Panels should fit tight and not rattle.

Builder Responsibility: The Builder should replace cracked panels. An exact match of the wood *grain* or color cannot be expected. The Builder should glue and shim loose panels.

Homeowner Responsibility: The Homeowner should treat stained cabinets like furniture and maintain the wood faces with low volatile organic compound (VOC) cleaning products.

Condition #9: Cabinet Plastic Laminate Surface Is Peeling

Potentially Impacting:

- Life of cabinet
- Structural integrity of the cabinet

Performance Guideline

Cabinets that are covered with high-pressure plastic laminate should not delaminate.

Comments: Over time and without proper care, plastic laminate cabinets can delaminate at joints and corners. This usually results from Homeowner negligence such as getting water into the core of the cabinet *door*.

Builder Responsibility: If plastic delamination is not the result of Homeowner negligence, the Builder should perform repairs to conform to the Performance Guideline.

Homeowner Responsibility: It is essential for the Homeowner to maintain proper care of the cabinets. Liquids should be removed immediately and not left on a surface, particularly at joints or corners. This creates the potential for the breakdown of the glues used to attach the surface to the *substrate*.

Condition #10: Cabinets Are Not Level

Potentially Impacting:

- Appearance

Performance Guideline

Cabinets should not have a deviation of more than 3/8 inch out of level over 6 feet of length.

Builder Responsibility: The Builder should perform repairs to conform to the Guideline. When finishing or refinishing, the Builder should attempt to match the original cabinetry.

Homeowner Responsibility: None.

Condition #11: Cabinet Doors Do Not Align When Closed

Potentially Impacting:

- Appearance

Performance Guideline

Gaps between abutting doors should not exceed 1/8 inch.

Builder Responsibility: The Builder should adjust doors to conform to the Performance Guideline.

Homeowner Responsibility: None.

Condition #12: Cabinet Finish (Paint or Stain) Is Irregular, Mismatched, or Blotchy

Potentially Impacting:
- Appearance

Performance Guideline

Irregularities of wood color in stained cabinets are considered acceptable unless two or more different stains were used. Painted cabinets should be uniform in color when viewed under normal lighting conditions at a distance of 6 feet.

Comments: Cabinet finishes are created two ways: 1) as a completely finished module that is either painted or stained in a factory; or 2) as a larger component that is made in a cabinet shop and painted or stained after it is installed in the Home. Cabinets that are stained to show the *grain* of the wood will have irregularities in the finish color. This is due to the fact that no two pieces of wood have exactly the same characteristics. Stain absorbs differently through flat surfaces, soft grains and ends. Painted cabinets are expected to be reasonably uniform in color because there is no intention to show the grain. Painted cabinets may be made of materials other than wood.

Builder Responsibility: The Builder should take corrective action to conform to the Performance Guideline.

Homeowner Responsibility: None.

Condition #13: Gaps Appear between Sections Where Cabinets Are Joined

Potentially Impacting:
- Appearance

Performance Guideline

Gaps where cabinet cases are joined together that are in excess of 1/32 inch for painted cabinets and 1/16 inch for stained cabinets, are considered unacceptable.

Builder Responsibility: The Builder should perform repairs to conform to the Performance Guideline.

Homeowner Responsibility: The Homeowner should be aware that painted cabinets may separate at the *stiles* due to normal drying out of the Home *frame*. Bathroom and laundry fans should always be operating when those rooms are in use.

Condition #14: Stain Grade Cabinets Show a Dark Band around Door and Drawer Openings

Potentially Impacting:
- Appearance

Performance Guideline

None.

Comments: This is a condition that can occur on light stained and whitewashed cabinets. It is due to the sun fading the exposed areas of the cabinets, while the part covered by a *door* or hardware edge remains the original stain color.

Builder Responsibility: None.

Homeowner Responsibility: None. If the Homeowner wants to achieve a uniform color, the doors and drawers can be left slightly open and exposed to the light. This procedure may take up to a year to achieve a uniform result.

Stairs and Railings

General Subject Information: Stairs are divided into two categories in this section: rough stairs, which are intended to be covered with another material, such as carpet, and finish stairs, which are not covered by any other material, such as hardwood stairs. (Note: some municipalities will not permit the Builder to deliver a hardwood stair without a non-slip covering or carpet.) Each stair category has different performance tolerances.

Condition #1: Stairs Have Gaps between *Treads*, *Risers*, and Skirt Boards

Potentially Impacting:
- Appearance

Performance Guideline

Rough stairs that will receive a covering may have gaps up to 3/8 inch between stair components. Finish stairs shall not have gaps between components that are in excess of 3/32 inch.

Comments: Finish stairs are considered a "fit and finish" item. The staircase may be tight at time of installation only to have gaps appear as the Home goes through seasons of changing humidity.

Builder Responsibility: The Builder should perform adjustments to conform to the Performance Guideline within the warranty period. Filling gaps with a matching wood filler or hardwood putty is acceptable as long as the gap does not exceed ¼ inch on rough stairs and 1/8 inch on finish stairs.

Homeowner Responsibility: None.

Condition #2: Stair Treads and Risers Are Uneven

Potentially Impacting:

- Appearance
- Tripping hazard

Performance Guideline

The "run and rise" of stairs are set forth in the building code. While there are some exceptions, in residential construction, treads are generally permitted to be no less than 10 inches deep. Risers are permitted to be no less than 4 inches and no more than 7 inches high. Further, riser height from one tread to the next cannot vary by more than 3/8 inch and the tread depth cannot vary by more than 3/8 inch from one tread to the next.

Builder Responsibility: The Builder should perform adjustments to meet the code.

Homeowner Responsibility: None.

Condition #3: Stair Tread Deflects Excessively

Potentially Impacting:

- Occupant safety

Performance Guideline

Stair tread deflection shall not exceed 1/8 inch under 200 pounds of vertically applied pressure.

Comments: If stair treads deflect excessively and it is not the result of a loose tread, it generally means that the stair carriage framing is undersized or the span between carriage supports is too wide.

Builder Responsibility: The Builder should reinforce the stair carriage to conform to the Performance Guideline. If the deflection is due to an overcut support, it may be possible to shim the support to stop the deflection.

Homeowner Responsibility: None.

Condition #4: Stair Treads Squeak

Potentially Impacting:

- Occupant comfort

Performance Guideline

Wooden stairs should not squeak excessively.

Comments: Stairs frequently squeak. The *treads* should not feel loose. The best method of application of treads to the stair carriage is to glue and then screw them to the carriage. Nevertheless, with changes in humidity and occupant use, squeaks may develop over time. Typically, this is a "fit and finish" item.

Builder Responsibility: Depending upon the warranty terms, the Builder should make a good faith attempt to eliminate or reduce stair squeaks.

Homeowner Responsibility: The Homeowner should be aware that even the most conscientiously built wooden staircase may develop some squeaks.

Condition #5: Stair Railing Deflects Excessively

Potentially Impacting:

- Occupant safety

Performance Guideline

Deflection of stair railings shall be within tolerances of the building code.

Comments: Stair railings must be able to withstand a concentrated load of 200 pounds per linear foot applied in any direction with a maximum 3 ½ inch deflection, or a uniform load of 50 pounds per linear foot, whichever results in the greatest stress on the stair rail and its supports.

Builder Responsibility: The Builder should secure guardrails and stair railings to conform to the tolerances of the building code.

Homeowner Responsibility: The Homeowner has a duty to take care of guardrails and stair rails and prevent anything that would cause them to become loose from their anchor points. This would include children playing on railings or several adults consistently leaning on deck rails which might exceed the code's mandated limits.

Moldings and Trim

General Subject Information: Interior *trim*, also called finish trim, is divided into two categories: standing trim and running trim. Standing trim is used for window and *door casings*. Running trim is used for baseboards, crown or chair molding. The application of trim or moldings is not structural in nature. However, the trim is a finished product of the Home and it should conform to the Performance Guidelines for manufacture and workmanship.

Condition #1: Molding Has Gaps at Joints

Potentially Impacting:

- Appearance

Performance Guideline

No separation should exceed 1/16 inch in width at the time the Home is delivered to the Homeowner.

Comments: Minor separation at the joints may occur as a result of expansion and contraction of the Home. This occurs as the lumber in the Home starts to dry out and stabilize. Expansion and contraction may also occur during seasonal changes with regard to humidity.

Builder Responsibility: If the gaps or splits are greater than the Performance Guideline at the time of the *walkthrough*, the Builder should perform repairs to conform to the Guideline. When finishing or refinishing, the Builder should attempt to match the original material.

Homeowner Responsibility: ***Maintenance Alert!*** During the first year of the life of the Home, framing lumber will shrink. This action is likely to cause some gaps in *trim* and molding. If the gaps are less than the Performance Guideline, the Homeowner should putty and/or *caulk*, sand and refinish in order to prevent any further splitting or separation at the molding or trim.

Condition #2: Nail Heads Are Visible in the Finished Woodwork

Potentially Impacting:

- Appearance

Performance Guideline

Finish nails or staples should be set below the surface; holes should be filled and finished. Finish nail holes should not be visible from a distance of 6 feet under normal light (daylight).

Builder Responsibility: If *trim* and molding does not meet the Performance Guideline, the Builder should perform the necessary repairs. When finishing or refinishing, the Builder should attempt to match the original materials.

Homeowner Responsibility: None.

Condition #3: Inside and Outside Corners Are Not Miter Cut

Potentially Impacting:

- Appearance

Performance Guideline

Inside and outside corners should be miter cut. There is an exception to this Guideline if the trim or molding is rectangular in cross section, butt joints may be used at the Builder's discretion.

Builder Responsibility: The Builder should perform repairs to conform to the Performance Guideline.

Homeowner Responsibility: Gaps in the joints at trim and molding are to be expected within the first year as the wood in the Home dries out. The Homeowner is responsible for caulking and painting these separations.

Condition #4: Molding or Trim Is Split or Checked

Potentially Impacting:

- Appearance

Performance Guideline

All finished woodwork should be smooth and without any surface marks at the time of the walkthrough. Caulking or filling gaps is acceptable as long as the filled area blends with the surrounding surface when viewed from a distance of 6 feet under normal light (daylight).

Comments: Hairline cracking is inherent in wood and is an acceptable condition. However, at the time of walkthrough, all *trim* and molding should be free of splitting or checking.

Builder Responsibility: The Builder should conform to the Performance Guideline at the time of the walkthrough. If the woodwork does not conform to the Guideline, the Builder should correct by replacing and/or filling, puttying, sanding and refinishing as necessary. When finishing or refinishing, the Builder should attempt to match the original materials.

Homeowner Responsibility: ***Maintenance Alert!*** Depending on the climate/environment, wood products, even interior woods, may need more than normal maintenance. If cracks occur, the Homeowner should seal the cracks by either *caulking* or puttying, then sanding and refinishing. This is very important in order to prevent any moisture from migrating to the unprotected backside of the wood, potentially causing twisting and warping.

Condition #5: Molding or Trim Has Hammer Marks or Other Mars

Potentially Impacting:

- Appearance

Performance Guideline

Hammerhead marks or other mars should not be visible from a distance of 6 feet under normal light (daylight).

Builder Responsibility: The Builder should perform repairs to conform to the Performance Guideline. When finishing or refinishing, the Builder should attempt to match the original materials and colors.

Homeowner Responsibility: None. However, the Homeowner should inspect all *trim* and molding work during the *walkthrough*.

Mirrors

General Subject Information: A mirror is a combination of high quality glass and a thin layer of silver or aluminum applied to the backside. The glass supports the metallic layer and will protect its shiny surface. Silvering quality glass is specially selected glass, which is exceptionally free of imperfections and other irregularities and is used in mirror and optical applications. A second grade is mirror glazing, which is also a superior glass for mirrors. Both silvering glass and mirror quality glass have very low distortion levels and must be smooth to within 1/25,000 inch.

Condition #1: Mirror Is Scratched

Potentially Impacting:

- Appearance

Performance Guideline

If scratches or imperfections are visible under normal lighting conditions from a distance of 3 feet or more, the mirror is considered unacceptable (providing the glass was not damaged as a result of Homeowner negligence).

Comments: Scratches do not constitute a safety concern, but tend to be more of a visual distraction. Cracked glass may present a safety issue and should be replaced by a professional glazing company as soon as possible.

Builder Responsibility: Mirrors should conform to the Performance Guideline. If the mirror does not meet the Guideline, the Builder should replace the mirror.

Homeowner Responsibility: At the time of the *walkthrough*, the Homeowner should thoroughly inspect all mirrors for any irregularities within the glazing. It is much harder to have the Builder respond to a complaint months after the Homeowner has taken possession of the Home.

Condition #2: Mirror Backing Is Deteriorating

Potentially Impacting:

- Appearance
- Function

Performance Guideline

When viewing the mirror from the front, there should be no visible imperfections, peeling, flaking and/or discoloration within the metallic backing material of the mirror.

Builder Responsibility: If the mirror does not conform to the Performance Guideline, the Builder should replace the mirror.

Homeowner Responsibility: At the time of the *walkthrough*, the Homeowner should thoroughly inspect all mirrors for any irregularities within the glazing and its metallic backing. It is much harder to have the Builder respond to a complaint months after the Homeowner has taken possession of the Home. ***Maintenance Alert!*** When cleaning a mirror, use caution with cleansers that contain ammonia or vinegar. Ammonia and vinegar are excellent glass cleaners, however they can be extremely damaging to the metallic backing of the mirror. Do not allow cleaners to go over the top, sides or to get into the track at the bottom of the mirror. Manufacturers often recommend applying cleaning agents to a cloth and then wiping down the mirror.

Condition #3: Bathroom Mirrors Are Glued to the Wall

Potentially Impacting:

- Life of the silver mirror backing
- Removal of mirror for replacement or remodeling

Performance Guideline

Mirrors in bathrooms should be installed on hangers or clips so there is a small air space behind them. Mirrors should not set directly on the top of a vanity backsplash.

Builder Responsibility: The Builder should install the mirror to conform to the Performance Guideline.

Homeowner Responsibility: None.

Shower and Tub Enclosures

Condition #1: Glass/Plastic Enclosure Is Scratched

Potentially Impacting:

- Appearance

Performance Guideline

At the time of walkthrough, shower and tub enclosure glass or plastic panels should not be scratched. To be considered unacceptable, scratches must be noticeable from a distance of 3 feet.

Builder Responsibility: The Builder should replace scratched glass or plastic panels observed at the time of walkthrough.

Homeowner Responsibility: None. However, the Homeowner should be aware that claims for scratched shower and tub enclosure panels may not be honored by the Builder after the walkthrough.

Condition #2: Shower or Tub Enclosure Leaks

Potentially Impacting:

- Flooring surface life
- *Underlayment* and frame integrity

Performance Guideline

Shower doors should not leak through the frame. Shower enclosures should not leak through the joint between the door edge and the frame or at the door bottom.

Comments: Except under unusual cases where the plastic or rubber parts used to keep water inside the tub or shower are missing, leaks at the door or sliding panel are due to two causes: 1) the bather has directed the shower head at the joint between the door and the fixed panel, or 2) the sliding panels at the tub have had their direction reversed by the bather. The inside panel must be the one closest to the shower head for proper use.

USE A JUMBO PAPER CLIP TO CLEAN SHOWER DOOR TRACK WEEP HOLES

Builder Responsibility: The Builder should perform repairs so there is no leakage at the enclosure frame (this excludes the intersection of the two movable panels on a tub enclosure). If there is leakage at the shower enclosure door, the Builder should determine if it is improper installation or caused by the Homeowner directing the shower head at the door opening while showering.

Homeowner Responsibility: The Homeowner should become aware of the proper use of a tub and shower enclosure. Keep shower water directed away from the door and panels. Continuous leaking may result in rot of the underlayment and *subfloor*. Continuous leaking also creates an environment for mold and mildew growth and for termites. (Refer to "**Homeowner Maintenance Summary**" for proper care and additional details, page 254.) The enclosure track should never be used as a handle to pull a bather up into a standing position.

Condition #3: Fiberglass or Acrylic Tub Bottom or Shower Stall Enclosure Flexes When Occupied

Potentially Impacting:

- *Useful life* of fixture

Performance Guideline

Some flexing of tub and shower side walls and bases is permissible as long as the installation conforms to the manufacturer's guidelines.

Comments: Fiberglass, acrylic, and other synthetic materials used in tubs and showers will normally exhibit a certain amount of flex. Each manufacturer has specific installation instructions for support of their product. Installation of synthetic material (plastic) tubs is especially important because a tub filled with water, plus the weight of the bather, may cause the tub to pull away from its edges of support.

Builder Responsibility: If the tub or shower has been installed in accordance with the manufacturer's instructions, the Builder does not have any responsibility. If the tub or shower has not been installed in accordance with the manufacturer's installation instructions, the Builder should perform repairs to conform to the manufacturer's instructions.

Homeowner Responsibility: The Homeowner should learn how to care and maintain synthetic bath surfaces and should notify the Builder if the tub cracks or pulls away from its supports.

Condition #4: Shower/Tub Enclosures Are Not Tempered Glass

Potentially Impacting:
- Occupant safety

Performance Guideline

If glass is used in shower and tub enclosures, it must be tempered. If plastic panels are used, they must be approved by the local Building Official.

Comments: Tempered glass has a small tempering "logo" or mark permanently placed on the panel by the glassmaker. Before the use of tempered glass became common, many enclosures were made of glass containing a wire grid. "Wire glass" is no longer permitted.

Builder Responsibility: Unless approved plastic panels are used in shower and tub enclosures, all glass panels should be tempered.

Homeowner Responsibility: None.

Condition #5: Top Rail of Shower/Tub Enclosure Is Not Screwed to the Frame

Potentially Impacting:
- Occupant safety

Performance Guideline

The top rail of a tub or shower enclosure should be screwed to the frame or mechanically connected in a manner approved by the local Building Official.

Comments: Many shower and tub enclosures are sold as a "snap together" kit. While the sidepieces screw to the tub or shower wall, the top piece (known as a rail) snaps into the top end of the sidepieces. This is not a tight connection and the bather could dislodge the entire top rail while getting in or out of the shower or tub. This action could cause the *door* panels to fall out of their tracks and break.

Builder Responsibility: The Builder should take corrective measures to conform to the Performance Guideline.

Homeowner Responsibility: None.

Condition #6: Grout Is Cracked between the Tub/Shower and First Row of Tile

Potentially Impacting:

- Watertightness of the assembly
- Appearance

Performance Guideline

The bottom course of tile between the tile and the tub/shower pan should never be grouted. This joint should be sealed with a flexible water-resistant caulk to permit movement between the tub or shower pan. The exception to this is when the shower is 100% tile or stone and there is no pan.

Comments: The first row of tile around the shower floor or the top of the tub is susceptible to cracking and is primarily a Homeowner maintenance item.

Builder Responsibility: At the time of *walkthrough*, the installation should conform to the Performance Guideline. The Builder should perform repairs as necessary if *grout* cracks are noted at walkthrough.

Homeowner Responsibility: ***Maintenance Alert!*** The Homeowner should seal tile grout prior to use using a silicone-based sealer that can be purchased at any hardware store. Grout should be cleaned frequently and should be kept free of mold and mildew. When significant cracking first appears, the cracks should be sealed with a caulking compound made for bathroom use. Many grout manufacturers also make flexible sealants, both standard and smooth, to match their grouts. Old caulk or grout should be dug out and discarded. The Homeowner should not apply new caulk over old caulk.

A WATERTIGHT JOINT BETWEEN THE TUB OR SHOWER AND THE FLOOR PREVENTS MOLD AND DRY ROT

Condition #7: Water-Resistant Backing Improperly Installed at Tub or Shower Surrounds

Potentially Impacting:

- Life of structure

Performance Guideline

If backing is to be used at tub and shower surrounds, it must be water-resistant. Materials such as cement board or special water-resistant paper may be used. Lath and mortar are preferred. Water-resistant gypsum board known as "blueboard" or "greenboard" is not a code-permitted alternative.

Comments: Because water splashes on tub and tile surround surfaces (even though they may be tile or some other water-resistant finish), water and water vapor can penetrate the surface. Over time, such water penetration may cause underlying wood or ordinary *drywall* to fail and/or grow mold and mildew. Except in the case of fiberglass or plastic tub and shower surrounds, water-resistant materials, properly sealed, flashed and *caulked*, should be used as backing for surface finishes. Water-resistant drywall, commonly used as tub and shower surround backing in the past, is no longer accepted by the Gypsum Association for this purpose. On fiberglass tub and shower assemblies, it is not necessary to place backing behind the fiberglass walls (unless required by local code).

Builder Responsibility: The Builder should use an appropriate water-resistant backing material at tub and shower surrounds and water-resistant drywall only at other potentially damp locations.

Homeowner Responsibility: The Homeowner should make certain that a coat of premium enamel paint is maintained on the drywall surface. Maintain the caulking between the tubs or *shower pan* and the first row of tile (see "**Homeowner Maintenance Summary**", page 254). Use the vent fan when bathing and showering to reduce humidity.

Condition #8: Towel Bar Is Not Level or Secure

Potentially Impacting:

- Appearance

Performance Guideline

Towel bars shall be level within 3/16 inch. Towel bars shall be secured to the wall by mounting into the wood or steel Home frame or by using anchors that penetrate the drywall and secure the fastener behind the drywall.

Builder Responsibility: The Builder should conform to the Performance Guideline.

Homeowner Responsibility: None, but the Homeowner should be aware that even the most secure towel bar can come loose from overloading or mistreatment.

Chapter Seven

UTILITY SYSTEMS

includes:

Heating

Cooling

Electrical

Plumbing
Piping
Faucets
Sinks
Tubs/Showers
Toilets
Water Heaters

Mechanical Ventilation

Fire Sprinkler System

Telephone/Internet

Cable TV and Satellite TV

References for this chapter:

- *ASHRAE Handbook: Fundamentals, American Society of Heating, Refrigerating and Air-Conditioning Engineers*
- *Residential Construction Performance Guidelines*, NAHB 2011 ed.
- *Code Check Electrical 6th ed.*, Taunton Press
- *Code Check Plumbing and Mechanical 4th ed.*, Taunton Press
- *Residential & Light Commercial Construction Standards*, by Don Reynolds
- *National Electric Code 2011,* National Fire Protection Association (NFPA)
- *International Building Code 2012,* International Code Council
- *International Residential Code 2012,* International Code Council
- *Indiana Quality Assurance Builder Standards 2009,* Indiana Builders Association
- *NASCLA Residential Construction Standards 2009,* National Association of State Contracting Licensing Agencies
- *California Building Code 2013,* California Building Standards Commission
- *Homeowner Handbook 2003,* Greater Atlanta Homebuilders Association
- *New Home Warranty Program 2010,* State of New Jersey Department of Community Affairs
- *South Carolina Residential Construction Standards 1997,* Residential Builders Commission of the South Carolina Department of Labor
- *Uniform Plumbing Code 2012,* International Association of Plumbing and Mechanical Officials

A comprehensive list of references by author and publisher is found in the Bibliography section.

Chapter Seven

Utility Systems

Heating

General Subject Information: While there are several systems available to heat the Home, the focus of this chapter will be on the two most common systems: forced air systems and radiant systems. Forced air systems consist of a gas, fuel oil, or electric *furnace* and a network of large pipes in the *attic* and *crawl space* known as ducts. Ducts supply warm air to the ceiling, floor, or walls of the Home. The forced air system also has a return air component that circulates the air back to the heat source. Forced air furnaces may use natural gas, bottled gas, fuel oil, or coal as a source of heat. Natural gas is the most common fuel. Less frequently used systems are heat pumps and electric furnaces. Electric furnaces operate solely with electricity. Heat pumps are reverse air conditioners. Heat pumps take heat from the air outside a Home and transfer it to inside the Home. Even on very cold days, there is a small amount of heat present in the outside air. In the summertime the heat pump operates like a standard air conditioner.

Radiant heat systems use either tubing filled with warm fluid or electrical wires that are heated to transmit radiant energy into the living space of the Home. Systems that use tubing circulate a warm fluid, usually water or light oil, through the tubes. They may be located along the baseboard or embedded in a *concrete* floor. Like a forced air system, the heat source for the fluid comes from burning natural gas or fuel oil. Flames heat the fluid in a small boiler and a pump circulates the hot fluid to a heat exchanger that transfers heat to tubing in the Home.

Radiant systems using electricity rely upon electrical resistance (much like the wires inside an ordinary household toaster) to create heat. The electrical heat strips are found in either the floors or ceilings of a Home. While the electrical resistance system is low cost to install, it is rarely used today except in bathrooms because of high operating costs.

Radiant systems provide quiet operation and uniform warmth, but they do not circulate air through the Home as a forced air system does. A thermostat controls the temperature of both types of systems. There is at least one thermostat in the Home, perhaps more depending upon how many zones are created for heating within the Home.

Many factors control interior comfort for heating a Home. Some factors include:

- The orientation of rooms in the Home;
- The amount of window area in a room;
- Whether the windows are shaded with a drapery that could provide additional *insulation;*
- The amount of insulation installed;
- The type of windows and *exterior doors* installed;
- The ceiling height or “volume” of the rooms.

Condition #1: Some Rooms Are Comfortable, While Others Are Cold

Potentially Impacting:

- ♦ Occupant comfort

Performance Guideline

The heating system should be designed to meet the local design temperature. Every room that is supposed to be heated should achieve a temperature of 68°F when the temperature of the Home has stabilized. Measurements should be made 2 feet from exterior walls and 3 feet up from the floor according to code standards. A temperature variation of 4°F from room-to-room is considered acceptable. The fan switch on the thermostat can be set to "fan on" to increase circulation and reduce room-to-room temperature differences.

Comments: Many factors affect the performance of heating systems. The most important is system design. Other factors include placement of furniture, solar orientation of the room and location of the room in the Home. For example, a room that is located above the thermostat will be warmer in winter than a room located below the thermostat. The downstairs room will be cooler in both summer and winter; this is because warm air rises to the ceiling and cool air falls down to the lowest level in the Home. Programmable, set-back thermostats should be used in every new home or remodel. Thermostats containing a mercury filled bulb should never be installed.

FIRST, YOU DETERMINE WHETHER THE FILTER IS IN THE ATTIC OR THE CLOSET... -THEN, REPLACE IT WITH THE SAME SIZE AND MERV.

Builder Responsibility: The Builder should design and balance the heating system to conform to the local design temperature. If the Homeowner has failed to cover large window openings so as to minimize heat loss or has blocked the system's airflow in any manner, the Builder is not responsible.

Homeowner Responsibility: The Homeowner should be aware that it is not possible to achieve a uniform temperature throughout the Home. A difference in temperature will exist between thermostat locations and other rooms, particularly if the rooms are located above or below the thermostat location. Large window areas should be properly draped or otherwise protected from heat loss, and no furniture or other devices should be placed in rooms that will impede the airflow from grills (registers). Most air supply grills have *dampers* that can be adjusted in rooms for the difference in the summer and winter temperature needs.

Maintenance Alert! The Homeowner should change or clean the *furnace* filter in accordance with the manufacturer's recommendations (usually no less than every six months). A dirty filter will reduce airflow and cause the system to use more energy.

Condition #2: Thermostat Does Not Work

Potentially Impacting:

- Occupant comfort

Performance Guideline

Thermostats should perform as designed throughout their useful life. A thermostat can vary 4°F from actual room temperature without being considered unacceptable.

Builder Responsibility: The Builder should replace unacceptable thermostats assuming that the condition does not result from Homeowner negligence or failure to change the batteries.

Homeowner Responsibility: The Homeowner should check thermostats periodically and change the batteries when it is indicated that batteries are weak. Do not leave dead batteries in a thermostat, especially during months when the system is not being used. Dead batteries can leak and corrode the thermostat.

Condition #3: Heating System Is Noisy

Potentially Impacting:

- Occupant comfort

Performance Guideline

Noise levels in bedrooms should not exceed 25 dB (decibels). Noise levels in other rooms should not exceed 40 dB.

Comments: The *air handler* fan (blower) will make noise as it blows warm air throughout the Home. Noise will also be heard as air flows back to the *furnace* through the return air system. The architectural design of the Home often puts restrictions on the design of the heating system. As a result, the system may have a noise level that is irritating to some occupants. A closed or partially closed warm air supply register can create noise.

Builder Responsibility: The Builder should control noise levels in the cooling and heating system in conformance with the Performance Guideline. Further, if part of the system is loose internally and rattles as the system is operating, the Builder should make adjustments to remove the rattling noise. Systems mounted in *attics* should be isolated from *frame* members.

Homeowner Responsibility: The Homeowner should keep all warm air supply registers open to avoid noisy, whistling sounds.

Condition #4: Heating System Makes Booming Noise When First Turned On or When Cooling Down (Effect No. 1)

Potentially Impacting:

- Occupant comfort

Performance Guideline

The Builder should minimize booming noise to the extent reasonably feasible, but it may not be possible to completely eliminate the noise.

Comments: The booming noise created in forced air heating systems in Effect No. 1 is known as the “oil canning” effect. This effect may occur when a large area of sheet metal is rapidly heated or cooled.

Builder Responsibility: The Builder should make all reasonable attempts to minimize this effect.

Homeowner Responsibility: None.

Condition #5: Heating System Makes Booming Noise When First Turned On (Effect No. 2)

Potentially Impacting:
- Safety of occupants
- Occupant comfort

Performance Guideline

All furnace burners should ignite quickly and smoothly as designed, without delay, and should not permit excessive accumulation of unburned fuel gases. The time for burner ignition should be no more than 15 seconds and the start up time for the furnace blower should be 45 to 120 seconds after burner ignition.

Comments: The booming noise in Effect No. 2 is likely to be caused by a delay when the furnace burner ignites too late. A larger than designed volume of gas accumulates and is not ignited (burned) soon enough, creating a small explosive effect in the furnace.

Builder Responsibility: The Builder should adjust the burner ignition device to conform to the Performance Guideline.

Homeowner Responsibility: If a booming noise is heard when the furnace is turned on, the Homeowner has a duty to notify the Builder of this condition. The Homeowner should maintain the furnace annually. If any problems are observed with burner ignition or blower start-up, the Homeowner should notify the Builder during the warranty period. After the warranty period, the Homeowner should notify a qualified heating and cooling contractor or the local gas utility company.

Condition #6: Floor Has Cold Spots (Radiant System)

Potentially Impacting:
- Occupant comfort

Performance Guideline

Radiant heating systems should not leak or become clogged during their useful life.

Comments: The radiant heat system using oil or water to transfer heat from the boiler to the *slab* is known as a *closed loop system*. Fluid is heated in the boiler and pumped to the floor or baseboard. There, it gives off its heat, and then the cooler fluid is returned to the boiler to be reheated.

Builder Responsibility: The Builder should perform repairs within the warranty period to assure the system provides continuous and uniform heat. However, beyond the initial charging of the system, the Builder is not responsible when unapproved fluids are added (such as *hard water* that may be used to recharge the system).

Homeowner Responsibility: ***Maintenance Alert!*** A radiant heating system requires routine annual maintenance. If make-up fluid constantly needs to be added to the system, there may be a leak. The Homeowner should report leaks to the Builder immediately, since they can cause the underlying soil to swell and heave or undermine the slab. Leaks can also affect the structural integrity of the *frame*.

Condition #7: Duct Work Has Separated

Potentially Impacting:
- Occupant comfort

Performance Guideline

Duct work should be continuous and should not have gaps, breaks, or holes. Ducts should be sealed tight and comply with applicable energy codes.

Builder Responsibility: The Builder should secure and repair all separated duct work and repair any holes provided that the unacceptable condition was not caused by the Homeowner or by an after-market contractor (such as cable installer, alarm installer, termite inspector, etc.).

Homeowner Responsibility: None. However, the Homeowner should be aware that pest control companies and after-market contractors who install alarm systems have well deserved reputations for tearing and squashing duct work in *attics* and *crawl spaces*. When having work of this nature done, the Homeowner should inspect the crawl space or attic both prior to and after the work is completed, to ensure that all duct work remains intact.

Condition #8: Duct Work Is Not Insulated

Potentially Impacting:
- Occupant comfort
- System performance
- Energy costs

Performance Guideline

Duct work should be insulated in all non-conditioned areas and comply with applicable energy codes.

Comments: Non-conditioned areas are parts of the Home that are not normally heated or cooled by the *furnace* or air conditioner. They include the garage (except for very cold climates), unheated *basements*, *crawl space* and *attic*. Duct work that is run through these areas should be insulated to avoid heating and cooling loss.

Builder Responsibility: The Builder should ensure that duct work conforms to the Performance Guideline.

Homeowner Responsibility: None.

Cooling

General Subject Information: Regional climates may vary significantly from communities near sea level which have little or no need for central air conditioning, to communities in the plains and valleys which experience many days in excess of 100°F. Another factor is relative humidity which tends to be higher in states that are east of the Mississippi River and in the southern states. Typically, central air conditioning systems are primarily installed as part of the indoor comfort package of the Home.

Most central air conditioning systems share the same *air handler*, duct work, and return air systems as the heating system. Note: Homes that are built with air conditioning or are "prepped" for future air conditioning will have larger ducts than Homes that are built for heating only. If the Home was built for heat only, the Homeowner should not assume that air conditioning could be installed successfully at a later date. The difference between a Home that has central air conditioning and one that does not is the addition of a circular or box-like unit called the condenser that is outside the Home (or sometimes on the *roof*). A cooling coil is also added inside the *furnace*. Almost all central air conditioning systems use electricity as their power source.

Another type of cooling system used less frequently in residential construction is the evaporative cooler, commonly known as the "swamp cooler". Like central air conditioning systems, evaporative coolers use some of the same components of the heating system such as the duct work. The evaporative cooler is usually mounted on the roof and the cooling effect is a result of air being *drawn* through wetted filter pads. While evaporative coolers are cheaper to operate than central air conditioning, they are less able to achieve comfort levels in periods of extreme heat.

Homes that are heated with radiant heating typically do not have central air conditioning, as there is no duct work system to deliver cool air into the rooms. Central air conditioning can be installed in Homes with radiant heating using duct work, *air handlers*, and condensers, but the system is totally separate from the heating system. Because of the expensive installation, Homes that have central air conditioning and radiant heat typically are custom homes.

Condition #1: Air Conditioner Does Not Cool the Home

Potentially Impacting:

- Occupant comfort

Performance Guideline

Central air conditioning shall be capable of meeting the local design temperature. Typically, this is a maximum difference between outside and inside temperatures of 20 degrees. To provide an accurate measurement of this differential, the air conditioning system must have been operating for 12 hours.

Comments: Installed air conditioning systems are required to meet state or local design temperatures. Typically, every city or county is assigned a design temperature for both heating and cooling data based upon historic temperature records. On extremely hot days, it is not possible to turn the system off during the day and then turn it on when returning from work and expect the Home to be cool by bedtime. Because Homes built today are well insulated and well sealed, once they are heated, the rate of cool down in a typical new Home will depend upon how long it takes to dehumidify it. As an example, if the outside temperature is 100°F, a Home in Arizona will cool faster than a Home in Florida because Florida has a much higher relative humidity. (See "**Heating and Cooling Tips**" below.)

Homes that are currently being built can have central air conditioning systems installed that offer Seasonal Energy Efficiency Ratings (SEER) of 13 to 22. Air conditioners with a higher SEER are more efficient. Air conditioning systems installed today are much more efficient than those installed just a few years ago. They are designed to operate continuously without the repeated on and off cycles that are characteristic of older models. The continuous operation actually results in lower energy costs.

Builder Responsibility: If the air conditioning system does not meet the design and performance requirements of the design criteria or the local or state energy standards, the Builder should perform repairs or replace the system to conform to the Performance Guideline.

Homeowner Responsibility: (See "**Heating and Cooling Tips**" below.)

Heating and Cooling Tips

1. The "Away" setting on a thermostat should be no more than 4°F higher than the "Return" setting. Turning the system off when leaving for work and then on upon return is not likely to achieve the desired temperature by bedtime;
2. The system is designed to operate continuously. Repeated on-and-off cycles do not remove the humidity from the Home and result in higher energy costs;
3. All windows and sliding glass *doors*, particularly those facing south and west, should have insulating drapes or shades that are closed during the hottest times of the day;
4. Sunrooms, solariums and similar spaces that gather light also gather heat. These areas should be separated from the rest of the Home by doors that block heat from moving into the main rooms of the Home; and
5. Do not place any tinting material on the inside pane of the dual or triple pane windows. This can cause excessive heat to buildup between the panes of glass and result in a rupture of the seals between the two layers of glass. Also, it is likely to void the warranty provided by the window manufacturer. (Refer to Preface: "**Ten Most Common Mistakes Made by New Homeowners**", page 20.)

Condition #2: Some Rooms Are Hotter (Or Colder) Than Others

Potentially Impacting:

- Occupant comfort

Performance Guideline

A temperature variation of 4°F from one room to another is considered acceptable. In two story Homes, a temperature variation of 8°F between the first and second floor is considered acceptable.

Builder Responsibility: The Builder should balance the system to conform to the Performance Guideline.

Homeowner Responsibility: In order to achieve more uniform cooling (and heating) between rooms and floors, the Homeowner should turn the fan switch on the thermostat from Auto to On. This will result in the fan running continuously and keeping the inside air circulating and mixing.

Condition #3: Refrigerant Line Leaks

Potentially Impacting:

- System efficiency
- Occupant comfort

Performance Guideline

Refrigerant lines should not leak. They are part of a closed loop system.

Builder Responsibility: The Builder should repair the leak and recharge the system assuming the Homeowner or after-market contractor did not cause the leak.

Homeowner Responsibility: None. However, the Homeowner should prevent children from playing around air conditioning condensers. The Homeowner should also maintain the manufacturer's recommended clearance between the condenser and any landscaping, fencing or other structures. Refer to the manufacturer's warranty and the annual maintenance requirements. Typically, shrubs should not be permitted to grow within 1 foot of the outer sides of the condenser.

Condition #4: Condensate Line Is Plugged

Potentially Impacting:

- System performance

Performance Guideline

This is a Homeowner maintenance item.

Comments: The *condensate line* is typically a white plastic or copper pipe that comes out of the *air handler* portion of the *furnace* and discharges through an outside wall. Because the water is cool and the discharge is slow, the condensate line provides a great environment for algae to grow. Systems are installed with a primary line and secondary condensate lines. The primary line goes through a *trap* and then discharges near the outside foundation (or in some locations into a sewer trap). The secondary condensate line discharges above a window or *patio door* (if the air conditioner coil is in the *attic* furnace) or in the garage or other prominent place (if the air conditioner is located in the furnace in that area). The reason why the secondary condensate line is located in a prominent and visible location is to give notice of a malfunction since it should only discharge when the primary line is plugged.

Builder Responsibility: None.

Homeowner Responsibility: ***Maintenance Alert!*** The Homeowner should inspect the condensate lines twice a year: at the beginning of the air conditioning season and also at the end of the season. If a trickle discharge is reduced to an occasional drip, it potentially means that the condensate line is in the process of becoming plugged. Another symptom of a plugged condensate line is cold water droplets blowing out of the air supply grills in the Home. If water is observed dripping in front of a window or patio door or onto a garage floor, it is likely that the primary condensate line is plugged. If this occurs, the Homeowner should shut off the air conditioner and schedule the system for service.

Condition #5: Compressor Fails

Potentially Impacting:

- System performance
- Occupant comfort

Performance Guideline

Compressor should not fail within the manufacturer's warranty period.

Builder Responsibility: The Builder should arrange for the replacement of the failed compressor if it fails within the warranty period.

Homeowner Responsibility: None.

Condition #6: System Fails to Turn On When First Activated in Spring/Summer

Potentially Impacting:
- System performance
- Occupant comfort

Performance Guideline

Air conditioning systems should turn on as intended. This is typically a Homeowner maintenance item.

Comments: Homeowners often encounter a situation where a functioning air conditioning system shut off in the fall will not start when it comes time to turn it on in the spring. Typically, this condition can be traced to one or two blown fuses. When the compressor remains idle during the winter months, its internal parts become resistant to turning. This resistance often results in a blown fuse when first turned on in springtime.

Builder Responsibility: None. Typically, air conditioner condensers are warranted by their manufacturer.

Homeowner Responsibility: ***Maintenance Alert!*** Once every two months, on warm winter days, the Homeowner should start the air conditioner and run it for a few minutes to keep the internal parts clean and lubricated.

Condition #7: Compressor Unit Is Out of Level

Potentially Impacting:
- *Compressor useful life*

Performance Guideline

Compressor units should be set level to a tolerance of 1 inch in any direction unless otherwise stated by the manufacturer.

Builder Responsibility: The Builder should set the compressor to conform to the Performance Guideline.

Homeowner Responsibility: None.

Condition #8: Evaporative Cooler Blows Warm Air

Potentially Impacting:
- Occupant comfort

Performance Guideline

Evaporative coolers should not blow air that is the same temperature as the outside air. The cooler should provide cool air in accordance with the manufacturer's specifications.

Builder Responsibility: If the evaporative cooler does not meet the manufacturer's performance specifications, the Builder should repair or replace the unacceptable cooler. The Builder is not responsible for service problems arising from poor water quality.

Homeowner Responsibility: ***Maintenance Alert!*** Evaporative coolers need to be kept clean and free of mineral build-up in order to operate properly. Depending upon local water quality, the Homeowner should treat and backwash the evaporative cooler periodically.

Electrical

General Subject Information: The electrical system in new homes is installed in compliance with the National Electric Code (NEC). Most cities and counties in the United States have adopted this code and it is effectively a national code. Among many other things, the NEC deals with wire size, circuits, *breakers* and placement of outlets.

Condition #1: Lights Flicker When Appliances Are Turned On

Potentially Impacting:

- System *useful life*

Performance Guideline

If the circuit is not overloaded by the Homeowner, the lights flicker continuously, and the breaker does not trip, the circuit is unacceptable.

Comments: Flickering lights can indicate a possible overload or poor connection somewhere in the branch circuit. If a heavy-duty motor driven appliance is plugged into a wall outlet, it is likely to cause momentary flickering of the lights when it is first turned on. If the Home was wired in accordance with the National Electric Code, the Builder is not responsible for this condition. Compact florescent lights often will flicker or glow when first turned on.

Builder Responsibility: The Builder should inspect the circuit, determine the problem and perform repairs. The Builder is not responsible for momentary flickering when high capacity appliances are plugged into wall outlets.

Homeowner Responsibility: The Homeowner should avoid overloading circuits with multiple appliances and add-on outlets. If appliance wires feel warm to the touch, they should be unplugged and reinserted into a separate circuit. Note: circuit breakers are found in the service panel where the meter is located or in the *subpanel* (the gray metal panel typically located in the hallway, laundry room, or bedroom of the Home). The Homeowner should label each of the circuits inside the panels, if the Builder has not already done so.

Condition #2: Breakers Trip or Fuses Blow Frequently

Potentially Impacting:

- Electrical system performance
- Occupant safety

Performance Guideline

Circuit breakers that trip and fuses that blow frequently under proper design usage, are indications of an unacceptable circuit or a malfunctioning appliance.

Comments: Fuses and circuit breakers are electricity's safety valves. When a fuse blows it must be replaced. When a circuit breaker trips, it can be reset. Most Homes today are equipped with circuit breakers in the service panel (outside) or in a *subpanel* (inside). Special appliances like *furnaces* and air conditioning condensers have their own fuse boxes or circuit breakers. When frequent tripping occurs it is usually a sign that the circuit is being overloaded. As circuit breakers get older they tend to wear out and will trip more easily.

Builder Responsibility: The Builder should test circuits to determine their capacity and perform corrections if the circuits are found to be inadequate for expected normal usage by the Homeowner.

Homeowner Responsibility: The Homeowner should not overload circuits to the point where fuses blow or breakers trip. If frequent tripping occurs, the Homeowner has a duty to notify the Builder. **DO NOT replace a fuse or circuit breaker with one that has a higher amperage rating or one made by a different manufacturer! This action could result in a fire.**

Condition #3: Ground Fault Interrupter Trips Frequently

Potentially Impacting:

- Appliance performance at ground fault interrupter locations

Performance Guideline

Ground fault interrupters should be installed in accordance with the National Electric Code or other government adopted code in effect at that time.

Comments: A *ground fault circuit interrupter (GFCI)* is a device intended to detect electrical current flowing outside its intended path, such as a person receiving a shock, and to interrupt the flow of current. They protect people from electrocution. Receptacle outlets require GFCI protection when installed outdoors in garages, unfinished *basements*, *crawl spaces*, bathrooms, at kitchen countertops, and when installed within 6 feet of laundry, utility, or wet bar sinks. GFCI receptacles have a test and reset button. Newer GFCIs have an indicator light to show that power is being supplied to the receptacle. Appliances manufactured outside of the United States (although they may carry a *UL label*) are notorious for tripping GFCIs. Hairdryers frequently trip GFCIs. When a GFCI trips it can be reset at the outlet by pressing the small button or inside the sub panel if it is wired that way.

Builder Responsibility: None, assuming the installation was done pursuant to the applicable National Electric Code and that the GFCI device itself is acceptable.

Homeowner Responsibility: The Homeowner should test GFCIs monthly by pressing the test button. The Homeowner should never plug a freezer or refrigerator into a GFCI protected outlet. The tripping could cause the refrigerator contents to spoil.

TEST G.F.C.I. OUTLETS MONTHLY

Condition #4: ARC Fault Circuit Interrupter Trips Frequently

Potentially Impacting:

- Electrical system performance
- Usage by Homeowner

Performance Guideline

Arc-fault circuit interrupter (AFCI) breakers should trip when the test button is operated. They should reset and restore power after moving the breaker handle to the "off" position then to the "on" position. They should not have "nuisance" tripping.

Comments: *Arc-fault circuit interrupters* are also safety devices that provide additional protection against fires caused by electrical arcing. Depending upon local codes, they are required for any circuit that has outlets in bedrooms, living areas, hallways, closets, dens, dining rooms, and similar rooms. This includes circuits that supply lights or smoke alarms in those areas. Older AFCIs labeled "branch feeder type" on the breaker are no longer allowed. Only "combination" type AFCI breakers are allowed today. AFCI breakers will "nuisance trip" if mis-wired, including the combining of neutral conductors from different circuits. An AFCI that trips under normal household loads could indicate a wiring error or could indicate a fault in the wiring such as a nail through a cable.

Builder Responsibility: The Builder should test all circuits under load to determine that no nuisance tripping occurs. The Builder should repair wiring to eliminate nuisance tripping.

Homeowner Responsibility: If frequent tripping occurs, it is likely to be from an appliance that does not meet current Underwriter Laboratory (UL) standards.

Condition #5: Aluminum Wire, Not Copper Wire, Was Installed

Potentially Impacting:

- Usage by Homeowner

Performance Guideline

Home wiring should be installed in accordance with the National Electric Code or other government approved code in effect at that time.

Comments: Use of aluminum wiring is permitted in residential construction under the National Electric Code. When copper shortages occurred in the past, aluminum was used in its place. Aluminum conducts electricity better than copper, but aluminum requires special installation procedures that copper does not. Most new Homes are wired with a combination of copper and aluminum wire. Aluminum is likely to be the main wire from the street to the Home and also the wiring for electric ovens and electric dryers. Copper wiring is used in lower rated circuits.

Builder Responsibility: The Builder should install wiring to conform to the Performance Guideline.

Homeowner Responsibility: None.

Condition #6: Recessed Ceiling Lights Turn Themselves Off

Potentially Impacting:

- Occupant safety

Performance Guideline

Recessed light fixtures should operate as the manufacturer intended.

Comments: Recessed light fixtures are equipped with a thermal protection device that disables (turns off) the light when it gets too hot. Typically, there are two causes for this condition: the Homeowner has installed a light bulb of a higher wattage than specified by the manufacturer or there is ceiling *insulation* on top of the light housing. Some light fixtures are rated for contact with insulation while others are not. Fixtures are labeled as to whether they can be in contact with insulation.

Builder Responsibility: If the cans are not rated for contact with insulation, the Builder should verify that the *attic* or ceiling insulation is at least 3 inches away from the recessed light cans.

Homeowner Responsibility: The Homeowner should ensure that bulbs used in recessed lights do not exceed the manufacturer's maximum wattage that appears on a label inside the fixture.

Green Tip! Convert from incandescent bulbs to compact florescent or LED bulbs that operate cooler, save energy and last much longer. Do this with all household lights.

WHEN REPLACING BURNED OUT CFLS, BE SURE TO RECYCLE OR PLACE IN A HAZARDOUS WASTE RECEPTACLE. CFLS CONTAIN MERCURY, WHICH SHOULD NEVER GO IN THE TRASH.

Condition #7: Light Fixture Is Tarnished

Potentially Impacting:
- Appearance

Performance Guideline

Light fixtures should not be tarnished at time of walkthrough.

Comments: Light fixtures, especially ones with a bright brass finish, will tarnish. The rate of tarnish depends upon outdoor and indoor air pollution and the degree to which the finish was coated with a protective film. It is very important not to use a higher wattage bulb in a light fixture than the wattage recommended by the manufacturer.

Builder Responsibility: The Builder should conform to the Performance Guideline at time of walkthrough.

Homeowner Responsibility: The Homeowner should inspect fixtures during the walkthrough and check with fixture manufacturers regarding the warranties. ***Maintenance Alert!*** The Homeowner is responsible for the routine maintenance of cleaning and polishing fixtures, especially bright brass, which requires frequent polishing.

Condition #8: Light Switch and Outlet Plate Protrude Too Far From Wall

Potentially Impacting:
- Appearance

Performance Guideline

Switch and plug plates that protrude more than 1/16 inch from the finished wall are considered unacceptable. Further, the rough opening voids in the drywall or plaster around an electrical box cannot exceed 1/8 inch as measured on all four sides per the National Electric Code.

Builder Responsibility: The Builder should adjust switches and outlet plates to be flush and level in the wall. For minor protrusions less than 1/16 inch, caulking is an acceptable repair. For drywall or plaster overcuts in excess of 1/8 inch, the Builder should fill the voids with joint compound.

Homeowner Responsibility: None.

Condition #9: Light Switch Sticks or Must Be Jiggled to Turn On

Potentially Impacting:
- Appliance performance
- System *useful life*

Performance Guideline

Light switches that stick or require tapping or jiggling to turn on lights or appliances are defective and unacceptable.

Builder Responsibility: The Builder should replace light switches that operate in an unacceptable manner.

Homeowner Responsibility: None.

Condition #10: Wall Outlet in Bedroom Does Not Work

Potentially Impacting:

- Use of lights or appliances

Performance Guideline

A bedroom must have an overhead light or a wall outlet that is turned on from a switch by the door.

Comments: If a bedroom does not have a ceiling light, the Builder is required by code to connect at least one wall outlet (one receptacle only, not both) to a wall switch near the door. Unless the switch is on, any light or appliance plugged into the outlet will not operate. Homeowners often mistake this condition as unacceptable outlet. Often times, this designated outlet is intentionally installed upside down. This outlet is also called a "half hot".

Builder Responsibility: None, assuming that the Builder has properly wired the outlet to a switch.

Homeowner Responsibility: None.

Plumbing

General Subject Information: The liquid plumbing system in the Home consists of three main components: water supply piping, wastewater and vent piping, and fixtures. Gas piping is a separate system used to convey natural or LP gas to appliances such as *furnaces*, water heaters, stoves, cook tops, ovens, fireplaces, and barbeques.

Both copper and plastic are used for water supply piping in new homes. Plastic has overtaken copper as the most prominent material used. Older homes were piped with galvanized steel, but due to corrosion problems, galvanized steel piping is no longer used in residential construction. Waste piping, which carries wastewater from the fixtures in the Home to the sewer, is typically black plastic piping called acrylonitrile-butadiene-styrene (*ABS*). This piping can also be white piping called polyvinyl chloride (*PVC*). Alternatively, some municipalities require waste piping to be copper or cast iron or a combination of both. Unless the Home is connected to a septic tank, wastewater flows in a sewer to a local sewage treatment plant. Wastewater piping also has pipes that protrude in through the roof of the Home. These are called *vents* and their purpose is to allow wastewater to flow through the pipes without becoming "air locked". The vents also help to dissipate odors. Fixtures are items like toilets, bathtubs and sinks. Nearly all plumbing fixtures have *traps*, which prevent sewer gases from backing into the Home. Traps can be seen under the sink and are a U shaped part of the piping where wastewater sits and blocks the flow of sewer gases. Toilets have traps built into the bowls.

Some water suppliers do not recommend the installation of water softeners as they may make the water more corrosive and lead to early pipe deterioration. Check with the Builder or water supplier prior to any water softener installation.

Depending upon local regulations, the Home may be fitted with a fire sprinkler system. The system consists of water under continuous pressure in pipes that in the event of fire will spray water through the sprinkler heads located in the ceilings and walls. Unless there is a fire or excessive source of heat, the fire sprinkler system remains passive. Routine testing and certification of the fire sprinkler system is very important. (Refer to the **"Fire Sprinkler System"** section of this chapter, page 221.)

Condition #1: Plumbing Vents Are Located within 18 Inches of a Valley, Hip, or Ridge of the Roof

Potentially Impacting:

- Occupant safety
- Plumbing system performance

Performance Guideline

Plumbing vents on the roof must be located more than 18 inches from any valley, hip or ridge.

Comments: Vent performance can be affected by wind currents that can occur in valleys, hips and ridges of roofs. A flow of air can pass down the vent instead of upward.

Builder Responsibility: The Builder should take corrective measures to relocate the vents that are closer than 18 inches.

Homeowner Responsibility: None.

Condition #2: Water or Gas Pipe Leaks

Potentially Impacting:

- Structural integrity
- Contents of Home
- Health and safety of occupants

Performance Guideline

Water supply piping, gas piping, wastewater piping, and fire sprinkler plumbing should not leak. Piping must contain and convey 100% of the liquid or gas that it is intended to convey.

Builder Responsibility: The Builder should perform repairs to leaking pipe systems. The Builder should not be responsible for piping leaks caused by hurricanes, tornados, earthquakes, shifts in the structure, or other acts of nature that were not caused by the Builder.

Homeowner Responsibility: The Homeowner has a duty to notify the Builder upon noticing any gas or liquid leaks in piping no matter how small. Failure to give timely notice can result in health hazards, personal injury, and structural damage. ***Maintenance Alert!*** The Homeowner (if applicable) should have the fire sprinkler system professionally tested every two years (or more frequently if required by the local fire authorities) to determine that the system will operate as designed in the event of a fire.

Condition #3: Water Pipe Freezes

Potentially Impacting:

- Water supply
- Structural integrity
- Contents of Home

Performance Guideline

In geographic areas where freezing weather is normal, water supply and waste piping should be protected from freezing. For geographic areas where freezing weather is rare, unprotected pipes are considered acceptable.

Comments: In most geographic areas of the country, freezing weather occurs frequently. Unprotected pipes may leak at valves and joints in areas where freezing weather is common and part of the normal weather pattern. In areas where temperatures normally drop below freezing, the water supply piping should be installed in a manner that safeguards against freeze damage. Some safeguards include: bringing the water supply line into the interior of the Home below ground level (*crawl space* or *basement*, not an outside wall); using deep seat valves on hose bibs; wrapping pipes in unheated areas with thermostatically controlled heat tape; and providing a drain down valve at the lowest accessible part of the water supply system.

Builder Responsibility: The Builder should protect all pipes from freezing weather if the Home is constructed in an area where freezing weather is normal and customary. If the Homeowner does not maintain minimum heat, the Builder is not responsible for leaking pipes due to freezing that occurs in portions of the Home intended for heat.

Homeowner Responsibility: To protect against pipe freezing, the Homeowner can purchase protective materials such as pipe *insulation* and electric resistance heat tape at any local hardware store. If the Homeowner will be gone for a period of time during possible freezing weather, the thermostat should be set on “Heat” at its minimum setting.

Condition #4: Water Tastes Funny, Smells, or Is Discolored

Potentially Impacting:

- Occupant health
- Occupant comfort

Performance Guideline

Water should be of good quality. However, the Builder may not have control over the quality of water supplied by the local water district. Water quality requirements are overseen by the appropriate state agency and the Federal Environmental Protection Agency.

Comments: In many subdivisions, the Builder installs the water system subject to specifications and inspections by the local water agency. Upon final testing, the water agency takes over responsibility for the water supply, including pressure and quality.

Builder Responsibility: None, unless the Builder is responsible for creating the water supply to the Home. This does not mean installing the water piping system that is to be taken over by a municipal authority. If the Builder is responsible for supplying the source of water, the Builder should provide water that meets minimum quality standards as set by the governing agency, such as the local County Department of Health or the State Department of Water Quality. The Builder is not responsible for changes in water quality if the initial water quality complies with the local or state set standards. For example, a change in nearby agricultural uses or mining activity subsequent to construction may cause changes in water quality that are not the Builder's Responsibility.

Homeowner Responsibility: If water quality standards are met by the Builder and/or the local water supply agency and are still unacceptable to the Homeowner, consider a Home filtration system or use of a drinking water service company.

Condition #5: Toilet and Drains Back Up

Potentially Impacting:

- Interior finishes and furnishings
- Occupant health

Performance Guideline

At the time of the walkthrough, all fixtures should operate as intended and all drains should flow freely. The Builder should demonstrate this to the Homeowner.

Comments: Backed up drainage systems, particularly toilets, are a frequent complaint of new Homeowners. For the vast majority of such incidents, occupants of the Home have caused the condition. In some infrequent cases, the main line has received construction debris during the construction process. This can usually be determined within the first week of occupancy. It is very important that each toilet is flushed and the water be turned on to each fixture during the walkthrough process.

Federal law requires that all toilets installed in new construction flush with 1.6 gallons of water or less. These include dual flush toilets that use only one gallon to flush non-solids. Homeowners who are used to larger capacity toilets (3.5 or 7 gallon flush) sometimes have difficulty making the transition to low flush toilets, and consequently require at least another flush.

Builder Responsibility: The Builder should ensure that the fixtures conform to the Performance Guideline at the time of walkthrough. The Builder is not responsible for conditions after the walkthrough unless it is determined that the cause of the blockage was from construction related activity.

Homeowner Responsibility: ***Maintenance Alert!*** The Homeowner should keep sink, tub, and shower *traps* clear of debris as part of routine maintenance. Material such as hair, toothpaste, etc., may accumulate in the traps and could eventually cause a backup. It is important to keep these materials from getting into the trap in the first place. Use a drain cleaner every 6 months to keep the traps scoured out and free from debris build-up. The Homeowner should learn the proper use of a low-flush toilet and how to clear a sink trap.

Condition #6: Water Pressure or Flow Is Low

Potentially Impacting:

- Use of plumbing fixtures

Performance Guideline

For Homes that are connected to a municipal water system or mutual water system serving 10 Homes or more, the Home piping system should be designed to operate between pressures of 40 pounds per square inch (psi) and 80 psi. For Homes that are connected to a well or a mutual water system serving 10 Homes or fewer, the water pressure is subject to the capacity of the well and the output of its equipment.

Comments: Water pressure problems arise from two sources: 1) inadequate pressure in the piping system of the water supply agency; or 2) the piping system in the Home is undersized. Most plumbing systems are designed to operate within the range of 40 psi and 80 psi measured at the point where the water supply pipe enters the Home. High water pressure can be a problem because it creates a condition known as *water hammer* and causes noise and banging of the pipes. Washing machines and dishwashers are equipped with electric valves that open and close quickly. These valves may produce a water hammer effect. High water pressure can be reduced with a special pressure-reducing regulator. Low water pressure can be increased with the use of a booster pump. It should be noted that all showerheads and most sink faucets are required to have flow restrictors placed in them for water conservation purposes. Reduced flows from flow restrictors may give a mistaken impression of low water pressure.

Builder Responsibility: None, provided the Builder has met the state-adopted or local code for proper water pipe system design. If water pressure exceeds 80 psi, the Builder should install a pressure reducing regulator.

Homeowner Responsibility: In areas where the water service is at the lower end of the allowable pressure range, water flow from fixtures will be less. This condition is beyond the control of the Builder and should be addressed with the agency that supplies the water. If the problem persists, the Homeowner should consider installing a booster pump to increase pressure. Using several fixtures simultaneously may also result in low water flow and a decrease in pressure. If a pressure reducing regulator is installed, the Homeowner should clean the sediment screen if there is a decrease in water pressure.

Condition #7: Sewer Gas Smell Coming from Drain

Potentially Impacting:

- Air quality
- Occupant health

Performance Guideline

This is a Homeowner maintenance item unless the sewer gas is coming from a cracked pipe.

Builder Responsibility: None.

Homeowner Responsibility: Sewer gas smells coming from drains typically indicate a lack of water in the *trap*. This occurs when a drain is not used for long periods of time and the water evaporates from the trap. If the Homeowner pours a large glass of water into the drain, it should fill the trap sufficiently.

Condition #8: Copper Water Pipe or Black Gas Pipe Is Wet on the Outside

Potentially Impacting:

- Appearance

Performance Guideline

Condensation on the outside of water lines is a normal condition.

Comments: In geographic areas where humidity is high, condensation may form on the outside of cold water lines, gas lines and toilet tanks. Cold water inside the pipe or gas moving through the pipe creates a cooling effect. Water in the surrounding air then condenses around the pipe.

Builder Responsibility: The Builder should install pipe *insulation* on cold water pipes (as well as hot water pipes in non-heated areas for energy conservation purposes) where there is a likelihood of condensation and mold growth.

Homeowner Responsibility: None.

Condition #9: Faucet Drips

Potentially Impacting:

- Water consumption
- Occupant comfort

Performance Guideline

At the time of the walkthrough all washers and cartridges should seat tightly and faucets should not leak.

Comments: Faucets are manufactured with either washers or cartridges to prevent leakage when the faucet is turned off. Cartridges have approximately 10 times the *useful life* of washers. The quality of the water supply affects the useful life of both cartridges and washers. Both municipal water and well water contain a certain amount of very small particles of solid material. Over time, these particles may affect the performance of washers and cartridges.

Builder Responsibility: The Builder should perform repairs on faucets that leak at the time of the walkthrough.

Homeowner Responsibility: ***Maintenance Alert!*** The Homeowner should replace washers and cartridges when dripping is first noticed. Many cartridges have a five year to lifetime guarantee on parts. Most current bathroom and kitchen faucets are made with cartridges and require only infrequent replacement. Hose bibs (the valves that a hose is connected to on the outside of the Home) are made with washers. Depending upon the amount of use, hose bib washers may need to be replaced as frequently as every six months or as infrequently as every three years. If leaking occurs at the "stem" or handle of the valve (often at the hose bib or water heater), the nut at the base of the stem can be tightened or repacked to solve this problem.

Condition #10: Sink/Tub Is Chipped

Potentially Impacting:

- Appearance

Performance Guideline

Fixtures should not be chipped at time of the walkthrough. Chips, mars, or discolorations 1/32 inch or less are considered acceptable.

Builder Responsibility: Chips, mars, or discolorations, observed at the time of the walkthrough that do not conform to the Performance Guideline should be repaired by the Builder.

Homeowner Responsibility: None.

Condition #11: Shower Head Pipe/Tub Spout Is Loose

Potentially Impacting:

- Watertightness of structure

Performance Guideline

At time of walkthrough, shower head pipes and tub spouts should be secured so they cannot move in or out (no movement at all). This applies to control valves as well.

Builder Responsibility: The Builder should perform repairs to conform to the Performance Guideline, if an unacceptable condition is noted at time of walkthrough.

Homeowner Responsibility: The Homeowner should avoid hanging heavy objects such as shower caddies full of bathing shampoos and lotions on the shower head pipe. The Homeowner should not pull on the tub spout or use it as a handle.

Condition #12: Shower/Tub Enclosure Leaks

See "**Chapter Six—Interior Components, Shower and Tub Enclosures**", Condition 2, page 188.

Condition #13: Fiberglass Tub/Shower Flexes When Occupied

See "**Chapter Six—Interior Components, Shower and Tub Enclosures**", Condition 3, page 188.

Condition #14: Water Drains from Sink/Tub When Stopper Is Engaged

Potentially Impacting:

- Use of sink/tub

Performance Guideline

Water should not drain past the stopper mechanism at a rate which allows the depth of water in the sink or tub to decrease by more than 1 inch per hour.

Comments: Sink and tub stoppers are not designed to create a perfect seal. A perfect seal is not necessary for customary and usual use. Sink and tub stoppers easily get out of adjustment through continuous use and can be affected by debris trapped in the drain.

Builder Responsibility: The Builder should adjust or replace sinks and tubs which drain more quickly than permitted under the Performance Guideline and whose stoppers have been properly maintained.

Homeowner Responsibility: The Homeowner should clean the edges of stoppers monthly.

Condition #15: Brass Bathroom Faucet and Drain Are Tarnished

Potentially Impacting:

- Appearance

Performance Guideline

Brass fittings should be free of tarnish at the time of walkthrough; brass fittings that become tarnished subsequent to the walkthrough are acceptable.

Comments: Just as *concrete* is certain to crack, brass bathroom fittings are certain to tarnish. Most brass fittings are coated with lacquer. Eventually, the lacquer chips or is rubbed off, and the brass tarnishes. The degree of tarnish depends upon the amount of use, water quality, and pollutants present in the air. Some manufacturers offer a lifetime finish on their brass fittings.

Builder Responsibility: The Builder should replace bathroom brass fittings that are tarnished at the time of the walkthrough.

Homeowner Responsibility: ***Maintenance Alert!*** Brass is a beautiful but "soft" metal. It is easily scratched and tarnished. The Homeowner should follow the manufacturer's instructions when cleaning brass. The Homeowner should wipe brass finishes frequently and avoid abrasive cleansers and cleansers with ammonia that are likely to scratch and chemically attack brass finishes.

Condition #16: Toilet Runs Continuously

Potentially Impacting:

- Water consumption

Performance Guideline

When a toilet tank fills, it should shut off. Water should not run continuously through the overflow pipe or flapper valve.

Builder Responsibility: The Builder should adjust the toilet tank system so that the water shuts off when the tank is filled to the appropriate level.

Homeowner Responsibility: ***Maintenance Alert!*** Toilet tanks have mechanical parts inside and the parts wear out over time. Depending upon the amount of use and the water quality, replacement of flappers, floats, and valves can be required as frequently as once a year or as infrequently as every 10 years. Water supplies with high concentrations of minerals (known as *hard water*) will leave deposits inside the toilet tank and its parts. This condition will cause more frequent replacement of toilet parts than those areas that do not have high mineral content in the water supply. The Homeowner should not place tablets that contain chlorine (bleach) into the tank because they can corrode the fittings inside the tank.

Condition #17: Toilet Leaks at Floor

Potentially Impacting:

- Appearance
- Structural integrity
- Termite attraction
- Mold and mildew growth

Performance Guideline

Toilets should not leak at the floor.

Comments: The connection between the pipe, the floor, and the toilet base is made with a wax ring. This wax is the same inside diameter as the flange pipe. A portion of the wax ring fits tightly into the pipe and pressing the toilet onto the wax ring makes a complete seal. When a toilet leaks at the floor the chances are, that the seal of the wax ring has failed. Wax rings dry out and become brittle over time.

Builder Responsibility: The Builder should perform repairs to ensure a watertight flow between the toilet and the Home waste plumbing.

Homeowner Responsibility: The Homeowner should notify the Builder of a leaking toilet or a toilet that rocks from side to side before additional damage occurs. Toilets that are permitted to leak will cause structural damage if the toilet is located over a wood *subfloor*. A toilet that leaks creates a condition for termites to enter the Home, regardless of whether it sits on a wooden subfloor or a slab. It is important to note that a toilet that rocks back and forth or moves side-to-side may be leaking even though no leak is visible.

Condition #18: Lack of Hot Water

Potentially Impacting:

- Occupant comfort

Performance Guideline

The Builder should provide a hot water system, either gas, electric, or solar, that meets the energy code and supplies hot water to all appropriate fixtures in the Home. Generally, accepted industry practice does not require that all hot water pipes that pass through unheated spaces (such as garages, crawl spaces, and attics) should be insulated, provided that the Builder has installed other energy conserving devices that make the entire Home code compliant. It should be noted that some local and state codes require that both hot and cold water pipes be insulated.

Comments: In many Homes, the source of hot water is a tank type water heater. In recent years, another type of water heater has come to market: the tankless water heater. There are also solar water heaters and waste gas recovery heaters that link to the *furnace*. The source of heat for both the tank and tankless type of water heaters is likely to be gas. In areas where gas is not available, electric water heater types are permitted. Gas is a more efficient method of heating water than electricity. There are several factors that could contribute to a lack of hot water: a power failure that cuts off the supply of gas or electricity; the pilot light has gone out; a low capacity water heater; a temperature setting too low on the water heater; and heat loss through the piping system, particularly at far ends of the Home. Typically, the water heater installer will set the water temperature between a low of 120ºF and a high of 140ºF. Since dishwashers only operate with hot water, 140ºF is considered hot enough to effectively kill bacteria that may be present on dirty dishes.

Builder Responsibility: The Builder should perform repairs to conform to the Performance Guideline.

Homeowner Responsibility: Frequent demand over short time periods (such as morning showers by an entire family) can result in a lack of hot water until the water heater has had time to recover; this is not a Builder responsibility. To increase water temperature, the Homeowner can adjust the control dial on most tank type water heaters. Electric water heaters are often pre-set and cannot be adjusted. However, it is very important the Homeowner recognizes that the higher the temperature setting, the greater the danger of scalding. **CAUTION!** Before entering the tub or shower, the Homeowner should always turn on the water and adjust it to a safe and proper temperature. Children and the elderly (or any person) should never be placed in a tub or shower before the water is turned on and the temperature safely adjusted. Although many gas water heaters have automatic ignition systems, the Homeowner should become familiar with how to manually light a water heater pilot light.

Condition #19: Water Heater Is Not Earthquake Secured

Potentially Impacting:

- Occupant safety

Performance Guideline

Tank type water heaters should be strapped or secured in code approved manner to prevent tip-over during an earthquake. This Guideline also applies to water heaters that have been installed in areas of historically identified seismic zones where earthquakes occur infrequently, but nevertheless, have previously occurred.

Builder Responsibility: The Builder should strap or secure the water heater to the *frame* of the Home in a manner prescribed by code. The Builder should connect the straps to the Home frame and not just through *drywall*.

Homeowner Responsibility: None.

NOTE: To prolong the life of a tank type water heater, accumulated sediment should be removed from the heater tank once a year. This task can be performed by attaching a thick wall garden hose to the drain spigot at the bottom of the tank and draining out no more than two gallons. **Since the water being drained is very hot, be very careful that the hot water does not come into contact with persons, animals, plants, or any material that could be damaged by scalding water (120ºF to 160ºF).**

WATER HEATERS
SHOULD BE SECURELY
STRAPPED TO THE
HOUSE FRAME TO
AVOID TIP-OVER

Condition #20: Electric Water Heater Circuit Breaker Trips Continuously

Potentially Impacting:
- Occupant safety
- Occupant comfort

Performance Guideline

Electric water heater breakers should not trip. Tripping is an indication of an electrical problem within the heater or the wiring to the heater.

Builder Responsibility: The Builder should take corrective measures to eliminate electric water heater breaker tripping.

Homeowner Responsibility: None. However, as electric water heaters age, their heating element can wear out and fall to the bottom of the tank. If this condition occurs, the circuit breaker cannot be reset and the Homeowner will need to replace the water heater.

Mechanical Ventilation

General Subject Information: Other than by windows and *doors*, Homes can be ventilated by numerous other means. These devices include humidistat and whole house fans, as well as fans in the bathroom, laundry room, fireplace, *attic*, *basement*, *crawl space*, and kitchen hood. Dryer vents are included in this category, although their primary purpose is to pass warm moist air from the dryer. Forced air *furnace* fans, known as *air handlers*, also provide circulated ventilation.

Houses built today are much "tighter" and often require a whole house ventilation system to bring in fresh air while discharging stale air to the outside. These systems are known as Heat Recovery Ventilators (HRV) and Energy Recovery Ventilators (ERV). Both systems have filters that must be changed or washed periodically.

Condition #1: Bathroom/Laundry Fan Is Noisy

Potentially Impacting:
- Occupant comfort

Performance Guideline

Bathroom and laundry fans can be noisy. This is not a condition of non-performance unless the sound is a result of fan blades hitting part of the housing. Many state or local municipalities now have maximum noise level in their codes.

Comments: The amount of noise from exhaust fans varies by manufacturer. Exhaust fans are required to change over a certain volume of air in the room per hour. As long as the plastic or metal fan blades are turning freely, they are likely to be operating as intended. If the fan blades are hitting something solid, like the fan housing, they will make a distinct battering noise.

Builder Responsibility: None, unless the fan blades are hitting the housing or other solid object. If this is the case, the Builder should perform repairs to conform to the Performance Guideline.

Homeowner Responsibility: The Homeowner should not disconnect the bath or laundry fans because they create an annoying noise. Moist air must be exhausted to the outside; otherwise, mold and mildew can form on the walls and ceiling. The Homeowner should always operate the fans when bathrooms and laundry rooms are in use.

Condition #2: Fan Discharges to Attic, Crawl Space, or Basement

Potentially Impacting:

- Occupant health and safety

Performance Guideline

Fans that are designed to move air from a room or closet shall discharge only through an exterior wall or roof. Fans that discharge to the face of a foundation vent or eave vent are unacceptable.

Builder Responsibility: The Builder should conform to the Performance Guideline by exhausting all fan ducts to the outside through an exterior wall or the roof.

Homeowner Responsibility: The Homeowner should not disconnect bathroom fans.

Condition #3: Fan Pushes Hot or Cold Air Back Into the Room

Potentially Impacting:

- Occupant comfort

Performance Guideline

All ventilation systems should have back draft dampers either on the fan itself or at the point of discharge through the wall.

Builder Responsibility: The Builder should conform to the Performance Guideline by installing fans that have a back draft *damper* in the system. The Builder should also verify that the output of the fan has been properly sized to the square footage of the room or the area to be ventilated.

Homeowner Responsibility: The Homeowner should check the vent discharge covers annually to ensure that birds are not nesting in the vent cover.

Condition #4: Dryer Duct Is Assembled with Sheet Metal Screws

Potentially Impacting:

- Occupant health and safety
- Dryer efficiency

Performance Guideline

Sections of dryer ducts shall be joined with sheet metal tape and no fastening device shall penetrate the duct sections. Dryer ducts shall discharge through an exterior wall or the roof at a termination cap that has a damper and not an insect screen. Dryer duct ventilation material needs to be fire rated per code.

Comments: Dryer ducts shall not be assembled using sheet metal screws because they penetrate the inside of the duct. This penetration catches lint and can cause dryer duct fires. Similarly, nothing should be attached to the duct termination cap, like an insect screen, that would impede the flow of lint.

Builder Responsibility: The Builder should conform to the Performance Guideline by removing any penetrating fasteners and screen covered termination caps.

Homeowner Responsibility: The Homeowner should clean the dryer lint trap after every use.

Condition #5: Improper Termination of Dryer Duct

Potentially Impacting:

- Occupant health and safety

Performance Guideline

Dryer ducts shall terminate through an exterior wall or roof with a termination cap approved for dryer ducts. Dryer ducts shall not discharge into an attic, a crawl space or a basement.

Builder Responsibility: The Builder should ensure that all dryer ducts meet the Performance Guideline.

Homeowner Responsibility: None.

Fire Sprinkler System

General Subject Information: Many state and local jurisdictions in the country require automatic fire sprinklers to be installed in new homes. Usually, the Homeowner does not find out if and how the system works, until it is needed. However, periodic testing of the system and alarms must be done, subject to local regulations.

Condition #1: Fire Sprinkler Pipe or Fitting Leaks

Potentially Impacting:

- Surrounding finishes
- Mold and mildew growth
- Alarm performance

Performance Guideline

Fire sprinkler systems should not leak.

Builder Responsibility: The Builder should perform repairs of leaking pipes, fittings, etc., to eliminate leaks. The Builder should notify the pipe manufacturer if plastic piping appears to be defective.

Homeowner Responsibility: The Homeowner should not paint any fire sprinkler heads or covers, or hang any objects from the head. Be aware that if the *drywall* is removed from the ceiling, such as in a repair or remodel, plastic sprinkler pipes could melt if exposed directly to a fire while the ceiling was open.

Condition #2: Sprinkler Head and Escutcheon Do Not Fit Flush to Wall, or Are Out of Line with Drywall Opening

Potentially Impacting:

- Appearance
- Function

Performance Guideline

All sprinkler heads and their escutcheons should fit neatly and tightly to wall and ceiling finishes. Escutcheons should not protrude more than 1/8 inch as measured from the back of the plate beyond the wall surface.

Comments: This condition can be the result of poor workmanship or more infrequently because the *frame* of the building has shrunk or settled. If copper pipes are used in the sprinkler system, the pipes will be rigid and will not settle with the building. To some extent, a similar condition may occur with plastic piping, but plastic has some flexibility. Once the shrinkage has run its course, the building will be stable and this condition should not recur.

Builder Responsibility: The Builder should conform to the Performance Guideline by correcting sprinkler heads that are out of line or do not fit neatly to finish surfaces.

Homeowner Responsibility: None.

Telephone and Internet

General Subject Information: Telephone wiring in homes today can range from a simple two pair wire system to a complex, high-tech fiber optic system for voice and data transmission. The wiring of the telephone system within the Home is likely to be done by a specialty contractor hired by the Builder and not by the company providing the telephone service. The telephone service comes into the Home in a box called the *interface*, located on an outside wall. The company providing telephone service takes responsibility from the street to the interface and the Builder or the Homeowner takes responsibility from the interface throughout the inside of the Home. When telephone problems occur, it is often difficult to determine the area of responsibility.

Condition #1: Phone Has Static or No Dial Tone

Potentially Impacting:

- Intended use of telephone

Performance Guideline

A clear signal (dial tone) should be provided from the interface to all jacks within the Home. The maximum signal loss between the interface and any jack should not exceed 6 dB (decibels).

Builder Responsibility: If the telephone service provider identifies the problem as being on the Home side of the interface, the Builder should take corrective measures to conform to the Performance Guideline.

Homeowner Responsibility: None, however, the Homeowner should be aware that after-market alterations to the phone system may affect the performance of the original wiring.

Cable TV and Satellite TV

General Subject Information: Cable TV, or CATV as it is commonly known, is the acronym for Community Antenna Television. The cable service provider receives TV transmission in a large satellite dish at the company facilities and retransmits it via cable to the individual subscriber's Home. Most cable service companies provide high speed internet service as well. Satellite TV operates on a similar principle, except that the satellite dish is located on the subscriber's Home. In many areas of the country that do not have cable wiring, satellite TV is the only option to receive a wider variety of channels.

For cable and satellite TV, like the telephone system described in the previous section, there is an *interface* on the outside of the Home. The cable and satellite service providers take responsibility for the quality of the cable signal to the interface. From the interface throughout the Home is typically the responsibility of the Builder or the Homeowner. In most cases a specialty contractor working for the Builder installs the cable wiring within the Home. A simple system is run directly from the interface to wall outlets. A more complex system involves a panel within the Home and an amplifier that boosts the signal to the various rooms in the Home. Cable and satellite boxes that unscramble the signal are part of the package.

Condition #1: TV Reception Is Snowy, Wavy, or Unclear

Potentially Impacting:

- Intended use of television

Performance Guideline

If the cable wiring within the Home is installed by the Builder, there should be a clear, uninterrupted signal to each outlet with a maximum signal loss of 8 dB (decibels) between the interface and any one outlet.

Builder Responsibility: Upon report of a problem by Homeowner and a statement by the cable provider that the problem is on the Home side of the interface, the Builder should perform corrective measures to conform to the Performance Guideline.

Homeowner Responsibility: None, but if the Homeowner adds after-market splitters, boosters, and other cable enhancing devices, the system may not perform as originally intended. The Builder is not responsible for any conditions created by after-market changes.

Chapter Eight

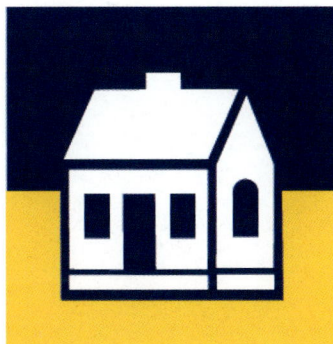

GROUNDS

includes:

Drainage

Landscaping

Irrigation

Retaining Walls

Fencing

References for this chapter:

- *Code Check Building 3rd ed.,* Taunton Press
- *Operating Cost Manual for Homeowners Associations*, CA Department of Real Estate
- *Residential Construction Performance Guidelines*, NAHB 2011 ed.
- *Residential Water Problems*, by Alvin Sacks
- *Sunset Western Landscaping,* by Kathleen Brenzel, Oxmoor House, 2006
- *Lowe's Complete Landscape,* Sunset Publishing Corporation, 2008

A comprehensive list of references by author and publisher is found in the Bibliography section.

Chapter Eight

Grounds

General Subject Information: Water must be kept away from *foundations* and *basements* in order to reduce the potential for structural and interior damage. Not only can seeping water cause interior damage, it can cause the foundation to move. There are several potential causes for these conditions:

1) Lack of *gutters* and *downspouts* (downspouts should be piped either to the street or away from the foundation). See "**Chapter Five—Exterior Components, Gutters and Downspouts**", page 115;
2) Lack of required *slope* away from the foundation;
3) Overwatering landscaping near the foundation. Site drainage that may be the responsibility of a Homeowners Association should be subject to good irrigation practice and maintenance. Soil movement is discussed in "**Chapter One—Foundations, Landslides, Sinkholes and Other Soil Movement**", page 35.

Drainage

Condition #1: Water Does Not Drain Away From Foundation

Potentially Impacting:

- Interior finishes and furnishings
- *Foundation* integrity

Performance Guideline

The grade of soils that surround the foundation of a building should slope a minimum of 6 inches within the first 10 feet from the foundation. This required slope must be maintained for a minimum of 10 feet away from the foundation unless water is diverted from the foundation into an approved structure (such as concrete drainage ditch or graded swale). Hard surfaces such as walkways and patios should slope 1 inch in 4 feet. Any water that is standing or ponding within 6 feet of the foundation must dissipate within 24 hours after rain.

Comments: Keeping water away from the foundation is one of the most critical responsibilities of the Homeowner. When water has an opportunity to pond (stand), it can lead to severe interior damage to both finishes and furnishings. Water vapor can migrate through concrete as well as through cracks beneath the foundation and through *basement* walls. All "soils" should maintain a minimum vertical distance of 6 inches from finished floors and any portion of the wood floor that is subject to decay to the top of finished soil. The 6 inch distance can be reduced to 2 inches if the surface that surrounds the foundation is a hard surface, for example concrete, asphalt or *pressure treated* wood.

Builder Responsibility: At the time of the *walkthrough* the Builder should ensure that foundation slope conforms to the Performance Guideline.

Homeowner Responsibility: ***Maintenance Alert!*** The Homeowner has a responsibility to maintain conditions that conform to the Performance Guideline. The Homeowner may be out of compliance with the Guideline in one of two ways: 1) during the installation of landscape materials, the existing *grade* is modified by leveling it out, causing either a *negative slope* or a flat slope; or 2) the Homeowner hires a landscape company that modifies the grade during soils preparation and planting, causing either flat or negative slope. It should also be noted that if *gutters* and downspouts are not installed, the Homeowner should assume responsibility either to install them or have them installed. If downspouts are installed, water should discharge on to approved *splash blocks* or into a pipe collector system.

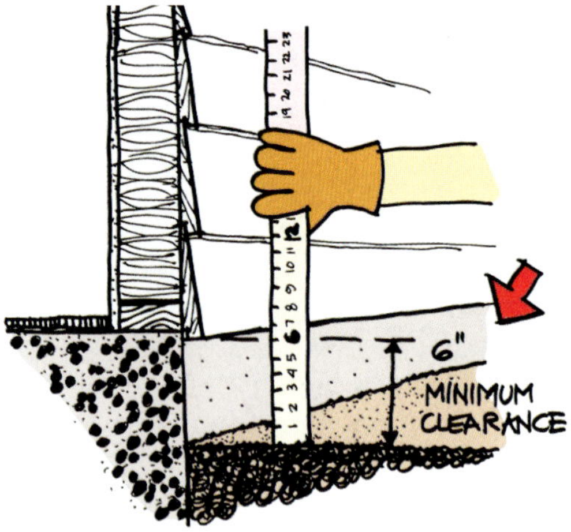

SEPARATION BETWEEN WOOD AND SOIL

(USE CARE WHEN INSTALLING PATIOS AND DECKS)

Condition #2: Improper Site Drainage (Areas beyond 10 Feet of the Perimeter of the Foundation)

Potentially Impacting:

- Adjoining properties
- *Foundation* integrity

Performance Guideline

Existing grades and swales are not allowed to drain onto adjoining properties. Water that is transferred via yard drains, swales, or sump pumps may require 48 hours to drain.

Comments: Under extreme weather conditions, *ponding* or standing water may take longer to dissipate. Water that stands or ponds under extreme conditions is considered acceptable and is not the responsibility of the Builder.

Builder Responsibility: The Builder should establish the proper grades prior to the *walkthrough*.

Homeowner Responsibility: The Homeowner should keep swales and drains free of silt and other debris.

Condition #3: Soil Settling around the Foundation

Potentially Impacting:

- Site drainage
- Integrity of *concrete* walks and *foundations*
- Watertightness of structure

Performance Guideline

Soils that settle and cause water to stand or pond within 5 feet of the foundation perimeter and do not dissipate within 24 hours after rain are considered unacceptable.

Comments: If soils that surround the foundation (within the 5 foot perimeter) settle more than 3 inches in depth in any one area larger than 3 feet in diameter, the Builder is responsible for correcting the settlement, provided that the soil settlement is not a direct result of actions of the Homeowner.

Builder Responsibility: The Builder should ensure that soils surrounding the foundation are reasonably compacted in order to conform to the Performance Guideline.

Homeowner Responsibility: *Maintenance Alert!* The Homeowner is responsible for maintenance issues that involve soils that conform to the Performance Guideline. Repair of erosion caused by a rainstorm is the responsibility of the Homeowner.

NOTE*:* If the Homeowner modifies existing *grades* that surround the foundation and this causes the soils to subside in any manner, the Builder is not responsible.

Condition #4: Soil Settling and Water Ponding at Utility Trenches

Potentially Impacting:

- Integrity/use of *driveways*, *walkways*, *patios*, streets
- Occupant safety related to tripping hazard
- Utilities

Performance Guideline

Trenches in landscaped areas should not settle more than 6 inches or cause water to pond within 5 feet of the foundation perimeter. Water that does not dissipate within 24 hours after rain is considered an unacceptable condition. Trenches that are overlaid with concrete or asphalt are considered unacceptable if water ponds for more than 48 hours after rain. If a paved-over trench subsides more than 1 inch from the surrounding pavement, it is unacceptable, whether it drains or not.

Builder Responsibility: The Builder should perform repairs of utility trench conditions that do not conform to the Performance Guideline.

Homeowner Responsibility: None.

Landscaping

General Subject Information: The addition of landscaping is a significant positive amenity at any individual Home or housing project. In the case of individual Homes, the Builder either: 1) does not provide the landscaping; 2) the Builder provides a minimum package in front to satisfy the requirements of a local planning agency; or 3) the Builder may install a more complete landscape package and irrigation system. Alternatively, in most *condominium* or townhouse projects, the Builder typically provides the entire landscape installation. Care taken in the initial installation of landscaping and proper maintenance afterwards is essential for keeping the property looking well kept and attractive.

Condition #1: Improper Soil Preparation

Potentially Impacting:

- Growth of planted materials
- Life expectancy or failure rate of planted materials
- Heavy weed growth

Performance Guideline

Soils should be prepared according to generally accepted local conditions as specified by a landscape architect or as recommended by a soils test report.

Builder Responsibility: If the Builder installed the landscaping, the Builder is responsible for reasonable and proper soil preparation in accordance with generally accepted local procedures prior to the installation of plant materials. This includes placing amendments into high clay soils.

Homeowner Responsibility: The Homeowner should maintain soils by periodically adding the proper amount of nutrients, for example fertilizer, mulch, humus, and minerals required for the particular type of planting.

Condition #2: Plants Die within the Warranty Period

Potentially Impacting:

- Appearance
- *Slope* erosion

Performance Guideline

Plants that die within the warranty period must be replaced, provided that the plant death is not due to improper maintenance or irrigation by the Homeowner.

Comments: The Builder should provide a written warranty agreement for any planted landscape materials. Typically, trees, shrubs and ground cover have different warranty periods. Common grounds of large developments with a Homeowners Association should have a start-up maintenance schedule with their independent maintenance company, followed by a standard yearly maintenance schedule.

Builder Responsibility: If the Builder installed plants, shrubs, trees and/or sod, the Builder should issue a warranty and maintenance schedule (usually provided by the actual landscape installer) regarding the planted vegetation. This should include the length of the warranty period and any inclusions and exclusions to the warranty. If plants die within the warranty period and this is not a result of improper care and/or maintenance, either by the Homeowner, the Homeowners Association, or both, the Builder should replace plants that die or appear unhealthy.

Homeowner Responsibility: The Homeowner or Homeowners Association should provide the required maintenance to ensure that plants stay healthy and are not overwatered. Any water that is standing or *ponding* 30 minutes after watering is a sign of overwatering. If there are no specific instructions as to the proper maintenance of the plants, then the Homeowner should consult an expert, such as a nursery, the Builder, or a landscape maintenance contractor. All plants, shrubs, sod and trees should be maintained properly to ensure their healthy growth and survival.

Condition #3: Weeds Grow in Landscaped Area

Potentially Impacting:

- Appearance
- Plant life

Performance Guideline

Minimal weed growth is to be expected; "minimal" is defined as less than 10% of the planted area.

Comments: Even after applying *pre-emergent* weed control, it is still virtually impossible to guarantee against some weed growth in planted areas.

Builder Responsibility: The Builder should ensure that proper weed control has been provided prior to and immediately after planting.

Homeowner Responsibility: The Homeowner or Homeowners Association should provide proper maintenance regarding weed control.

Irrigation

Condition #1: Improper Design or Installation of Irrigation System

Potentially Impacting:

- Exterior wall integrity
- Structural framing integrity
- Drainage
- Plant health

Performance Guideline

Irrigation water should not spray directly onto the Home. Minor overspray and wind driven overspray are acceptable. The irrigation system should be designed so all areas receive the intended amount of water.

Comments: Particular attention should be taken regarding sprinkler head location. Water should not spray directly onto the Home, walls, masonry, *walkways*, or metal and wood fencing. Many landscape professionals recommend *drip irrigation* at the *foundation* perimeter to eliminate overspray.

Builder Responsibility: The Builder should ensure that the irrigation system is designed to supply the proper amounts of water needed for the landscape (sod, shrubs and trees). All irrigation and planting should be installed according to generally accepted industry standards and local *building codes*. It should be suitable for the geographic region and microclimate as well.

Homeowner Responsibility: ***Maintenance Alert!*** The Homeowner should avoid overwatering the landscape. *Ponding* or standing water that accumulates at and around foundations can cause serious structural damage, insect infestation, and plant root rot. The Homeowner is responsible for adjusting the watering times on the irrigation controller to avoid overwatering as a maintenance item. At communities with Homeowners Associations, where landscape maintenance is likely to be done by a professional service, overwatering may be commonplace.

DO NOT ALLOW IRRIGATION WATER TO SPRAY AGAINST HOUSE WALLS AND FENCES.

Condition #2: Controller/Clock Does Not Operate

Potentially Impacting:

- Landscape health

Performance Guideline

The landscape irrigation controller/clock should operate as intended by the manufacturer within the warranty period.

Builder Responsibility: The Builder should perform repairs or replace the controller/clock if it fails within the warranty period.

Homeowner Responsibility: The Homeowner should change the backup battery (if the controller has one) once a year. The irrigation system should be turned off and blown out if freezing conditions exist in winter months.

Retaining Walls

General Subject Information: Typically, the most commonly used material in retaining wall construction is CMU (*Concrete* Masonry Unit) block. A masonry or concrete retaining wall, engineered for the intended application, will have steel reinforcement, an appropriately sized *footing*, in some cases a *waterproofing* or damp-proofing *membrane* applied to the backside and back and footing drainage. Other retaining wall types include open face modules that allow water to drain through each block and crib lock walls that also allow moisture to drain through each level. In many localities retaining walls more than 3 feet high are required to have a building permit and be constructed according to plans, which include a civil engineer's stamp. When retaining walls fail, water is one of the most common causes of failure. There are two ways that water attacks retaining walls: 1) surface water; and 2) sub-surface water. Surface water should be directed into concrete *swales* or *brow ditches* to a proper drainage area. *Subsurface water* should be diverted through a sub-drainage system, for example *trench drain*, and directed to a proper drainage discharge location.

Cement products can and often do crack which can permit water to pass through them. However, walls that are designed to retain soil or gravel may have a waterproofing product or membrane applied to the side of the wall that is against the hillside. Along with the waterproofing membrane, a protection board is also often applied to protect the membrane from damage when soils are placed against it. A swale or *berm* is often utilized in order to transfer surface water away from the wall. In order to remove any sub-surface water from the hillside, a trench drain or *weep holes* over a concrete swale are generally used as a method to remove subsurface water via a pipe to a designated discharge location. Some walls, notably the loose block variety (*blocks* not held together with *mortar*), are designed to have groundwater pass through the joints.

Condition #1: CMU Wall Leaks

Potentially Impacting:

- Structural integrity
- Appearance

Performance Guideline

Water that leaks or migrates through a masonry wall is unacceptable, except through weep holes that are intentionally designed for that purpose.

Comments: If the retaining wall leaks and is structurally sound, the cause can often be a result of several things: 1) a *waterproofing*/damp-proofing *membrane* was not installed; 2) the membrane was improperly installed; or 3) the *subdrain* system has failed, for example, the *trench drain*.

Builder Responsibility: The Builder should perform repairs to ensure that the masonry wall conforms to the Performance Guideline.

Homeowner Responsibility: The Homeowner should maintain the system installed to divert surface water away from the wall, either through a *concrete swale* or *berm*. The Homeowner should also inspect where the trench drain (provided that one was installed) *daylights* in order to determine whether the drain system is functioning correctly during heavy rains.

Condition #2: Wall and Mortar Joint Is Cracked

Potentially Impacting:

- Appearance
- Structural integrity

Performance Guideline

Cracks greater than ¼ inch are considered unacceptable.

Comments: Wall cracks are generally considered acceptable up to ¼ inch, as long as there is no dislocation of the plane of the wall and no vertical dislocation. Cracks should not be left open to the weather. They should be filled with an epoxy sealant or be filled with expandable *grout*.

Builder Responsibility: Provided that the Homeowner has not modified the *slope* above the retaining wall, the Builder should perform repairs to ensure that the wall conforms to the Performance Guideline.

Homeowner Responsibility: The Homeowner should repair cracks up to ¼ inch in a timely fashion. On long slopes that are relatively steep, the Homeowner should divert surface water away from the top of the wall to prevent conditions that could lead to cracking.

Condition #3: Wall Is Discolored with a White, Chalk-Like Substance

Potentially Impacting:

- Appearance
- Integrity of the reinforcing steel

Performance Guideline

This is a normal condition and is considered acceptable.

Comments: *Efflorescence* is a white, chalk-like powder that appears as a result of moisture migrating through the *mortar*, dissolving salts within, and leaching to the surface. Salts in the brick or block itself or high alkali content in the cement may also cause efflorescence. In geographic areas where high concentrations of sulfates are in the soil, there may also be a chemical attack on the *concrete*.

Builder Responsibility: The Builder is not responsible for common efflorescence. However, if there is severe efflorescence, where the entire face of the wall has a coating of white powder and is *spalling*, the Builder should investigate the condition further. If there is a large recurring area, it is possible that the *waterproofing membrane* was improperly installed or is missing. It may also be possible that a *subdrain* failed or was not installed.

Homeowner Responsibility: The Homeowner can remove common efflorescence by brushing or by applying a high-pressure water spray.

Condition #4: Wall Is Out of Plumb

Potentially Impacting:

- Appearance
- Occupant safety
- Slope

Performance Guideline

The outward lean of a wall should not exceed ¾ inch out of plumb in a 6 foot vertical direction.

Comments: Brick or masonry walls do not need to be perfectly plumb or level to function acceptably. Many wall types, such as *criblock*, or stacked concrete modules, *slope* back into the hillside.

Builder Responsibility: If the wall does not conform to the Performance Guideline, the Builder should perform repairs and replace all landscape materials damaged in the repair process.

Homeowner Responsibility: None, provided that the Homeowner has not built something on top of the wall or altered the slope in a way that would compromise the performance of the wall.

Fencing

Condition #1: Wood Post, Picket, or Panel Is Rotting

Potentially Impacting:

- Useful life of fence
- Security
- Privacy

Performance Guideline

Fence posts should be made of rot-resistant pressure treated wood rated for direct ground contact, or heartwood of cedar, or redwood. Bottom rails and pickets or sideboards should maintain a minimum clearance of 2 inches to finished grade. Posts should be set in concrete above grade so that water does not accumulate against the post.

Comments: The *building codes* usually do not specify requirements to prevent decay of fencing. However, by maintaining adequate clearance between fence-to-finished grades, the useful life of the fence may be drastically increased.

Builder Responsibility: The Builder should furnish a completed fence with the appropriate clearance between wood and finished grade. If the fence (railings, pickets or *siding*) is in contact with soil, the Builder should perform repairs to conform to the Performance Guideline.

Homeowner Responsibility: The Homeowner should not change the finished grade in any way that would adversely affect the clearance recommended in the Performance Guideline. If natural conditions (for example, rains washing soils down onto the fence) cause the clearances described in the Guideline to be compromised, it is the Homeowner's responsibility to perform the appropriate corrections. Planting shrubs whose foliage is in constant contact with the fence may also potentially reduce the life of the fence boards.

Condition #2: Fencing Is Prematurely Weathered or Rusted

Potentially Impacting:

- Appearance
- *Useful life* of fence

Performance Guideline

Wood fence surfaces are expected to weather unless they are painted at the time of installation. For information on "wrought iron", see Comments below.

Comments: True wrought iron fences are seldom installed today. What is referred to as "wrought iron" is really square or round tubular steel. Because the tubes are hollow, they can be more susceptible to rust at the welds. Any fence will need regularly scheduled maintenance in order to maximize the full *useful life* of that fence. There are many different factors that play a part in determining how often the Homeowner should maintain a fence, such as:

- Site-specific location of the fence - is it located in an area of direct harsh sunlight or is it in a wet and shady area;
- Type of material - metal, wood or masonry;
- Is there a finish or not - stains, sealers, paint;
- Geographic location - coastal, desert, inland or mountain environments.

NAILING A FENCE BOARD TO THE SIDE OF THE HOUSE IS AN OPEN INVITATION FOR TERMITES TO MOVE IN.

Builder Responsibility: The Builder should ensure that wrought iron or ornamental iron fences and weld joints are completely painted upon installation.

Homeowner Responsibility: *Maintenance Alert!* The Homeowner should direct irrigation sprinklers to spray away from fences. The Homeowner should inspect fences semi-annually and paint every three years. Wrought iron fences should be painted when rust is evident.

Condition #3: Fence Board Has Warps, Knots and Cracks

Potentially Impacting:

- Appearance
- Security value of fence

Performance Guideline

Fence boards that have loose or dislodged knots covering more than 25% of the width of the board are considered unacceptable. Boards that are split top to bottom with a split 3/8 inch wide or more are considered unacceptable. Boards that warp more than 1 inch in 6 feet of length are considered unacceptable.

Builder Responsibility: The Builder should replace boards that do not conform to the Performance Guideline.

Homeowner Responsibility: In order to prolong the *useful life* of the fence, the Homeowner should keep the fence in good repair by periodically re-nailing loose boards and painting and sealing wood fences every three years.

Chapter Nine

MISCELLANEOUS

includes:

Ice and Snow

Noise Transmission

Mold and Mildew

Septic Tanks

Smoke and Carbon Monoxide Alarms

Wood Destroying Insects

Radon

References for this chapter:

- *500 Terrific Ideas for Home Maintenance and Repair*, by Jack Maguire
- *Fire Resistance Design Manual*, Gypsum Association
- *National Electric Code 2011,* National Fire Protection Association (NFPA)
- *Mold in Residential Buildings*, NAHB
- *Residential Construction Performance Guidelines*, NAHB 2011 ed.
- *Residential Water Problems*, by Alvin Sacks
- *California Building Code, 2013 ed.,* The California Building Standards Commission
- *Building Radon Out,* EPA/402-K-01-002m April 2001
- *Homebuyer's and Seller's Guide to Radon,* EPA January 2009
- *The Consumer's Guide to Radon Reduction,* EPA
- *Guidelines on Assessment and Remediation of Fungi in Indoor Environments,* New York Department of Health, November 2008

A comprehensive list of references by author and publisher is found in the Bibliography section.

Chapter Nine

Miscellaneous

Ice and Snow

General Subject Information: Most Homes in the country are built where ice and snow are prevalent. Even in geographic areas where ice and snow are not common, it is important to recognize that occasional periods of below freezing weather can affect the performance of the Home. Good design and construction practices are important. In general, there are three areas of concern related to ice and snow discussed in the following conditions.

Condition #1: Roof Sags or Fails under Snow Load

Potentially Impacting:

- Structural integrity
- Occupant safety

Performance Guideline

Roofs should not fail under normal snow loads for the region; roofs may sag or deflect by only the amount permitted under the state or local code.

Comments: Accumulations of snow will add substantial weight to the structure of a Home, particularly to roofs and decks. Homes built in geographic areas subject to snow are required to accommodate these additional loads. However, storms may exceed normally predicted ranges, producing excessive snow accumulations. This can result in unacceptable deflection of *beams* and *rafters*, which may lead to cracking of interior finishes and in extreme circumstances, to structural collapse.

Builder Responsibility: Prior to construction, the Builder should ensure that the snow load requirements are met. The Builder should perform repairs to conform to the Performance Guideline.

Homeowner Responsibility: The Homeowner should remove the accumulation of snow from the roof during periods of exceptionally heavy snowfall. Except in isolated areas, the Homeowner should employ a company to perform this service. This is the safest approach for the Homeowner.

Condition #2: Doors and Windows Are Blocked With Snow

Potentially Impacting:

- Occupant comfort

Performance Guideline

This is a Homeowner maintenance issue.

Comments: During periods when heavy snow and icing occur, access *doors*, *garage doors* and even windows can be blocked. Proper "snow country" design should provide reasonable protection at essential openings, such as exit doors and garage doors. Reasonable protection would include overhangs and orientation away from customary storm exposure. Snow and ice accumulations can also create hazards from snow loads falling from roofs and heavy icicles from overhead projections.

Builder Responsibility: None.

Homeowner Responsibility: ***Maintenance Alert!*** When garage doors, access doors and windows become blocked, the Homeowner should take preventive measures to keep repetition of these problems to a minimum. More frequent shoveling is a first step toward minimizing accumulation. The severity of this condition depends upon the geographic location, Home design and orientation to the weather conditions.

Condition #3: Ice Dams Cause Eaves to Leak

Potentially Impacting:

- Interior finishes
- Structure

Performance Guideline

Ice dams should not cause eaves to leak.

Comments: When snow melts and then re-freezes, ice may form dams at areas such as roof eaves and deck perimeters. Subsequent melting or rainfall can accumulate behind such dams and the depth of resulting ponds can exceed the height of *waterproofing* systems. When this happens, water can enter the interior of roof and wall systems causing damage. In addition, *ponding* water on flat roofs and decks can exceed their design loads.

Builder Responsibility: The Builder should construct the roof assembly to conform to the requirements of the state *building code* and/or local code amendments with respect to ice dam elimination. The Builder should perform corrections if ice dams persist under normal weather conditions. If a structural or other type of failure occurs because of extreme weather conditions, the Builder is not responsible. (See the appropriate conditions in "**Chapter Four—Roofs**" for further information, page 65.)

Homeowner Responsibility: The Homeowner should be aware of the causes of ice dams and take steps to prevent their occurrence. ***Maintenance Alert!*** The Homeowner should keep *gutters*, drains, deck openings and major catch basins free of debris and other obstructions. If there are publicly owned drainage facilities nearby that are subject to blockage, the Homeowner should contact authorities to request maintenance. Failure to do this could result in localized flooding during periods of rapid snowmelt, with consequent property damage.

Noise Transmission

Condition #1: Sounds Can Be Heard through Walls and Floors (Condominiums and Townhouses)

Potentially Impacting:

- Occupant comfort

Performance Guideline

1. Party walls (also referred to as common walls) and floors between units: Sound transmission must be limited by code to meet a Sound Transmission Coefficient (STC) Standard of 50. Measurement of sound transmission can only be made using specialized equipment. The STC Standard of 50 is a laboratory test standard. When an approved wall or floor assembly is tested in the field, an STC rating of 45 is considered acceptable.

2. Devices (fans, etc.) should be of the quiet operating type. Water and plumbing waste lines should be installed in a manner that minimizes transmission of noise directly from pipes to the structure of the building.

3. Interior walls and ceilings: insulate vertical waste lines; use sound-absorbing underlayment at floors (particularly hard surfaces such as tile and uncovered hardwood floors) when units on different floors are not under control of the same owner.

4. The Performance Guideline regarding noise transmission between walls and floors of detached single-family Homes does not apply.

Comments: To prevent sound transmission between adjoining units from exceeding Performance Guidelines, walls must be assembled in accordance with industry accepted cross-sections (for example, those published by the Gypsum Association) or their established equivalents. Prior to granting a building permit, the Building Inspection Department should check to see that the floor and wall design meet an approved design standard. If it does not, the Builder or architect is required to prove that their design will satisfy the requirements of the code. Some common measures that should be used to diminish noise transmission include avoidance of plumbing lines within party walls, offsetting of electrical outlets so that none are back-to-back, and *insulation* of all necessary openings at such walls (for example, electrical outlets and switches). The structural *frame* of the building should not be continuous, but should be interrupted between adjacent units. Sprayed urethane insulation is also an effective way to increase the STC.

Builder Responsibility: The Builder should correct any deviations from STC standards where identified. The Builder should inform the Homeowner that it is impossible to totally eliminate noise transmission in party walls and common floor housing.

Homeowner Responsibility: The Homeowner should avoid any changes that affect the assembly of sound-insulating party walls or ceilings and avoid making new openings in walls and floors. A common Homeowner error is to install a speaker system in the party walls of a townhouse or *condominium*.

Mold and Mildew

General Subject Information: Mold and mildew (fungi) and the *spores* by which they reproduce are present everywhere in the environment, including indoor air and surfaces. Usually the small numbers of these tiny organisms do not cause any problems. However, high levels of moisture combined with organic materials provide conditions that can result in their rapid growth. In high concentrations, some of these fungi may consume wood and other building materials sufficiently to cause decay and rot. Others may produce stains and unattractive coatings on interior and exterior surfaces. Some people can develop allergy symptoms if exposed to mold. While it is quite difficult, if not impossible, to entirely eliminate these organisms in normal residential environments, control of interior humidity and preventions of leaks limits their growth and minimizes any resulting effects.

There are several thousand types of molds and mildews. A limited number of varieties are commonly associated with damage to buildings. Under conditions favorable to growth, these fungi can form dense colonies that may be visually unattractive. Of all the known varieties of mold and mildew, only a few are believed to pose health hazards. Among these few are "stachybotris chartarum" which can produce mycotoxins. In the few varieties of mold and mildew that are believed to produce adverse health effects, concentrations must be relatively high to affect most healthy individuals. It is important to note that at the present time there are no accepted Federal, state, or local health-based standards concerning exposure to mold and mildew. Nevertheless, whether it is believed that the potential for ill affects is little or large, it is universally accepted that Homes should be kept free from mold.

Some *common areas* for mold and mildew growth in the typical residential environment are: 1) around window frames. Two major reasons for this are condensation and leaks. Condensation often occurs at window frames if the residence is tightly sealed and inadequately ventilated, and if the temperature is colder outside than inside; 2) at and near toilets, sinks, and tubs (anywhere water splash and leaks are likely to occur); 3) in *basements* and other spaces which are below ground level, when drainage and/or *waterproofing* of walls is not adequate or is failing due to age or lack of maintenance; 4) anywhere two or more pieces of wood are tightly fitted together and water can get between them. Typical examples are unflashed and *uncaulked* wood *trim* around windows and *doors*, wood railings and caps with open miter joints; and 5) in poorly ventilated and damp enclosures.

Sometimes mold will grow in enclosed (not visible) locations such as the cavities at exterior walls. If the building construction or lack of maintenance allows water to leak into wall cavities, mold can grow in the affected areas. Resulting damage can progress unseen for some time. Aside from gray or black stains and blotchy patches that are readily identifiable as mold, signs that should help identify some potential problems include softness in *drywall*, water stains at walls and ceilings, damp carpets, buckling or swelling of exterior surfaces, and a persistent musty odor. These are possible indications, but do not prove that mold or mildew exist. The actual existence of mold and mildew must be established by visual observation and in some cases by appropriate testing and expert inspection by an industrial hygienist.

Homeowner Responsibility: The Homeowner should become familiar with how to identify, minimize, and prevent mold growth. The Homeowner should observe and eliminate condensation on walls, around windows, and other cool places. Indoor humidity should be kept low by the proper use of ventilation devices. Generally, a relative humidity of 60% or less should limit condensation-caused mold.

The Homeowner should seek help if they are concerned about possible indications of mold and mildew. Some sources for help include biology departments of major universities, city and county health departments, and the organizations to which health and hygiene specialists belong, such as the American Conference of Governmental Industrial Hygienists (ACGIH). This group can be contacted through their website: http://www.acgih.org.

Homeowner Guidelines to Prevent Mold

1. Inspect and maintain air conditioning and heating systems on a periodic basis. Clear out or repair the condensate line if the air conditioner drip pan overflows.
2. Promptly dry any damp or wet indoor areas. This includes shower stalls and tubs.

3. Always use vent fans in baths, kitchens, and laundries. Keep the vent fans running for 15 minutes after room use to assure adequate removal of condensation.
4. Promptly remove mold or mildew growing around the edges of window frames (where condensation is the cause) with a bleach/water mixture and a disposable rag.
5. Establish/maintain roof drainage into *gutters* and *downspouts*. Maintain the ground slope away from the Home foundation.
6. Repair leaks as soon as they are discovered. Keep in mind that mold can grow within 24 hours after the start of a leak. Proper Homeowner inspections and prompt maintenance are essential.
7. Do not store organic materials (such as paper, wood, cardboard, books, or clothes) in damp locations.
8. Promptly and thoroughly clean areas affected by a flood or sewer overflow.
9. If mold and mildew are suspected to exist, the most important thing to do is to stop the source of water if possible, and to notify the Builder immediately if the condition is believed to be Builder-caused.

Condition #1: Mold and Mildew at Leak Site

Potentially Impacting:

- Appearance
- Life of building materials
- Air quality

Performance Guideline

No condition should be permitted to exist, such as a rainwater leak, plumbing leak, or use of excessively wet framing lumber, which fosters the growth of mold and mildew.

Comments: Prevention and elimination of leaks is discussed in other sections of this Manual (see Chapters on Walls, Roofs, Exterior Components and Utility Systems). Nevertheless, where leaks *do* occur it is possible that mold and mildew may follow. If mold and mildew are present as a result of leaks, the repair of leaks should include removal of materials that are stained, coated or otherwise adversely affected by such organisms. Because removal of moisture can arrest the growth of these organisms and because surfaces that are not significantly damaged can be cleaned or treated, it may be possible to retain some or all affected building components during the repair process. In severe cases, removal or retention of building components is a technical matter that is best handled by a mold and mildew specialist. The specialist will determine whether the types of molds and mildews present are a potential health hazard, and if they are, the best way to remove them.

Builder Responsibility: The Builder should perform leak repairs that result from improper construction to eliminate sources of water intrusion and remove and arrest the growth of mold and mildew.

Homeowner Responsibility: The Homeowner should promptly address any leaks, and if caused by the Builder, report the leaks to the Builder so preventive repairs can be accomplished before significant damage occurs. If leaks are corrected quickly, mold and mildew may not flourish, and repairs and clean-up will be much easier.

Condition #2: Mold and Mildew around Windows, Doors, Baseboards, Bathroom Surfaces, without an Obvious Leak

Potentially Impacting:

- Appearance
- Air quality
- Life of materials

Performance Guideline

No condition should be created as a result of construction practices that foster the growth of molds or mildews. Absent of leaks, this is a Homeowner maintenance item.

Comments: Most molds and mildews that appear around window frames and *doors*, in tile *grout* at tubs, showers and kitchens, as well as other interior items, are the result of the Homeowner's lifestyle. Occasionally, interior humidity may rise sufficiently so that moisture condenses on cool surfaces (such as windows, doors, and walls). These conditions provide a fertile environment for the growth of molds and mildews, which most frequently appear around window and door frames and at the joint between frames and surrounding *drywall* and wood *trim*. Because of their warm and moist conditions, shower stalls and tub surrounds are also ideal places for mold and mildew to grow. Most of these conditions are controllable through appropriate use and maintenance of the Home.

TOWEL DRYING TUBS AND SHOWER SURROUNDS AFTER USE HELPS TO PREVENT MOLD.

Builder Responsibility: The Builder should perform repairs on conditions that may result from improper construction and which cause mold and mildew growth.

Homeowner Responsibility: *Maintenance Alert!* The Homeowner should do the following to minimize and prevent the growth of mold and mildew around Home components:

- Routinely clean and dry showers and tubs after each use;
- Periodically clean window frames and joints;
- Use a mildewcide if mildew or mold is observed to prevent and retard growth (available at any cleaning supply or hardware store);
- Air out rooms on a frequent basis;
- Ensure that all exhaust fans and other air circulation devices are functioning properly and used routinely;
- Avoid installing air deflectors over heat supply grills;
- Open draperies often during rainy periods to allow air to circulate around windows;
- Limit the use of atomizers or humidifiers;
- Open windows or operate vent fans while showering or bathing;
- Clean window tracks and *weep holes* at least twice yearly.

Condition #3: Mildew on Wood and Vinyl Siding, Stucco and Other Exterior Surfaces

Potentially Impacting:

- Appearance
- *Useful life* of exterior surfaces

Performance Guideline

1. The installation of siding should be made so that it prevents water from entering behind siding;

2. The design and location of Homes that are clad in hardboard or OSB siding should provide for adequate exposure to sunlight and ventilation and should avoid unusually damp surroundings;

3. Interior spaces should be adequately ventilated and protected by vapor barriers to avoid excessive condensation build-up that may result in the growth of mildew, mold and fungi.

Comments: The appearance of mildew or fungi on siding may result from three principal sources: 1) leaks that allow water to enter between the siding and the material behind the siding; 2) an environment that is excessively damp, shady and lacks air circulation; and 3) condensation of moist air on interior surfaces.

Builder Responsibility: The Builder should install or construct exterior surfaces to conform to the Performance Guideline. Once the Builder has complied with the Guideline, there is not much the Builder can do to prevent mold and mildew from occurring on outside walls. Variations in orientation, weather, and the air spore count can all have an effect on the growth of mold and mildew on exterior walls.

Homeowner Responsibility: ***Maintenance Alert!*** The Homeowner should keep siding sealed and painted and prevent landscape sprinklers from spraying on masonry, siding, and stucco. If mold and mildew grows on outside walls, the Homeowner should promptly use a mildew-killing spray and brush with soap and water to arrest or reverse mildew conditions. The Homeowner should also avoid planting shrubs or vines that will block sunlight and ventilation from the siding.

Condition #4: Mildew or Mold in Heating and Ventilating Duct Work

Potentially Impacting:

- Indoor air quality

Performance Guideline

The design and installation of heating and ventilating duct work should be accomplished in a manner that does not encourage the growth of organisms within the enclosed system.

Comments: Mildew or mold should not be allowed to remain in the heating and ventilating systems. The problem usually results from moisture getting into the duct work, either from a leak or condensation. Improperly insulated duct work can also be a cause. It may be difficult to identify the presence of mold or mildew in duct work, although a musty odor can be an indicator.

Builder Responsibility: The Builder should install properly assembled and insulated heating and ventilating systems and perform repairs on conditions that result from improper installation.

Homeowner Responsibility: The Homeowner should promptly notify the Builder of a suspected mildew problem.

Condition #5: Mildew or Mold near Enclosed Plumbing Pipes

Potentially Impacting:

- Indoor air quality
- Structural integrity

Performance Guideline

Cold water pipes in wall cavities and other interior spaces subject to moist, warm air should be insulated.

Comments: This condition is caused by moisture when interior air condenses on cold water pipes.

Builder Responsibility: The Builder should install pipe *insulation* on cold water pipes where there is a likelihood of condensation and mold growth.

Homeowner Responsibility: None.

Septic Tanks

General Subject Information: A typical private waste system works in the following manner: waste is piped out of the Home and into a watertight holding (dosing) tank. There, bacteria break the waste down into solids, liquid and scum. The sludge settles into the bottom of the tank, the scum rises to the top, and the liquid flows into: 1) a distribution box, which channels through *perforated pipes* that leach out into a field of loose gravel, known as the leach field; or 2) a separate pit through solid pipes.

Condition #1: Sewer System/Drains Not Operating Properly

Potentially Impacting:

- Occupant health
- Interior finishes and furnishings

Performance Guideline

All septic or waste systems should be capable of operating as designed, under normal use without any stoppage or backup.

Comments: Under certain conditions sewer systems can fail or overflow as a result of saturated leach lines, freezing, change in *water tables*, or excessive use of plumbing fixtures. Use of high phosphate detergents and overuse of detergents can result in leach field failure.

Builder Responsibility: At the *walkthrough*, the Builder should demonstrate that the septic system is operating as designed. If a clogged sewer line/drain is the result of improper installation by the Builder, then the Builder should repair the unacceptable condition so it conforms to the Performance Guideline. The Builder is not responsible for sewers and drains that are clogged because of Homeowner negligence or misuse.

Homeowner Responsibility: ***Maintenance Alert!*** The Homeowner should pump out the tank every 2-3 years depending on the size of the system and the number of people living in the Home. The local health department may require more frequent pumping. The following items are examples of Homeowner negligence regarding septic tanks:

- Pouring paint thinners, pesticides, motor oils, or chemicals down drains or in toilets;
- Disposing of grease, fat, paper towels, or feminine sanitary products in toilets;
- Drain cleaners should be used with caution and sparingly. Drain cleaners kill bacteria that break down sewage;
- Use of dyed toilet tissue. Dyes are harmful to the bacteria in the tank;
- *Compacting* the leach field by driving on it;
- Allowing storm water to either run into or be pumped into the dosing tank.

Condition #2: Septic Tank Emits Foul Odor

Potentially Impacting:

- Air quality

Performance Guideline

Septic tanks should not emit unreasonably foul odors given proper Homeowner use and maintenance.

Comments: The odors that come from a septic tank are largely the result of use and maintenance. A septic tank that is overused (beyond its capacity) and a septic system that has not been regularly pumped out will develop a terrible odor.

Builder Responsibility: None.

Homeowner Responsibility: ***Maintenance Alert!*** The Homeowner should pump out the tank on a regular basis and periodically add a bacteria-enhancing agent (sold at any hardware store). If the number of persons using the system increases, the Homeowner should consider expanding the system.

Smoke and Carbon Monoxide Alarms

General Subject Information: According to the national code, smoke alarms and carbon monoxide alarms are required to be installed in every new Home, need to be interconnected with each other, and maintained in an operating condition. New installations of smoke and carbon monoxide alarms must be wired to the Home electrical system as well as have a battery operated backup. If one smoke or carbon monoxide detector alarm sounds, all should sound.

While smoke alarms have been required in new homes for the past 20 years, the requirement for carbon monoxide alarms is relatively recent. Carbon monoxide is a tasteless, odorless gas that is very toxic to humans and animals. Carbon monoxide is produced as the result of incomplete combustion of any carbon based fuel: natural gas, gasoline, kerosene and charcoal briquettes, to name a few. The automobile, *furnace*, water heater, space heater, catalytic heater, dryer (gas), cook top (gas), oven, and back yard barbeque are all potential sources of carbon monoxide.

Condition #1: Alarms Sound during Use of Fireplace/Kitchen

Potentially Impacting:

- Occupant comfort

Performance Guideline

Smoke alarms are designed to be smoke sensitive; this is for the protection of the occupants. In all likelihood when smoke alarms sound at the time of cooking, the room has been overloaded with cooking vapors. If the alarm sounds each time a fire is built in the fireplace, there may be a ventilation problem. *(See "**Chapter Six—Interior Components, Fireplaces**", page 133, or "**Chapter Five—Exterior Components, Chimneys and Flues**", page 113.)*

TEST BUTTON
TEST SMOKE ALARMS AND CARBON MONOXIDE ALARMS MONTHLY

Builder Responsibility: The Builder should install a code-compliant alarm system. If the alarms sound at inappropriate times, and the fault lies with poorly constructed ventilation systems, the Builder should correct the unacceptable condition.

Homeowner Responsibility: The Homeowner should operate fireplaces and cook in a manner that does not generate undue quantities of smoke within the Home. The Homeowner should not disable the alarm because of frequent activation.

Condition #2: Alarms Do Not Operate When Tested

Potentially Impacting:

- Occupant safety

Performance Guideline

All smoke and carbon monoxide alarms should operate as intended by code and in compliance with manufacturer's specifications. Smoke and carbon monoxide alarms that do not operate because the battery is dead are considered a Homeowner maintenance item.

Builder Responsibility: In the event that an alarm malfunctions, the Builder should conduct an investigation to determine the cause and correct the unacceptable condition.

Homeowner Responsibility: ***Maintenance Alert!*** The Homeowner should test alarms once a month using the alarm test button. All newly installed alarm systems operate both from the Home wiring and from battery backups. The Homeowner must ensure that the batteries are changed on a regular basis so the backup system will function in the event of a power failure. It is a good idea to change all of the batteries at the same time, even though just one alarm is signaling a low battery beep. Another good idea is to write the date of the battery change on a piece of tape adhered to each battery. If one alarm consistently uses more battery power than the others, it may be defective. If that is the case, the Homeowner should replace the defective alarm. Typically, the *useful life* of an alarm is 10 years unless otherwise stated by the manufacturer.

Wood Destroying Insects

General Subject Information: Wood destroying insects can feed on, nest in, and otherwise invade a Home. They can cause significant unseen damage if allowed to flourish. These insects can enter the structure through the soil by flying, or from furniture or other wood items brought into the home. Once inside the Home, these insects most often will feed on wood or wood products and cause damage if gone unnoticed. The most important methods of preventing and controlling wood-destroying insects are preventative maintenance and periodic inspections. The Homeowner can perform both of these tasks by becoming aware of the conditions that invite these insects into the Home and learning to recognize the signs of insect infestation. The Homeowner should consult a pest control company to perform a professional inspection if unsure about the signs of infestation.

Condition #1: Wood Destroying Insects Are Present in the Home

Comments: There are five typical species of insects that can invade a Home or other wood structures:

1. **Subterranean termites—**Subterranean termites travel from the soil into the wood framing members of the Home. Indicators of the presence of subterranean termites are mud tubes in the soil through which they enter the Home. These mud tubes can run up the *concrete foundation* or be free standing like soda straws. Another sign of subterranean termites is what appears to be “bubbles” on interior wall paint. This occurs as a result of termites eating the paper from the *drywall* inside the Home.

2. **Dampwood termites—**Unlike subterranean termites, dampwood termites do not travel via mud tubes. Instead, dampwood termites get into the Home by boring into damp wood materials. Any part of the wood structures that are in direct contact with the earth, such as attached fencing, wooden porch steps and landscape dirt piled up against the *siding* provide a direct route into the Home for dampwood termites. These locations are where the termites colonize and continue to feed on the wood. Locations of common dampwood termite infestation also include areas near plumbing leaks or wood members with excessive moisture. Indications of dampwood termites are difficult to recognize since the openings through which they enter a structure are often sealed with wood products. The two best ways to detect dampwood termites are: 1) annually probe wood pieces that are close to the earth with an ice pick or 2) schedule an annual termite inspection with a pest control company.

3. **Drywood termites—**Drywood termites are flying insects and can be introduced into the Home through open windows and *doors* or through vent openings. Drywood termites can also enter the Home through cracks or openings in the *foundation* or siding and *trim*. Drywood termites become detectable as they emerge by flying away from the wood. Further signs of these termites are the small emergence holes that are slightly larger than a thumbtack hole.

4. **Wood boring beetles—**Wood boring beetles are also flying insects that can invade a Home via open windows, doors, or through vent openings. These insects and similar beetles feed

on floors, cabinets, and furnishings, as well as other wood materials. Another way wood boring beetles can enter a Home is from items brought into the home, for example cabinets, furniture and picture frames. This is especially common if the items are from overseas. Indications that wood boring beetles may be present in a Home or in a wood product are the emergence holes. These holes can range from the size of a pinhead to the size of a pencil eraser. The Homeowner should carefully inspect all furniture, picture frames, etc. to make sure there are no emergence holes. If emergence holes are discovered, or little piles of sawdust are observed, the Homeowner should schedule an inspection with a pest control company.

5. **Carpenter ants**—Unlike the other insects mentioned, carpenter ants do not actually feed on wood products. Instead, they create tunnels and galleries inside wood members and then nest inside. Carpenter ants commonly enter a Home from shrubs that grow against the Home or from tree branches that closely overhang the structure. Carpenter ants and termites can also enter a Home from tree stumps whose roots grow under the Home. As the ants travel through wood they create a network of tunnels that can weaken the internal structure of wood. If a carpenter ant infestation is large enough, the structural integrity of the Home may be compromised and significant damage may occur. Indicators of carpenter ants include piles of wood shavings typically with small insect parts within the shavings.

Builder Responsibility: None.

Homeowner Responsibility:

Exterior –

- Periodically inspect all exterior *siding* for cracks. Seal cracks with a good 25+ year *caulking* to keep the siding watertight. Be sure to include wood *trim*, *eave* openings, and *fascia* boards in this inspection and maintenance routine.

- Twice a year inspect interior and exterior *foundation* walls and *basement* walls to look for termite tubes.

- Make sure there is a waterproof *membrane* between any installed planters and the Home walls. If the planter is wood, it should have a metal lining, and it should be raised off the deck or *patio* with spacers.

- Make sure *concrete* patios or decks are installed with a 2% positive *slope* (away from the Home). If the patio or deck is poured too high, water can be *drawn* back up into the siding, causing decay and providing a route for termites to enter the Home.

- Avoid attaching to the Home any untreated wood that has direct contact with soil. This includes patios and decks. Any wood that has direct contact with or is near soil by 6 inches should be *pressure treated*.

- Do not nail or otherwise attach any part of a fence to a Home wall unless a metal termite shield is installed between the exterior of the Home and the fence.

IT'S TIME TO CALL A PEST CONTROL COMPANY!

Interior –

- Never place any wood or cellulose (paper, cardboard, certain fabrics, or actual wood products / pieces) on *crawl space* soil or *basement* floors. If this area is to be used for storage, have a *concrete* or masonry barrier installed between the soil and storage surface. Always elevate the stored material from the soil or *slab* by 6 inches using bricks or concrete blocks. Inspect semi-annually for termite activity.

- Make sure the crawl space / basement area receives proper ventilation. Do not block any *vents*.

- Keep all plumbing in proper repair and do not allow leaks to go unrepaired. This is also a good practice to prevent mold.

- In garage areas, avoid storing materials over a *control joint* (the joint intentionally cut in concrete slabs to control where concrete cracks). If this area is used for storage, periodically move the items and inspect for signs of infestation. Termites can travel through cracks between concrete and through the control joint-*foundation* wall intersection.

Radon

General Subject Information: Radon is a naturally occurring radioactive gas that is produced by decaying thorium and uranium. Radon typically comes from rocks containing uranium and thorium like certain granites or shale. The gas, which is colorless and odorless, can be found in the air, or it can be absorbed into groundwater and then subsequently released in the air. Radon is considered to be chemically inert, meaning it does not readily combine with other chemicals. However, certain levels of radon exposure can be hazardous to human health.

Radon is classified as a human carcinogen by the Environmental Protection Agency (EPA). It is a leading cause of lung cancer among non-smokers and the second leading cause among smokers. However, any cancer resulting from inhaling radon is not likely to become apparent for at least 20-30 years after initial exposure. The level of radon exposure, duration of exposure, and use of tobacco (smoking) are factors in determining the risk of developing lung cancer. Exposure to radon does not result in acute respiratory symptoms such as colds, asthma, or allergies.

A standard unit of measurement for radon is picocuries per liter of air (pCi/L). In the United States, the average level of radon found indoors is 1.3 pCi/L, but can range from 0.25 to over 3,000 pCi/L. There is insufficient data to define a "safe" or harmless level of radon, though it is accepted that the greater the level of exposure and the longer duration of exposure, the greater the health risk. The EPA guideline states that radon levels should not exceed 4 pCi/L indoors. If the radon level of a Home measures above 4 pCi/L, the Homeowner should consider a radon mitigation system.

Comments: Radon gas enters the Home through the soil from cracks and openings in *concrete slabs*, *crawl spaces*, floor drains, sumps, and concrete blocks. Generally, living areas that are closest to the soil will have the highest levels of radon as compared to living areas or rooms on second stories. Radon can also be present in tap water as it can be absorbed into the groundwater from soil containing radon. Radon present in water can be released when showering, washing dishes, or washing clothes. Radon can also be present in water when the water source is a well that is exposed to uranium and thorium rock strata. Radon is more of a concern when it comes from this type of source. Granite is a source of radon, but a granite counter top is not considered harmful because of its low emission levels.

Builder Responsibility: Within certain counties of the following states the Builder is required to install an approved radon mitigation system: Florida, Maine, Maryland, Michigan, Minnesota, New Jersey, Oregon, Virginia, and Washington. Each state has slightly different requirements and more states are expected to follow as the harmful effects of radon become more widely known. The Builder is not responsible for the presence of radon.

Homeowner Responsibility: Whether the Home contains a radon mitigation system or not, it should be tested. It is not possible to test for radon on a lot before the Home is built. Results can vary from Home-to-Home and from street-to-street.

- To test for radon in a Home, purchase an inexpensive test kit at a home improvement store or buy one online. Follow the instructions and mail the kit to the laboratory to get the results. If the results are in excess of 4 pCi/L, a radon mitigation system should be installed.

- Homeowners may also consult a government agency to help them determine the amounts of radon present in the Home and any recommended subsequent actions. To get more information on radon testing call 1-800-SOS-RADON.

- A water test should be considered especially if the indoor air levels of radon are at or above the EPA guideline of 4 pCi/L. The water company that supplies the Home should have information about the source of the water and any radon tests performed. If the Home has water supplied by a well, homeowners should contact a laboratory certified for radon testing to perform a water test.

- For more information on radon, refer to www.epa.gov.

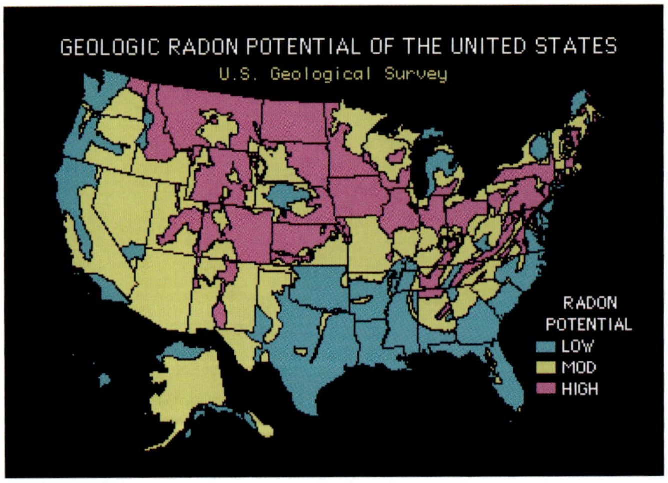

This map, from the US Geological Survey, is to be used as a guide and reference. This map should not be used to determine a homeowner's actual risk of radon exposure or to determine actual radon levels in their home. Homeowners should consult a government agency or certified laboratory to determine the actual radon levels in their home or within the region they live. Additional maps can be found on www.epa.gov.

RECOMMENDED MAINTENANCE SCHEDULE

MAINTENANCE ITEM	PURPOSE	FREQUENCY	DIFFICULTY	DATE PERFORMED		
AIR CONDITIONER	Start twice during winter months; keeps mechanical parts from sticking. Service professionally.	2Y Y4	● ◆			
BATHROOM CAULK	Seal joints that are subject to being wetted; prevent leaks, dry rot, mold and mildew.	2Y	▲			
CERAMIC TILE GROUT	Seal grout with silicone based sealer; cracked grout should be caulked with a caulk specifically made for filling grout. Improves appearance, prevents leaks.	Y	■			
CHIMNEY CLEANING	Remove buildup of tar and creosote from the flue; prevents flue fires.	Y2	◆			
DECKS	By inspecting deck surfaces for cracks in coating, loose boards and surface sealers, minor maintenance and repairs extend deck life.	Y	●			
DOORS	Vacuuming tracks and lubricating hinges and latches keeps parts smooth.	M/Y	●			
DRAINAGE	Keep drain from backing up and flooding during the rainy season. Make sure debris is removed from ditches and swales. Maintain positive drainage away from buildings.	Y	●			
DRYWALL (CRACKS AND NAIL POPS)	Set nails, caulk and paint. Improves appearance of finished interior wall surfaces.	Y	■			
ELECTRICAL (GFCI TEST)	Safety of electrical circuits. Test GCFI circuits (kitchen, bath, garage and outdoor) monthly.	M	●			
EXHAUST FANS	Vacuuming accumulated dust from bathroom and laundry fans for proper air flow.	2Y	●			
FENCE (INSPECTION AND REPAIR)	Retains privacy and security. Prolongs life of fence. Wrought iron schedule is 2Y.	Y	■			
FURNACE FILTER CHANGE	Helps remove dust and pollen from interior air; improves furnace efficiency; less energy consumption.	2Y	●			
GARAGE DOOR SYSTEMS	Lubrication promotes smoother, less noisy operation; extends systems life. Tighten keepers to avoid sag on one piece doors.	2Y	●			
GARBAGE DISPOSAL	Fill with ice and operate. Cleans and sharpens.	Y	●			
GROUNDS	Inspect for pavement breaks, heaving sidewalks and tree roots, dry rot at decks and blockage of drainage system. Avoids more expensive repair costs.	Y	■			
GUTTERS AND DOWNSPOUTS	Prevent overflow onto walls; prevents eve leaks; extends gutter life.	2Y	●			
INSECT CONTROL	Detected and treated early will prevent structural damage; controls annoying pests. If found, treatmonthly.	Y	▲ ◆			
IRRIGATION SPRINKLERS	Direct water spray properly. Eliminate excess watering, staining of exterior walls and dry rot of structures.	Y	■			
KITCHEN EXHAUST HOOD	Wash kitchen hood grease filters in the dishwasher.	Y	●			
ROOF INSPECTION / MAINTENANCE	Detect and correct conditions that can lead to leaks and premature roof replacement. Be sure to read Chapter Four to learn the process for inspection and repair.	Y	■ ◆			
SINKS	Inspect under sinks in kitchen, bath and laundry/utility for leaks. Early detection avoids greater damage and expensive repair. Clean sink traps to avoid backups and plugged drains; promotes sanitation. Use only cleaners recommended by manufacturer. Clean faucet aerators to maintain water flow.	4Y	●			
SMOKE DETECTOR	Replace batteries for safety and keep clean.	Y	●			
TRIM SIDING AND STUCCO	Caulking and painting keeps system water tight; improves appearance, extends major maintenance periods; reduces chance of mold and mildew. Paint all exterior wood trim, siding and stucco.	Y	◆			
WATER HEATER (PARTIAL DRAIN)	Extends water heater life; provides more efficient operation; uses less energy.	Y	■			
WINDOWS (TRACKS AND WEEP HOLES)	Keep windows sliding freely. Avoid water standing in tracks and potential leaks.	W/Y	■			
WINDOWS (SEALS-DUAL PANE)	Appearance, broken seals reduce insulating ability. Replace when foggy.	Y	◆			

KEY

FREQUENCY:

Weekly = W
Monthly = M
Yearly = Y

Twice a year = 2Y
Four times a year = 4Y
Every two years = Y2

Every three years = Y3
Every four years = Y4
Every six years = Y6

DIFFICULTY:

● Easy, no special skills required.

■ Some skill required.

▲ Good idea to get instruction on this item from a local improvement store.

◆ This task should be performed only by a qualified professional.

Refer to Homeowner Maintenance Summary for additional details.

Homeowner Maintenance Summary

The following list summarizes minimum maintenance requirements that should be performed by the Homeowner (or Homeowner Association) along with the Schedule. For more specific details, each maintenance item is referenced to a section within the Manual. This work should be done either by the Homeowner or by a maintenance person who is experienced and insured. A maintenance person who holds a contractor's license is typically better qualified. Failure to adequately maintain the following areas may eliminate or reduce the Builder's Responsibility if problem conditions arise.

→ **Bathroom Caulk:** *Caulk* joints in bathrooms need to be inspected and re-caulked (if necessary) every six months. This includes the joint at the bottom of the shower, the joint between the tub and the wall, the joint where the tub or *shower pan* meets the floor, and vertical inside corners and seats. It is very important that these joints do not pass any water; otherwise *dry rot* and mold can accumulate unseen for years. (Refer to "**Chapter Seven—Utility Systems, Plumbing**" for additional details.) Joints should be cleaned of old caulk before re-caulking. Any mold or mildew found growing in bathrooms (or other places in the Home) should be removed immediately with a mildewcide, available at most hardware stores. The cause of the mold or mildew should be discovered (for example a leaky window or failure to use vent fan while bathing) and the cause subsequently eliminated.

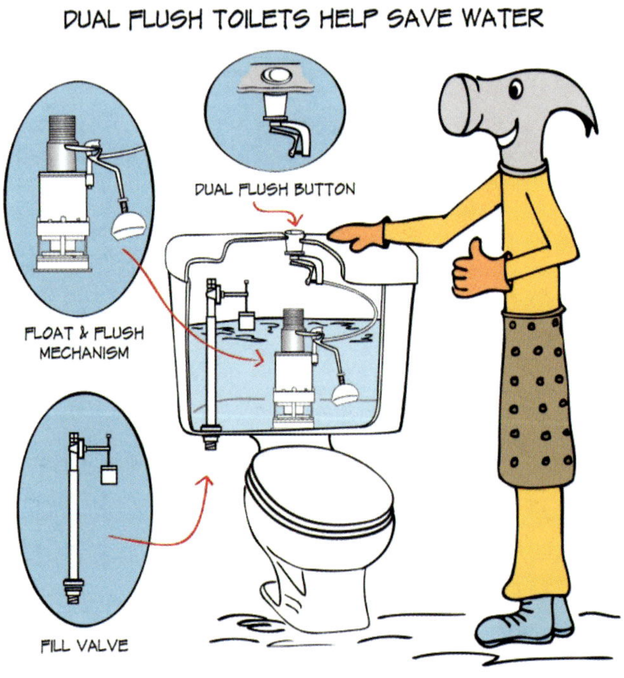

Green Tip! Prevent leaks. One leaking toilet can waste 1000 gallons of water in a month.

→ **Ceramic Tile Grout:** Re-grout or color caulk all cracks after the first year. Once the Home *frame* reaches equilibrium (in less than two years), frequent re-grouting or caulking should not be required. Tile *grout* should initially be sealed with a silicone based sealer the first year and then every two years following. (Refer to "**Chapter Six—Interior Components, Countertops**" for additional details.)

→ **Chimney Cleaning:** An all-fuel chimney *flue* should be professionally cleaned every two years if there are more than 50 wood fires per year or if there are more than 25 fires per year using manufactured fire logs made of wax and sawdust; subject to any restrictions or requirements of the manufacturer. (Refer to "**Chapter Five—Exterior Components, Chimneys and Flues**" for additional details.)

→ **Decks:** Annually, the Homeowner should inspect the surface sealer and also look for cracks in coating, loose boards and dry rot. (Refer to "**Chapter Five—Exterior Components, Decks and Patios**" for additional details.)

→ **Doors:** *Patio* sliding *doors* should have their tracks (bottom *sill*) swept and vacuumed monthly. The *weep holes* should also be inspected and cleaned as needed. Dust and dirt build-up in slider door tracks will interfere with the proper operation of the small wheels that the doors slide on. For swing doors, the hinges and *latches* should be lubricated annually with a dry lubricant specifically made for locks and latches. (Refer to "**Chapter Five—Exterior Components, Windows and Patio Doors**" for additional details.)

→ **Drains:**

- **Deck and Patio:** Deck and patio drains should be flushed with a garden hose and should show evidence of free-flow after the fall leaf drop. (Refer to "**Chapter Five—Exterior Components, Decks**" for additional details.)
- **Yard:** Yard drains should be flushed with a garden hose after the fall leaf drop and should show evidence of free flow at the curb or at the sump (if applicable), or at other points of discharge into a storm system. (Refer to "**Chapter Eight—Grounds, Drainage**" for additional details.)
- **Subdrains:** If the Home is equipped with a subterranean drainage system around the *foundation* or through the foundation, the *cleanouts* (if applicable) of this *subdrain* should be flushed twice a year. There should be evidence of free-flow through the curb or into the sump. Clogged drains can be cleared with a rooter machine or high pressure water jets. (Refer to "**Chapter Eight—Grounds, Drainage**" for additional details.)

→ **Drywall:**

- **Cracks:** Minor cracks in *drywall* usually appear within the first 12 months of occupancy. These cracks typically occur around door frames, cabinets, and window frames and can be easily *caulked*. (Refer to "**Chapter Six—Interior Components, Plaster and Drywall**" for additional details on cracks and Performance Guidelines.)
- **Nail Pops:** Nails will sometimes back out of the drywall as the House *frame* dries out. This is not a structural problem, but the nails should be re-driven and the heads should be spackled and painted with touchup paint. (Refer to "**Chapter Six—Interior Components, Plaster and Drywall**" for additional details.)

→ **Electrical:**

- **GFCIs:** Ground Fault Circuit Interrupters and *Arc Fault Interrupters* should be tested monthly. When testing, pressing the TEST button should cause the RESET button to pop out. Push in the RESET button to restore the circuit. If the GFCI will not reset, it may be faulty or there may be an open circuit. Contact a licensed electrical contractor to check the circuit. (Refer to "**Chapter Seven—Utility Systems, Electrical**" for additional details.)
- **Closet Ceiling Lights:** Light bulbs in the closets must be covered with a lens or globe as part of the fixture. When changing bulbs in the closet light fixtures, do not exceed the manufacturer's recommended wattage for the bulb requirement and do not leave the fixture cover off. Lights left on in closets, especially with halogen bulbs, can generate a significant amount of heat and be a fire hazard. (Refer to "**Chapter Seven—Utility Systems, Electrical**" for additional details.)
- **Aluminum Wiring:** While most household small circuit wiring is copper, the larger wires (known as cables) are likely to be aluminum. All wires are covered with *insulation*. Aluminum

cables are often used to provide power to air conditioners, heat pumps, electric dryers, and electric ovens. Aluminum is a softer metal than copper. Over time it can deform, or "creep", where it is connected. When aluminum creep occurs, the connection is no longer tight and sparking jumps through the gap. Appliances will consume more power and *breakers* will trip. It is recommended that the terminal connections of aluminum cables be inspected and tightened if necessary by a qualified, licensed electrical contractor within the first two years after occupancy. (Refer to "**Chapter Seven—Utility Systems, Electrical**" for additional details.)

→ **Fencing:**

- **Wood:** The condition of wood fences should be inspected every spring. Look for nails that have backed out of boards, fence posts that are leaning and kick boards (at the bottom) that have rotted. All leaning posts should be straightened, all loose boards should be re-nailed and if the kick boards have rotted significantly, they should be replaced. (Refer to "**Chapter Eight—Grounds, Fencing**" for additional details.)
- **Wrought Iron:** Wrought iron gates and fences should be inspected twice a year to check for rust, particularly at the base of all posts. If rust is discovered, it should be scraped away and the section should be painted with rust-resistant touchup paint. (Refer to "**Chapter Eight—Grounds, Fencing**" for additional details.)
- **Stucco:** *Stucco* fencing (patio fencing) should be inspected annually, in the springtime. Cracks on the top of the fence should be *caulked* and repainted and fence post bases should be inspected for *dry rot*. All dirt should be removed from the fence post bases. (Refer to "**Chapter Eight—Grounds, Fencing**" for additional details.)

→ **Garage Doors:**

- **One Piece:** One-piece *garage doors* (doors that raise and lower as one single piece) with automatic openers or garage doors without automatic openers should be lubricated at the hinge points every six months with 30w oil. The keepers (the long threaded rods that run across the top and bottom) should be kept tight to prevent the door from sagging in the middle.
- **Sectional:** Sectional doors (doors that roll up into the garage ceiling on tracks) should have the track rollers lubricated with 30w oil annually.
- **Automatic Opener:** The automatic openers, whether they are *chain drive* or *screw drive*, should have the drive mechanism (chain or screw) lubricated with a light grease annually.
- **Bolts:** Garage doors vibrate while opening and closing. It is important that an inspection be made every six months for the first year and then annually for bolts that can be wiggled or moved by hand. (For all of the above, refer to "**Chapter Five—Exterior Components, Garage Doors**" for additional details.)
- ***Weather stripping*:** Check flexibility and contact with floor.

→ **Grounds:** Annually, the Homeowner should inspect for pavement breaks, heaving sidewalks, tree roots and blockage of drainage system. (Refer to "**Chapter Eight—Grounds**" for additional details.)

→ **Gutters and Downspouts:** *Gutters* and *downspouts* should be cleaned and flushed twice annually. The first task is performed just after leaf drop in the fall and the second task is performed after the winter season is over. Prune branches that overhang roofs and gutters. (Refer to "**Chapter Five—Exterior Components, Gutters and Downspouts**" for additional details.)

→ **Heating and Air Conditioning:**

- **Air Conditioner:** If the Home has air conditioning, once every two months during warm winter days, the Homeowner should start the air conditioner and run it for a few minutes to keep the internal parts clean and lubricated. (Refer to "**Chapter Seven—Utility Systems, Cooling**" for additional details.)

- **Furnace Filters:** If the Home has heating and air conditioning, the *furnace* filters should be changed at least every six months or at the filter manufacturer's recommendation. If the Home has heating only, the furnace filters should be changed prior to the winter season. If the Homeowner lives in an area that has considerable wind driven dust, the above filter change schedule should be doubled. Replace the filter with the correct *MERV* rating. (Refer to "**Chapter Seven—Utility Systems, Heating**" and "**Chapter Seven—Utility Systems, Cooling**" for additional details.)

ENERGY SAVING THERMOSTAT
A PROGRAMMABLE THERMOSTAT SAVES ENERGY AND UTILITY BILLS

Green Tip! Always use programmable thermostats for maximum comfort and energy savings.

→ **Insect Control:** Insects, particularly termites and carpenter ants, can be harmful to the structure of the Home. An annual inspection should be made of the *foundation* (both on the outside and inside of the *crawl space* or *basement*). Look for brown termite tubes running up the foundation walls and bore holes of the carpenter ants on the exterior of the Home. Builders typically do not warrant against any type of insect invasion. Homeowners should pay close attention to pest control maintenance and should not hesitate to call a pest control service if destructive insects are suspected to be present. Firewood should be stored away from the Home in a structure or holder that is not in contact with the ground. Do not let vines grow on the Home; they will attract insects. If the geographic region is known to contain Louisiana or Formosan termites, professional inspections should be done twice yearly.

→ **Irrigation Sprinklers:** Irrigation sprinklers should be checked annually at the beginning of the growing period (usually March through May) to be sure that the heads are clean and do not spray against the Home and that the sprinkler lines have not broken during the winter. Spray patterns should also be checked during the growing season. (Refer to "**Chapter Eight—Grounds, Irrigation**" for additional details.) During periods of predictable rain irrigation controller times should be changed frequently to avoid overwatering and flooding.

→ **Locks:** Once a year or when they become stiff, apply a dry lubricant as directed into the lock. Use a lubricant specifically designed for locks. Graphite power lubricants work particularly well. Avoid use of popular oil synthetic sprays as they can form a gummy residue inside the lock.

→ **Roofing:** Roofing should be inspected for conditions that can lead to leaks and premature roof replacement. These inspections should be performed by a qualified professional annually. (Refer to "**Chapter Four—Roofs**" for additional details.)

→ **Sinks**

- **Garbage Disposal:** Homeowner should annually add ice and operate disposal in order to sharpen the blades while cleaning odor-causing bacteria.
- **Sink Traps:** Depending upon frequency of use, sink *traps* should be cleaned with a cleanser

approved for the type of plumbing pipes under the sink (plastic or metal). For a kitchen sink that receives daily use, a cleaning every 60 days should be sufficient. DO NOT put sink cleaner into a garbage disposal. It may corrode the cutting blade edges. Every four or five years, depending on use, sink traps will need to be removed and cleaned.

→ **Smoke and Carbon Monoxide Detector:** Homeowner should test smoke and carbon monoxide alarms once a month by using the alarm test button. Annually replace the batteries if needed. It is recommended to replace all the batteries at the same time even though just one alarm is signaling a low battery. (Refer to "**Chapter Nine—Miscellaneous, Smoke and Carbon Monoxide Alarms**" for additional details.)

→ **Solid Surface Countertops:** Do not apply countertop surface enhancers or cleansers such as Pledge™ or 409™ to a new solid surface countertop. These products will only attract and hold discoloring items such as coffee, wine, ketchup, etc., to the surface. The new solid surface countertop will remain in its natural state if it is simply wiped off with a soft sponge or cloth, with an ammonia based product such as glass cleaner, or with a mild soap and water solution. For integral solid surface sinks, use a mild abrasive such as Softscrub™ to cut any grease or discoloring buildup that has accumulated on the surface of the sink. Remove any harsh chemicals, such as nail polish remover, as soon as possible. Do not cut directly on the solid surface countertop or slide any rough edged objects across the countertop, since these items will create surface scratches in almost any type of countertop. To prevent shocking the surface of any type of sink, do not pour extremely hot grease or water into any sink without simultaneously running cool water. Do not place extremely hot items (such as sheet pans from a 450 degree oven) directly on the countertop or sink. (Refer to "**Chapter Six—Interior Components, Countertops**" for additional details.)

→ **Trim and Siding:** The term "*trim*" refers to the wooden trim either abutting the masonry, *stucco* or placed on the *siding* around windows and doors. The trim should be inspected each year prior to the start of the rainy season. If the trim has pulled away from the Home or the *caulking* has deteriorated, these areas should be re-caulked. If warping or twisting is severe (more than ½ inch), the trim should be replaced. (Refer to "**Chapter Six—Interior Components, Moldings and Trim**" for additional details.) Do not caulk the bottom gap of the trim piece over a window or *patio door*. Also, the siding should be inspected for warping and protruding nails. Inspections should be annual and prior to the start of the fall season. Warping should be caulked and painted, and protruding nails should be pulled and replaced with a slightly larger and wider nail. Use hot dipped galvanized box or common nails in exterior applications. Drive the nail head even with the siding; DO NOT drive the nail head into the siding. Driving the nail head into the siding may break the seal and cause the siding to swell and leak during precipitation. Touch up all work with caulk and paint.

→ **Vents and Fans:**

- **Dryer Vents:** Dryer vents must be kept lint free. Accumulation of lint will significantly reduce the efficiency of the dryer and under some circumstances, become a source of fire in the duct.

WHOLE HOUSE VENTILATION FAN - RUNS 24/7

A. TURN OFF BREAKER AND THEN GENTLY PULL DOWN COVER WITH YOUR FINGER TIPS

B. WASH COVER WITH MILD SOAP AND WARM WATER

C. VACUUM INSIDE OF FAN

Depending upon the degree of use and the length of the dryer duct, the dryer vent ducts should be cleaned every two to five years.

- **Exhaust Fans:** Bathroom and laundry fans should be vacuumed with a hose vacuum and crevice tool at least once a year.
- **Kitchen Exhaust Hood:** Kitchen hood filters should be removed and washed with a grease removing cleanser at least four times a year (depending upon use).

→ **Water Heater:** To prolong the life of a tank type water heater, accumulated sediment should be removed from the heater tank once a year. This task can be performed by attaching a thick wall garden hose to the drain spigot at the bottom of the tank and draining out no more than two gallons. Since the water being drained is very hot, be very careful that the hot water does not come into contact with persons, animals, plants, or any material that could be damaged by scalding water (120°F to 160°F).

→ **Windows (includes Patio doors):**

- **Seals:** Inspect for broken or breached window seals in dual or triple pane windows at least annually. Windows with broken or breached seals are identified by having a moist, foggy, or filmy condition between the two or three panes of glass. When this condition exists, the insulating value of the window is greatly diminished. The only repair is to replace the insulating glass unit. (Refer to "**Chapter Five—Exterior Components, Windows and Patio Doors**" for additional details.)
- **Weep Holes:** The *weep holes* at the bottom of windows and *patio doors* serve a purpose: to allow water to drain out from the track during rainstorms. Weep holes should be inspected at least annually to make sure that no debris has plugged the holes and that rainwater will drain freely from them. (Refer to "**Chapter Five—Exterior Components, Windows and Patio Doors**" for additional details.)
- **Tracks:** The tracks of windows and patio doors should be swept and vacuumed frequently to prevent dust and debris buildup. Clean window and *door* tracks allowing the sliding vent to move more freely, so that the drainage through the weep holes will not be impaired by any wet debris. In areas where there is ongoing construction or agricultural operations that generate dust, track cleaning should be done weekly. (Refer to "**Chapter Five—Exterior Components, Windows and Patio Doors**" for additional details.)

Glossary

A glossary of terms is an important tool for each Homeowner. Like almost every trade or profession, the homebuilding industry has, throughout time, developed a language all its own. Many of the industry used terms such as "heart, stud, cricket, jack, apron and chase" have completely different meanings in everyday life. While it is not possible to list all of the homebuilding terms and their meanings here, the ones most likely to needed by a Homeowner are defined below.

AAMA-American Architectural Manufacturers Association. A trade association that sets standards for window manufacturing.

ABS-black plastic pipe used to carry wastewater (sewage) from the various drains in the Home to a pipe known as the soil pipe. The soil pipe is located just outside the foundation of the Home. ABS pipe is also used for plumbing vents through the roof.

Aggregate-a mixture of small smooth rocks; an ingredient used in making concrete.

Air handler-the specialized fan inside the furnace or air conditioner that blows warm or cold air through ducts to the rooms.

Anchor bolts-bolts that hold the frame of the Home to the foundation. Anchor bolts, also known as J-bolts, are cast in the wet concrete of the foundation during the concrete pouring process to secure the mudsill to the foundation.

ANSI-the acronym for American National Standards Institute. This organization tests building components and determines if the components meet certain prescribed standards.

Apron-the small strip of trim wood that is underneath the windowsill. The windowsill is known as a stool in the homebuilding industry.

ARC Fault Circuit Interrupter-a specialized circuit breaker that provides additional protection against fires caused by electrical arcing.

ASHRAE-American Society of Heating, Refrigerating, and Air-conditioning Engineers. This Association establishes standards for heating and cooling equipment and systems, among other things.

Attic-the attic is the space in the Home between the ceiling of the top floor and the underside of the roof. The attic needs to be insulated over living areas and vented to allow proper air circulation from the Home in the summer and winter. Most Homes have an interior attic access panel, which can be located in the ceiling of a hallway, closet or bedroom, and allows access to the attic.

Backsplash-a part of the countertop in a bathroom and/or kitchen (and sometimes laundry room) that is a vertical piece of countertop material connected to the wall. A backsplash is typically 4 inches to 6 inches in height.

Baluster-the posts that support the handrails, located on the sides of stairs. The posts where the handrails start or stop are called the newell posts.

Barge rafter-a board attached to the edge of a roof that projects beyond the wall of the Home (also referred to as a varge board).

Batten-a strip of wood or plastic (usually 1 inch x 2 inches) that is applied to a roof to hold the concrete or clay tiles in place. Also, a batten is a strip of wood used to cover the vertical joints of panels of exterior siding.

Bead-see Corner Bead.

Beam-a horizontal piece of lumber, also can be glu-lam, composite-lam or steel, that is used to carry part of the weight of the Home. Beams are found at the roof, between floors, and between the basement or crawl space and the first floor.

Berm-a mound of dirt that is placed in landscaped areas to control the flow of storm water. Berms are also used in landscape beautification, to break up flat areas.

Bird stop-a metal, plastic, or wood insert found at the lowest point of a tile roof (typically the round or barrel shaped tiles). This is to keep birds and other creatures from nesting in the under part of the roof.

Bleed through-a term that describes a material that passes through another material and generally discolors the second material. An example of bleed through is redwood and cedar wood sap (tannins) that bleed through paint. It can also apply to rust from nails and staples that bleed through stucco.

Blocks-blocks are pieces of wood installed at the ends (and sometimes at intermediate points) of floor joists, to prevent the joists from twisting. By the use of blocks, the floor joists are tied together to create a more rigid assembly. Blocks are also found where floor joists lap one another (the joists cannot span the entire distance so a lap is created). Blocks are also used between studs to serve as fire stops. The blocks are typically made from the same material as the joists or the studs.

Breaker-a specialized switch found inside a panel (usually gray and known as a breaker panel) that will interrupt the flow of electricity in the event of a short circuit or an electrical surge. The act of interrupting is called "tripping". The small handle of a tripped breaker will be in the middle position between the markings OFF and ON. A tripped breaker will have to be turned off before it can be reset to the ON position. Breakers are usually found in groups in the panel and they are labeled as to identify which circuits they control.

Brow ditch-a ditch that sits just above and behind a retaining wall or cut slope. Brow ditches are designed to keep surface water from flowing behind and over the walls and cut slopes.

Building code-a set of written standards that are intended to protect the health and safety of building occupants. The codes can be general in nature, such as the International Residential Code, or specialty codes that cover subjects such as plumbing, electrical, heating and cooling, and energy to name a few.

Building Official-the person who is the head of the local department that issues building permits. This is usually a county or city agency. Building Officials, through their deputies, perform inspections and enforce the various Building Codes.

Building paper-a specially made thick paper that is stapled to the outside of the frame of a Home. Building paper is used prior to application of the exterior finish material (such as stucco, wood siding, shingles etc.). The paper is impregnated with a substance during its manufacturing process that makes it resistant to the flow of moisture. If the stucco or siding leaks, the building paper will serve as a secondary backup to prevent moisture from getting into the walls.

Bull nose-a piece of material that projects slightly past the supporting material and is rounded at its outer edge. Bull nosepieces can be found on roofing, interior trim, stair treads, and countertops to "finish off" flat surfaces.

Cant strip-a triangular piece of wood, fiberboard, or plastic that is typically applied between the intersection of a "flat" roof and adjacent wall.

Capillary action-the act of drawing a liquid, usually water, into another material. A good example of this is a sponge absorbing water. In the building industry, water can be drawn up into wood, stucco, or concrete by capillary action.

Casing-trim pieces that finish off an opening. Most commonly found at door openings. Sometimes mistakenly called frames. Casings can also be found around windows and shadowboxes.

Caulk-a gooey material used to seal joints for the purpose of keeping water out. Caulk is often found around bathtubs and is applied with a tool known as a caulking gun. There are many different types of caulks for various uses. It is critical to use the correct variety of caulk product for each situation.

Cement-one of the ingredients of concrete. Cement is the "paste" that binds sand and aggregate together. Because of its chemical composition and alkalinity, cement can burn human skin. Cement is not the same thing as concrete.

Chain drive-the mechanism that opens and closes garage doors and is part of automatic garage door openers. These automatic garage door openers operate with three types of drives, either chain drive, screw drive, or belt drive.

Chase-a horizontal or vertical enclosure in which a flue pipe, generally a chimney flue, is located. The chase is built around the flue and it extends above the roofline by an amount specified in the Building code. Chases can also contain plumbing pipes or wiring.

Cladding-the exterior "skin" of a Home. Examples of cladding are paneling, lap siding, brick, stone and stucco.

Cleanout-an opening in a plumbing waste line that allows access to the piping for the purpose of inspection and cleaning. Cleanouts are required by the plumbing codes and are typically found beneath kitchen sinks and just outside the foundation of the Home.

Closed loop system-any system that uses the same fluid or gases over and over and is returned to the source for heating or cooling.

Coffered ceiling-a ceiling that is not flat but has a portion of it lifted up to create a more dramatic architectural effect. The lifted portion is usually found in the middle of the ceiling.

Common area-areas that are owned in common by all members of a homeowners association. This term is associated with condominium projects and planned unit developments. They may include the exterior of buildings, landscape, driveways, recreation facilities and mailboxes. Common areas usually have their own legal description located in the deed to the condominium or individual lot, as applicable.

Compacting-the degree of solidity of the soil around and under the Home or behind a retaining wall. Areas requiring compact soil include foundations, driveways, walkways, and patios. Soil that is not compacted is often referred to as native soil or loose soil.

Compressor-a motor driven pump that compresses a gas as part of the air conditioning process.

Concrete-a mixture of sand, gravel (sometimes called aggregate) and cement. This mixture becomes concrete when it is mixed with water and is allowed to cure.

Condensate line-the plastic or metal pipe that comes out of the air conditioning part of the furnace. Condensate lines conduct water from the air conditioner coil to the outside of the House or to a trap.

Condominium-buildings, parts of which are owned in common with other people. This is a legal term and is often confused with an architectural style. Condominiums can include townhouses, flats and even detached homes, so long as part of the project is owned in common by all of the owners of the project.

Control joint-a linear separation made during the pouring of concrete made by troweling with a v-shaped tool. Its purpose is to provide a slightly weaker spot in the concrete so it will crack in a controlled manner along the joint. The joint can also be a groove made with a concrete saw at least one day after the concrete is finished pouring.

Corbel-a bracket having at least two sides at right angles and often ornately carved. This bracket may support a shelf or an element that projects out from a Home such as a bay window or a fireplace mantel.

Corner bead-a long strip of material that is applied vertically to "finish off" a corner. The corner may be a drywall corner or a stucco corner. Corner beads are usually made of metal, wire, and sometimes stiff paper.

Counter flashing-metal flashing that fits under the visible flashing on roofs, around chimneys and windows.

Crawl space-the space between the soil and the underside of the first floor joists. It is found in Homes that have a pier and grade beam foundation and do not have a basement. Building codes specify the minimum height of crawl spaces.

Criblock-a type of concrete or masonry wall that contains interlocking pieces similar to Legos™ or Lincoln Logs™.

Cricket-a section of the roof often found between the roof and a vertically projecting structure, such as a chase. The cricket is meant to deflect water away from the chase, where the chase and the roof meet. This is so that water does not accumulate and leak into the Home.

Crowning-a condition usually applied to wood and often hardwood floors. The wood takes on moisture and the center portion of the board becomes higher than the edges. The opposite of cupping. This condition can also apply to floor joists, where the center of the joist becomes higher than the ends.

Crown molding-a decorative architectural trim piece made of wood, plastic, plaster, or foam that covers the intersection of walls and the ceilings.

Cupping-a condition that occurs when boards (including flooring) dry unevenly and the edges become higher than the center.

Cure-the process of a building material drying and chemically bonding. A good example of curing is hardening of concrete. Concrete cures as it dries out. In the first three days, concrete is very weak. After 28 days concrete curing (when properly mixed) is said to reach 90% of its maximum strength. Other materials that cure are stucco, paint, deck coatings and fireplace linings.

Damper-a hinged flap of metal found above the firebox in fireplaces to close off the flue so that warm air does not escape from the room when there is no fire. The damper must be open when using the fireplace. It also prevents wind from blowing down the chimney when it is not in use. Dampers are also found in the ducts of heaters and exhaust fans.

Daylight-a condition where a covered or buried object protrudes through its cover and becomes visible. An example is the visible end of a buried pipe—at the point where the pipe becomes visible, it is said to have "daylighted".

Delaminating-the process by which two surfaces that are supposed to be tightly bonded together, separate from one another.

Displacement-refers to any horizontal or vertical movement of a building or the component within. More frequently it is used to describe the settlement or the heave of a foundation and the settlement of utility trenches that were once level with their surroundings.

Door-a movable structure used to close off an entrance to a room, building or covered enclosure. Consists of a panel of wood, glass, metal, or other building materials. An entire glossary could be written about doors. Here is a condensed version:

- **Exterior door-**a door that is on the outside wall of a Home. The door has been manufactured to be weather resistant, subject to proper maintenance.
- **Fire rated door-**a door that has been rated by an independent laboratory and has a label attached showing its rating. These doors can be made of many materials including wood, fiberglass, steel, and composite wood. A 20-minute fire-rated or 1-3/8 inch solid core door is generally required between the garage and Home and sometimes the entrances to condominium homes. The rating usually states that the door will withstand a fire for a certain number of minutes.
- **Flush door-**a door that has a front and back panel (also known as the skin) that is perfectly smooth.

- **French door-**a door or series of doors that are hinge mounted (as opposed to a patio door that moves on tracks) and provides access to a courtyard, patio or garden. French doors are often found with divided lites (small panels of glass in individual frames as opposed to one large panel). May also be used as interior doors between rooms.
- **Hollow core door-**refers to a particular method of door construction. These doors have airspace between the front panel and the back panel of the door. The airspace between the front and back panel often contains a cardboard "honeycomb".
- **Interior door-**a door that is found inside the Home and may include doors from one room to another as well as cabinet doors.
- **Overhead door-**also known as the garage door. May be constructed as a one-piece door or may be constructed in sections. A sectional door rides up into the garage ceiling on tracks whereas the one-piece door operates with springs and hinges.
- **Patio door-**an exterior door that is usually comprised of two panels, one sliding and one stationary. Patio doors are also known as sliding glass doors.
- **Pocket door-**a door that does not swing in or out, but slides across the opening from a "pocket" inside the wall.
- **Raised panel door-**a door that is manufactured with panels either individually inserted into the door or embossed into the face of the door as part of the manufacturing process. Raised panel doors can be solid core or hollow core.
- **Shower door-**a glass or plastic door that provides access to the shower.
- **Solid core door-**a door that has no airspace between the front and back panel, but is instead solid wood or some material that is glued or laminated to the front and back panels. Used in exterior applications and more custom interior applications.

Doorstop-the piece of trim that is put around three sides of a doorjamb to stop the movement of the door when it is closed and sometimes to provide a rudimentary seal against light, noise, and air.

Downspout-a specialized pipe usually made of aluminum, galvanized steel, or plastic that conducts storm water from the roof gutter down the wall and to the ground.

Draftstop-see Firestop.

Drain:
- **Deck drain-**located in a patio or elevated deck to control and direct rainwater away from that area.
- **French drain-**similar to trench drain, but there is no pipe at the bottom of the trench.
- **Overflow drain-**protects the structure in the event that the main drain plugs up. The overflow drain is typically 2 inches higher than the main drain. Overflow drains are also found on bathtubs and lavatory sinks.
- **Plumbing drain-**found at the low point of the plumbing fixture, such as a bathtub, shower, sink, etc.
- **Roof drain-**drains the roof area, including the hole in the gutter. If the drain is at the edge of a flat roof, it is called a scupper.
- **Trench drain-**often located in a yard or hillside area. Consists of a trench with a perforated pipe at the bottom and gravel filled on the top. The term is incorrectly interchanged with french drain.
- **Yard drain-**also known as an area drain or a site drain. This drains rainwater and irrigation run-off from landscaped areas.

Drainage plane-the assembly of components between (behind) the exterior cladding and the frame of the Home. Its purpose is to direct any unintended moisture away from the frame and discharge it at the weep holes at the base

Draw-the ability of a flue, chimney, or vent to pass air, smoke, or other vapors from the bottom, up and out the top. Unless impeded by some source, all vertical tubes have a natural draw due to a difference in atmospheric pressure.

Drip irrigation-a method of irrigating plants, shrubs and trees with a low pressure, low volume piping and tubing system. Drip irrigation significantly conserves water compared to conventional methods of irrigation.

Driveway-see Flatwork.

Dry rot-a condition of rotting wood (but sometimes paper and drywall) when the material is wetted repeatedly and dries between wettings. Wood that is dry rotted is internally infected by a fungus. The wood will often look almost in its original form, but it will have no structural value and can be easily pierced with a screwdriver.

Drywall-a gypsum based panel that is nailed or screwed to the studs that makes up the interior wall of the Home. These panels are also known as Sheetrock®. Drywall is typically finished by placing tape over the panel joints, applying drywall compound (known as taper's mud), and completed by spraying or troweling drywall texture onto the wall.

Dual pane-a type of window, skylight or patio door. Dual pane means that there is an outside layer of glass and an inside layer of glass separated by a spacer up to 5/8 inch in thickness and a dead air space between the two panes of glass. This is sometimes called insulating glass.

Dutch gutter-a rainwater diverter found on roofs, often over doorways or where the placement of a conventional gutter is impractical. It is usually inserted between rows of shingles or tile, and it protrudes up above the roofline by about 3 or 4 inches.

Eave-the underside of a section of the roof that extends past the walls of the Home.

Efflorescence-white powdery material that appears on the surface of concrete and stucco as the curing process occurs. Wet, winter weather may cause concrete and stucco to effloresce.

EIFS-an acronym for Exterior Finish Insulating System. This component system, when applied to the exterior of a Home, consists of building paper, foam insulation, wire mesh (lath) and a synthetic stucco product.

Elastomeric-coatings that have "stretch" characteristics and are applied to many decks and low-pitched roofs. Elastomeric components are mixed together and applied with trowels or rollers. Several coats are applied and if the surface is to be walked upon, often sand, pebbles or crushed walnut shells are applied in the final coat. Some elastomeric paints are made to be applied to stucco.

Escutcheons-a piece of circular trim, chrome, brass, plastic or wood that is used to finish off pipe penetrations through a wall or ceiling. They are usually round and 1 inch to 3 inches in diameter.

Expansion joint-a cut or gap that is deliberately left between sections of building materials to allow for expansion and contraction of those materials. Examples of expansion joints are found in large expanses of stucco walls, concrete driveways, garage slabs, and swimming pool and patio decks. Expansion joints that are trowelled into concrete when it is poured are also called control joints or cold joints. Since concrete frequently cracks, the cracks are supposed to occur at these joints to prevent cracking elsewhere.

Exposure-a measure for roofing, usually in inches, of the amount of roof shake, tile, or shingle that are exposed to the weather.

Fascia-the trim board that covers the edge of the rafters at a pitched roof. May also be incorporated with a gutter to collect rainwater from the roof.

Filter fabric-a textile made of synthetic threads that allows water to pass through but keeps particles of soil from passing through. Used to wrap underground drainage pipes and are placed underneath roadways in unstable soil areas.

Finish coat-the final coat of material applied to a Home. Examples are stucco, paint, drywall texture, deck coatings and other materials that require more than one application before being complete.

Firebox-the portion of the fireplace where the fire is actually built.

Firestop/Fire Block/Draftstop-material that is inserted into a wall to limit the spread of fire and smoke. Frequently used materials are sheet metal, wood, drywall, insulation and masonry block. Draftstops are found in chimney chases and between floors of multistory condominium units. They are often made of sheet metal.

Flapper valve-the rubber or plastic valve at the bottom of the toilet tank that keeps the water in the tank until the flush lever is pushed.

Flashing-strips of material, usually metal, that are used to direct water and wind from one surface to another. Flashing is placed where a roof and a wall intersect. It is also placed around the intersection of chimneys and roofs, where roof planes come together, and where trim pieces protrude from walls. Walls that terminate without being under a roof, such as a parapet, are flashed with cap flashing. Sometimes two flashing components work together, when one piece of flashing slides underneath the other; this is called counter flashing.

Flatwork-a broad-based term referring to concrete placement that is flat. Examples include driveways, patios and walkways.

Flue-the pipe protruding from the top of the firebox, furnace, water heater, or other gas appliance that carries the hot burned gases outside the Home.

Flush-to be in the same plane or level with another object.

Foundation-the lower most structural element of the Home that supports the weight of the Home. There are two primary residential foundation types: the raised footing and the slab on grade. There are several variations of the two primary foundation types:

- **Basement-**these foundations are a form of grade beam foundation, since the basement wall becomes the grade beam. Basement walls are founded on perimeter footing and a slab is poured between the footings to complete the basement floor.
- **Conventional slab-**this refers to reinforced building slab. Steel bars, called rebar, are crisscrossed to form a mat over which concrete is poured. In some cases, the reinforcing may be welded wire mesh.
- **Footing-**a term given to the underside of the grade beam or the underside of the edge of a slab. To provide additional foundation stability, foundations are made wider than the grade beam itself, and deeper than the thickness of the slab.
- **Grade beam-**concrete is poured in a form to allow a first floor framing of the Home to occur at least 6 inches higher than the surrounding ground. The grade beams comprise the exterior perimeter of the Home and sometimes the interior grade beams are also poured to support bearing walls.
- **Piers-**holes drilled into the ground typically between 6 and 18 feet deep, reinforced with rebar, and filled with concrete. Piers are typically connected to the underside of grade beams. Less frequently, piers independently support the underside of Homes. Even less frequently, piers are connected to the underside of slabs where unstable soil conditions warrant. The purpose of a pier is to provide additional stability to a foundation against upward and downward pressure.
- **Post tension slab-**a method of reinforcing where cables are crisscrossed in the slab area prior to pouring concrete. After the concrete is cured, the cables are tightened under extreme tension to provide a tight and dense foundation.
- **Slab on grade-**where the concrete is poured on top of the finished and prepared lot. The concrete slab then becomes the first floor of the Home. Slab foundations may have thickened edges or grade beams poured underneath them.

Frame-the skeleton of the Home. It contains the elements that support the weight and define the shape of the Home. The frame and the foundation are the most important structural components of the Home.

Furnace-a mechanical device located in, around, under the Home, or sometimes in the attic. The furnace is powered by either gas (natural or bottled), electricity, fuel oil, or a combination of power sources. The furnace provides a source of heat for the Home.

Furr out (or down)-to create a false or second wall or ceiling in order to hide plumbing pipes or heating ducts. Also used to correct misaligned walls.

Grade-the elevation of a particular lot above sea level and the degree of levelness of that lot. Finished grade is the elevation of the lot (sometimes known as the pad) after the grading operations have been completed. Grade is also describes the type, quality, and strength of lumber that is used in the frame of a Home.

Grade beams-the piers connected to low concrete perimeter and interior walls.

Grain-the naturally occurring lines of harder and darker wood that run though the field of a piece of lumber.

Greenboard-a special type of drywall that has moisture resistant characteristics. In the past its common application was around tubs and showers. Typically, it is either green or blue in color. Greenboard is no longer permitted for use around tubs and showers.

Ground fault circuit interrupter-a special electrical breaker (GFCI) that is more sensitive to electrical changes than standard circuit breakers. Areas that are subject to moist or wet conditions such as kitchens, baths, garages, and outdoor areas must have their electrical outlets connected to a ground fault interrupter.

Grout-material usually containing cement, sand, or a plastic polymer material, and a coloring agent, which fills joints between pieces of tile or marble. The joints between pieces of tile or marble are called grout joints. Stonework can also be grouted. Grout is also used to fill voids under foundation sills.

Gusset-a triangular piece of material often made of wood, plastic, or metal, which is used to strengthen intersecting corners. Gussets are used inside hollow core doors and inside cabinet frames.

Gutter-an open linear collector and distributor of water. Gutters may be found at the eaves of roofs, or can be associated with curbs and sidewalks in streets and parking areas. Another possible location for gutters is in the middle of driveways and streets.

Gypsum-a powdery mineral that is white in color, non-combustible, and is the primary ingredient in indoor plaster and drywall.

Gypsum board-see Drywall.

Hardboard-a variety of simulated wood products that are used primarily as exterior siding.

Hard water-water that is high in mineral content, mainly compounds of calcium and magnesium. Hard water prevents soap from lathering, and it can form deposits inside water lines and water heaters.

Header-a horizontal structural framing member made of wood or steel that spans the opening over a window or door.

Heart (Heartwood)-the grade of lumber, typically redwood. Heartwood is from the inner core of the tree trunk. It is considered the best lumber because it is more uniform in appearance. The opposite of heartwood is "sapwood", which refers to the lumber that is milled from the outer-most portion of the tree. Sapwood is usually lighter in color than heartwood.

Hold downs-structural metal straps that are embedded in the foundation at the time of pouring concrete and then are nailed to framing members during construction. Hold-downs can be comprised of anchor bolts, threaded rods, and metal gussets to tie the frame to the foundation in the event of an earthquake or loads (forces) caused by wind.

Holidays-a small area that the painter has missed or covered very lightly. Derived from the saying "it looks like the painter took a holiday".

Honeycombs-pockets of improperly mixed concrete where the gravel pieces are visible. Often seen in foundation walls.

HVAC-an acronym for Heating, Ventilating and Air Conditioning. Refers to the specialty work of contractors who install furnaces, fans and air conditioning systems.

Impermeable-the ability of a material to resist the passage of liquid through it. A plastic sheet or membrane that will not allow water to pass through it is considered impermeable. Semi-permeable membranes allow for the passage of some moisture.

Insulation-a material that keeps a Home from either gaining or losing heat. Normally insulation is put into walls, under the bottom floor, and into attic space during construction. Sometimes insulation is placed on the outside of slab foundations and is attached to the outer face of the studs before applying the exterior finish.

Interface-a point where two or more functions interact. For example, the telephone service company wiring meets and interacts with the Home telephone wiring at a box called the interface.

Jack-has four meanings in homebuilding: 1) the metal assembly on the roof through which plumbing vents and furnace flues pass through to the exterior. The jack may be a combination of metal and a rubber gasket to ensure a watertight seal. 2) a screw device that can remedy certain out of level conditions on foundation and floor frame members. 3) a “phone jack” at a wall plate into which a telephone cord is plugged. 4) any short filler in roof or wall framing such as "jack rafter" or "jack stud".

Jamb-the stationary component of a door assembly to which the hinges and latches are attached. The door assembly (excluding the door itself) is comprised of two jambs, a stop, a head, and casing.

Joist-the horizontal members of the Home frame that are the most common elements of a floor or ceiling system. While joists are the most common element of the floor system, other horizontal members known as beams or girders can also make up the floor system. Common joists have one nominal dimension, typically at 2 inches and the other nominal dimension at 8 inches, 10 inches, 12 inches, or 14 inches, depending upon how far they span. It is common practice today to use a manufactured component as a joist. This is called a truss; it is comprised of wood, metal or a combination of both. If a truss is used, it has been manufactured in a factory and approved for use by a structural engineer.

Kick-out (flashing)-the bottom-most piece of flashing between the roof and an adjacent wall. Instead of being flat, it is shaped with a “kicker” to direct rainwater away from the wall into the gutter.

Knocked down-a style of finished drywall texture that is applied coarsely with a texture spray gun. The bumpy surface is then “knocked down” with a large metal straight edge known as a texture knife.

Latch-the portion of the doorknob assembly that protrudes out from the door. Upon closing the door, it fits into the hole provided by the strike. The term can also generically refer to any part of a door, gate or opening mechanism that hooks into a receptacle designed to receive it.

Lath-a material to which plaster is applied. Lath is usually metal in the form of wire or mesh. It is applied over building paper to the exterior of the Home prior to plastering. The lath provides a surface for the plaster to hang onto during its wet application, and reinforces plaster much in the same way rebar reinforces concrete.

Leaf-a term given to the part of a door that swings in or out with another companion door, and which does not close into a jamb on the strike side. Good examples are French doors that connect to one another when closed. A leaf is also the flat part of a hinge.

Ledger-a horizontal piece of lumber or steel used to support beam joists and rafters. The wood ledger, which is at least 2 inches “nominal” thickness, may support joists by having them rest on top of the ledger or hang from the face of the ledger by metal brackets known as joists hangers. A common application for the ledger is in the construction of a deck attached to the outside of the Home.

Lippage-the difference in height between one piece of a finish component and the adjacent piece. For example: two hardwood floorboards; two sections of granite counter tops or two pieces of tile (unless the tile product is designed to have irregular surfaces).

Live load-the allowable amount of weight, usually expressed in pounds per square foot, that a floor, ceiling, wall, deck, or roof assembly can withstand. Includes the weight of the assembly itself (dead load) plus the weight of the occupants or other load like snow.

Membrane-a thin sheet of material used to prevent the passage of water or water vapor into an area that would be damaged by water. Often used under deck surfaces.

MERV-the acronym for Maximum Energy Reporting Value, a rating system for furnace filters.

Millwork-components that are generally part of the interior finish of the Home. They are manufactured in a mill or shop, rather than constructed at the site of the Home. Examples of millwork are cabinets, doors, crown molding, and baseboards.

Miter cut-a method of cutting wood (usually trim pieces) at an angle other than 90 degrees, but typically 45 degrees, so as to conceal the joint when the pieces of wood are placed together. Corner pieces of trim such as door casings and baseboards are often miter cut so that the cut end is not visible.

Mortar-a mixture of sand and cement. May be used for setting brick, stonework, and preparing a bed upon which tile is set. Unlike concrete, mortar does not have aggregate. Grout is a kind of mortar.

Mudsill-a 2x4 or 2x6 section of lumber that is bolted to the concrete foundation as the very first wood framing member. It must be pressure treated or foundation grade redwood.

Mullion-a strip that divides, or appears to divide, the panes of glass in a window. In many multi-pane windows, a false mullion is placed in the dead air space between the panes of glass to give the appearance of a multiple pane window. Also referred to as “grids”.

Negative slope-a slope or grade that runs in the wrong direction, causing water to flow in the opposite direction that is intended. See the definition of Slope for more information.

OSB-the acronym for oriented strand board. OSB is a manufactured wood product that comes in sheets that are 4 feet wide by 8, 9, or 10 feet in length. It can be part of the Home frame on the subfloor, walls, or roofs. It is always covered by the finish flooring, siding, or roofing material.

Pad-the level portion of a graded lot where the condominium or Home is to be built. A padded lot refers to a lot that has been graded flat in one or more levels and usually certified by a civil engineer. It is also the cushioning material installed under carpet.

Parapet-a low wall that extends above the level of a roof and is often referred to as solid guardrails on the sides of decks and balconies.

Particle board-a mixture of wood chips, sawdust and a glue-like binder called resin for creation of a synthetic wood product. It is manufactured in boards like lumber, or sheets like plywood, and has a broad range of applications. Examples are shelving, door cores, and backing (underlayment) for tile and vinyl flooring. A related product, called oriented strand board (OSB), is used as roof underlayment and shear panels.

Patio-see Flatwork.

Pavers-pieces of stone, concrete, or brick that are placed side-by-side to form walkways and driveways. Shapes can be square, rectangular, hexagonal or other geometric shapes. Depending on their specific use, pavers are set over a base of sand, concrete, or mortar.

Penny-a nail size measurement. Derived from Old English where copper was used for both pennies and nails. 10d = 10 penny

Perforated pipe-pipe with holes or slots through its sidewall. Permits the collection of subterranean drainage water or the discharge of wastewater into a septic tank system leach field.

Pier-a column of concrete that extends down into the ground and is often attached to the underside of the grade beam. Sometimes an “independent“ pier may be attached to the underside of subfloor joists in the crawl space. The purpose of the pier is to provide additional load carrying capacity at the foundation.

Pitch-also known as slope. The amount of drop (or rise) of a building component such as a roof or deck. For example a roof that has a 5 and 12 pitch means that for every 12 feet of horizontal measurement, the roof would rise up 5 feet in vertical measurement.

Plant on-an architectural feature that is usually glued to or fastened to the exterior of a Home to add dimension and character to walls and windows. Used frequently in stucco applications.

Plaster-see Stucco.

Plumb-a building component that is perfectly vertical. Out of plumb means that the component is tilted to some extent.

Ponding-a condition where flat surfaces that are supposed to drain collect water in depressed areas called ponds (also called birdbaths).

Post-a vertical structural element larger than a stud used in the framing of a Home. Posts are usually the vertical support for horizontal beams. Posts can also be found as a component in handrails.

Pot shelf-an architectural feature found on the inside and outside of some Homes, used to permit the placement of pots or decorations. Often found in hallways and in bedrooms above closets, as well as on the exterior in front of windows.

Pre-emergent-a chemical applied to landscape areas in winter and spring prior to the growth of weeds to prevent weed seeds from sprouting.

Pressure treated-a chemical treatment given to lumber that may or will come in contact with the ground. The process often gives a greenish or brownish color to the wood and linear perforations ("pickling marks") on the sides. Mudsills and fence posts are examples of lumber that should be pressure treated.

Primer-the base or initial coat of a liquid, usually paint, sometimes resin, which penetrates and adheres to the coated object and provides a compatible surface for finish coats.

PVC-a plastic pipe made from polyvinyl chloride. The most extensive use of this pipe is for irrigation supply lines. Other uses include storm and sewer piping. If the manufacturer adds another step to the process, called CPVC, the pipe can be used for cold water household use in most geographical areas.

R-Value-the measure of a material's resistance to heat flow. Insulation is rated by its R-Value. The higher the R-Value (like R-11, R-22, R-38 etc.), the greater ability to insulate.

Rafter-the common structural lumber used to create the frame of the roof. The rafters define the shape of the roof as well as the slope.

Rake-see Roof Rake.

Rain screen-a membrane installed behind masonry, siding, or stucco that directs unintended moisture down to exit at the bottom and to not migrate into the frame of the building.

Rebar-steel rods that are placed in a form, such as a foundation, to give added strength and resistance to prevent concrete cracking.

Refractory-ceramic or brick like material that is made to withstand high temperatures. Many fireplaces have precast panels of refractory material at the sides and back.

Repoint-the process of using a pointed masonry trowel to make repairs on mortar joints.

Resilient floor-another term for vinyl sheet flooring.

Ridge-see Roof Ridge.

Riser-the vertical, back piece of a stair step that separates one tread from another.

Roof-the upper most structural component of the Home or the building frame. A number of terms are associated with roofs:

- **Gable-**the portion of the end of a building that extends upward from the eaves to the ridge is referred to as a gabled roof. Typically the gable is triangular.
- **Hip-**a gable roof that has been clipped back at its outer end, and with a sloped roof added to the clipped area.
- **Mansard-**a small, steeply pitched portion found around the perimeter of low pitched or flat roofs as an element of architectural enhancement.
- **Rake-**the line of the roof running from the ridge to the eave. Rakes can occur at the ends of gables, or where two sections of roof join in a hip.
- **Ridge-**the highest horizontal part of the roof.
- **Shed-**a pitched roof where the upper most part terminates at a wall, or a pitched roof that starts at the top of a wall and is pitched in only one direction (as opposed to a gable roof which is pitched in two directions).
- **Valley-**the opposite of hip (see above definition). The low point where two roof planes intersect.

Roof cover-the material that gives the roof qualities of water shedding or water repellency. Examples of roof covers are:

- **Asphalt composition or shingle-**made primarily by combining fiberglass or felt with a petroleum product and finishing the outer surface with granulated sand, stone, or other hard substance. Applied in strips about 3 feet long.
- **Built-up roof-**also known as low pitch or flat roofs. The most common material used in this type of roof is hot asphalt (tar) mopped over a felt membrane and covered with gravel. Other materials used include rubber sheeting and elastomeric coatings, known as single-ply roofs.
- **Tile-**individual pieces made from mortar (called concrete) or terra cotta. The material can be colored in the manufacturing process and it is available glazed or unglazed. Shapes include flat pieces (known as shakes), interlocking "S" shapes, or semicircular barrels.
- **Wood shake or wood shingle-**usually made from split cedar logs and hand applied on the roof one at a time.
- **Other-**there are numerous other roof coverings that have limited use in new Home construction. These include metal shingles with granular material glued on them, shakes made of cement and fiberglass, and reconstituted wood shakes.

Rosette-the two circular end pieces (usually plastic) mounted on the inside of a closet. The purpose of a rosette is to provide the niche into which the closet pole is inserted. A rosette is also the round portion of the door hardware used to trim out the hole bored through the door.

Scalloping-the condition of finished boards (including flooring) where the saw has made irregular cuts or chips out of the surface of the board.

Screw drive-the method of operation of some garage door opener mechanisms. Also known as worm drive. The screw drive is a long steel rod that runs between the opener and the door header and it revolves in a clockwise and counterclockwise direction.

Scupper-an opening in the outside edge of a low slope roof or deck that allows rainwater to pass from the roof or deck over the side or into a downspout.

Seismic-frequently describes earthquake activity. Seismic design, for example making the Home stronger and less prone to damage in an earthquake, is a part of the Building code. Some seismic building methods include tying the Home to the foundation with long metal straps and using shear panels to keep the Home from moving back and forth during an earthquake.

Sheathing-the part of the roof that covers the rafters and provides the substrate for the roof covering system. Sheathing is usually plywood or Oriented Strand Board (OSB).

Sheetrock®-see Drywall.

Shower pan-the bottom part of a shower. It may have been installed as a single unit or tiled over a waterproofing system.

Siding-the exterior covering of a Home. Many materials can be used for siding, including wood, brick, vinyl, aluminum, plaster (stucco), and cement board.

Sill-the bottom of a window or patio door. This is often confused with the trim piece, known as the stool, which is placed on the sill. Another sill, known as the mudsill, is the first piece of horizontal framing that is bolted to the foundation. Mudsills are required to be termite resistant wood.

Slab-flat concrete often used with a foundation type known as slab on grade. Slab is also used in reference to the floor of a garage or basement known as the garage slab and basement slab.

Slope-the percentage or angle that a surface (such as a patio, driveway, or the grading around the Home) drops, as one moves outward from the Home. Sometimes referred to as pitch or "fall". When dealing with plumbing pipes the term "fall" is used, which means the percentage or degree of inclination of the pipe.

Soffit-a roof projection that has the underside enclosed so that the rafters cannot be seen. Overhead decks and walkways may be constructed in a manner so as to have soffits.

Sole plate-the 2x4 or 2x6 (sometimes 4x4 or 4x6) section of lumber that is laid flat on the slab or subfloor. The wall studs are attached to the plate. In the case of a concrete slab, the sole plate and the mudsill are the same.

Spalling-the chipping or flaking of the exterior surface of a building material, usually concrete, that deeply pits the surface of the material. Concrete is known to spall in cold climates where there is repeated wetting and freezing of the surface. Cement plaster (stucco) can also spall for the same reason. Spalling can also occur in concrete when it is allowed to dry out (cure) too quickly.

Spark arrester-a metal screen-like device that is mounted on top of the chimney to prevent hot ashes from passing into the air and creating a fire hazard.

Splash block-a shallow trough with one open end that is placed under the discharge of a downspout to direct rainwater away from the foundation. Splash blocks are usually made of cast concrete, but they can also be made of cast fiberglass, metal, and plastic.

Spores-microscopic organisms that are capable of rapid reproduction and give rise to a new adult molds, mildews, and fungi. Found in mushrooms, ferns, mosses, as well as other organic material.

Stile-the right and left side pieces of a door or cabinet that run from top to bottom.

Stool-the piece of trim that sits horizontally on the sill of a window. Often accompanied with a companion piece underneath it known as an apron. "Stool" can also refer to the lower piece of a toilet. Two-piece toilets have a tank to hold the flushing water and a stool to receive the waste.

Stoop-a step or series of steps, plus a landing that leads to the exterior door of a Home.

Storm collar-a piece of metal that looks like a collar and is attached to the chimney cap or vent from a gas appliance. The flue runs through the storm collar.

Strike-the portion of door hardware that is attached to the frame and receives the latch when the door is closed.

Stringer-the side boards on either side of a stairway. Unless the stairway is open, the treads run from one stringer across to the other.

Stucco-can be a form of mortar known as cement plaster (sand and cement) or it can be a more synthetic material consisting of plastic resins and materials to bind them together. Stucco is applied to the exterior of a

Home by troweling or spraying, to comprise a hard, weather resistant surface. Many final textures are available for stucco including skip trowel, sand float, and brocade.

Stud-the common vertical structural pieces, usually wood, sometimes steel, which support the walls of a Home. Studs are mostly 2 inches x 4 inches in cross dimension, although sometimes they can be 2 inches x 6 inches.

Subdrain-a drain that is placed underground to catch and divert subsurface water.

Subfloor-the flat flooring material that is connected to the floor joists. It is often made of plywood or several plywood substitutes. The finish floor, such as carpet, hardwood, tile, or linoleum, covers the subfloor.

Subpanel-a large electrical box with a metal or plastic door usually found mounted in the wall inside the Home or garage. The subpanel contains the circuit breakers or fuses of the branch electrical circuits. Homes may have more than one subpanel. The main panel is the box on the outside of the Home that contains the electric meter and possibly some circuit breakers.

Subsidence-see Displacement.

Substrate-a material that typically lies beneath the finish floor and serves as a support base for another material that covers it.

Subsurface water-water that passes underground through the soil, usually from a distant source. May cause soil to slide and swell, creating stability problems for Homes.

Sump pump-a submersible pump that is placed in a low location inside or outside the basement or crawl space walls to pump out excess groundwater to the street or nearby storm sewer. If a pump of this type is used to pump sewage, it is often called an ejector pump.

Swale-a surface path for seasonal water flow that can be natural or man-made. Often swales are cut around Homes as part of the finished grading process to allow rainwater to flow away from the Home and out toward the street.

Sweat-the process by which copper piping is joined together. Using a torch, the parts to be joined are heated and the solder flows into the joint. This process is known as "sweating" pipes.

Swing-sometimes known as "hand", the term describes whether a door swings to the right or the left as one faces it and opens it. Left hand doors open and swing to the left and right hand doors open and swing to the right. Swing is an important thing to know when replacing doorknobs.

Tack strip-a narrow strip of wood with specialized nails driven in the opposite direction of the anchor nails, designed to catch and hold the edge of carpet. Tack strips are about 1 inch wide and up to 8 feet long and are nailed to the subfloor or concrete floor around the perimeter of a room. These sharp and specialized tacks grab the carpet backing as the carpet is stretched toward the wall.

Tannins-a substance found in many plants and trees that is acidic and dark in color. Tannins will leach when the material is wetted or crushed. Two materials that contain significant tannins are redwood and oak wood.

Telegraph-a condition where the frame members or concealed joints are visible through the outer wall surface.

Threshold-a piece of wood, metal, or plastic that is placed on the bottom of the exterior door opening to provide a means of sealing the bottom and to direct water away from the opening.

Toe kick-a small piece of wood at the bottom of cabinets, usually about 4 inches high, which lifts the cabinet off the floor and is recessed behind the cabinet face.

Trap-the piece of waste pipe just below sinks (visible), and below tubs and showers (not visible), shaped like a "U" or a "P". Traps retain some of the wastewater and prevent sewer gases from backing into the Home.

Tread-the flat part of a step.

Trench drain-a subterranean drainage trench that contains a perforated pipe at the bottom and is filled with a gravel mix. The term is often mistakenly interchanged with "French Drain" which is a gravel filled trench without the pipe. (Also see definition of Drain.)

Trim-material that "finishes off" or dresses up a Home. Various examples of trim are baseboard, door casings, window stools and aprons, crown molding, wood applied to the exterior around windows, and material that is applied to the Home (usually wood) after the stucco or siding has been installed.

Truss-a structural component that has been engineered and manufactured to carry the weight of a floor or the weight of a roof. Trusses are often substituted for common floor joists and common rafters.

Tuckpoint-to use a pointed masonry trowel to make repairs on mortar joints.

UL label-a label affixed to electrical appliances that have passed the independent tests administered by Underwriters Laboratory.

Underlayment-sheet flooring material, usually plywood, particleboard, or cement board that is placed underneath the product it covers to give the top product rigidity. When used in roofing, the underlayment, if coated, can serve as a membrane (felt).

Useful life-how long a particular component or product is supposed to last. Useful lives are provided by manufacturers, by insurance companies, and by industry groups based upon actual experience and testing. If a product becomes obsolete, but is not worn out, it is also said that its useful life has passed.

Valley-see Roof Valley.

Vapor barrier-a sheet membrane that has numerous applications to keep moisture from entering (or in some cases leaving) a Home. Vapor barriers are installed on the exterior of the frame of a Home prior to the application of siding or stucco. Building paper serves as a vapor barrier prior to the installation of lath and stucco. Concrete slabs are poured over a plastic vapor barrier to keep moisture in the ground moving up through the concrete via capillary action. In colder climates interior vapor barriers are put in the inside of exterior walls and under the drywall to keep the humidity of the Home at a constant level.

Vaulted ceiling-a ceiling that is not flat, but rather follows the pitch of the roof, or the underside of the truss.

Veneer-a thin layer of finished material applied over a much thicker layer of core material. It is a common practice for door, cabinets, and furniture manufacturers to place a veneer of fine wood over a core of particle board as part of their manufacturing process. Veneers can also be brick or masonry products.

Vents-there are many types of vents found in Homes. Here are some of the more common ones:

- ❑ **Attic-**attic vents are usually louvered, often round, and found underneath the gables of a roof. Attic vents allow heat to escape during summer months.
- ❑ **Foundation-**foundation vents are installed with pier and grade beam foundations. These vents allow air to circulate and moisture to escape.
- ❑ **Plumbing-**plumbing vents are pipes that stick up through the roof and allow wastewater to pass through the Home plumbing without becoming air locked.
- ❑ **Soffit-**vents that are found on the underside of soffits. They may be round, rectangular, or narrow and long.
- ❑ **Window-**the portion of the window that opens and closes is called the vent.
- ❑ **Other-**examples of other vents are exhaust fans, water heater flues, and cooktop vents.

Walkthrough or Delivery-A practice used by Builders when a new Home is delivered to the Homeowner. A representative of the Builder walks through the Home with the Homeowner prior to delivery. Often the Builder will demonstrate the features of the Home and give the Homeowner instructions on care and maintenance. This event is a very important opportunity for the Homeowner to note any items that are not complete or appear to be unacceptable. For example, countertop scratches and marks on the walls will probably not be covered under a Builder's limited warranty once the Homeowner takes possession of the Home.

Walkway-see Flatwork.

Wall-the exterior and interior vertical component system of a Home. There are many types of walls and several examples are described here:

- **Bearing wall-**a wall that carries a portion of the weight of the Home. Most exterior walls are bearing walls. Some interior walls are also bearing walls.
- **Headwall-**not a wall in a Home, but a wall that has been constructed as part of a storm drain channel or piping system. The headwall is the concrete wall that serves as the beginning of a system where rain and storm water will flow from a channel into a system of piping.
- **Nonbearing wall-**a wall that is a partition between rooms, but does not carry the weight of any portion of the structure above it.
- **Party wall-**a wall where most likely two walls are constructed to separate one condominium from another or one townhouse from another. Also known as common walls, these walls must be constructed according to a specific standard in the Building code.
- **Rated wall (Ceiling)-**a wall that has been constructed to meet certain fire resistant and noise transmission standards.
- **Shear wall-**a wall of a Home that has been reinforced against back and forth movement (caused by earthquakes and wind forces) using sheets of plywood, oriented strand board, or other materials approved by the Building code.

Water hammer-the action of water under high pressure, rushing through pipes and hitting a turn in the piping or a closed valve. Water hammer makes a banging noise in the piping. It can eventually break the piping connections and cause the piping to come loose. A common water hammer problem is the electric valves on a washing machine closing quickly between cycles.

Water table-a trim piece that runs horizontally along an exterior wall that separates two different types of finish materials, such as brick and siding.

Waterproofing-the plastic and rubbery building materials that keep water from penetrating surfaces such as windows, retaining walls, and certain stucco surfaces.

Weather stripping-material made of plastic, felt, rubber, and metal that is placed around the frames of doors and windows to provide a final seal against the intrusion of wind and rain.

Weep holes-small holes found at the exterior side of most windows to allow rainwater to exit from the channel of the window onto the outside of the building.

Weep screed-strip of metal used to terminate the bottom of stucco applications, running parallel to the ground and about 6 inches off the ground. Rainwater that may enter behind stucco will run down the building paper and exit through the weep screed.

Index

If a component or condition is not listed above, refer to the Table of Contents or Glossary.

Bibliography and References

ASHRAE Handbook: Fundamentals, American Society of Heating, Refrigerating and Air-Conditioning Engineers, Atlanta, GA, 2006-2009.

Ballast, David Kent, *Handbook of Construction Tolerances*, McGraw Hill, New York, 1994.

Bliss, Steven, *Troubleshooting Guide to Residential Construction*, Journal of Light Construction, Washington D.C., 1997.

Brenzel, Kathleen, *Sunset Western Landscaping*, Oxmoor House, Tampa, FL, 2006.

Building Radon Out, EPA/402-K-01-002, 2001.

California Building Code, 2013 Edition, California Building Standards Commission, Sacramento, CA, 2013.

Concrete and Clay Roof Tile Installation Manual, Tile Roofing Institute, Chicago, IL, 2002.

Concrete Performance Standards-Appendix C, San Diego Regional Standards Committee, 2001.

Consumer's Guide to Radon Reduction, EPA, Washington D.C., 2010.

Fire Resistance Design Manual (FRDM), Gypsum Association, GA-600-12, Hyattsville, MD, 20th Edition.

Guidelines on Assessment and Remediation of Fungi in Indoor Environments, New York City Department of Health and Mental Hygiene, 2008.

Hansen, Douglas and Redwood Kardon, *Code Check Electrical,* Taunton Press, Newtown, CT, 6th ed.

Hansen, Douglas and Redwood Kardon, *Code Check Plumbing and Mechanical,* Taunton Press, Newtown, CT, 4th ed.

Home Buyer's and Seller's Guide to Radon, EPA, 2009.

Homeowners Booklet, New Home Warranty Program, State of New Jersey, Division of Codes and Standards, 2010.

Homeowner Handbook, Greater Atlanta Homebuilders Association, 2003.

Indiana Quality Assurance Builder Standards, Indiana Builders Association, 2009.

Installation Techniques Designed to Prolong the Life of Flat Glass Mirrors, Glass Association of North America (Mirror Division), Topeka, KS, 2012.

International Building Code, International Code Council, Washington D.C., 2012.

International Residential Code for One and Two Family Dwellings, International Code Council, Washington, DC, 2012.

Lowe's Complete Landscaping, Sunset Publishing Corporation, Menlo Park, CA, 2008.

Maguire, Jack, *500 Terrific Ideas for Home Maintenance and Repair*, BBS Publishing Corporation, New York, 1997.

Mold in Residential Buildings, NAHB Research Center, Inc., Washington D.C., 2001.

National Electric Code, National Fire Protection Association (NFPA), Quincy, MA, 2011.

New Home Warranty Program, State of New Jersey Department of Community Affairs, 2010.

NRCA Roofing and Waterproofing Manual. Vols. 1, 2 & 3. National Roofing Contractor's Association, Rosemont, IL, 2007-2009.

NASCLA Residential Construction Standards, National Association of State Contracting Licensing Agencies, Phoenix, AZ, 2009.

Operating Cost Manual for Homeowner Associations, California Department of Real Estate, Sacramento, CA, 2007.

Prescriptive Residential Wood Deck Construction Guide, American Forest and Paper Association, Inc., Washington, D.C., 2010.

Problems, Causes and Cures. National Wood Flooring Association, Ellisville, MO, 2002.

Residential Construction Performance Guidelines 3rd ed., NAHB Home Builder Press, Washington, DC, 2011.

Reynolds, Don, *Residential & Light Commercial Construction Standards*, R.S. Means Company, Inc., Kingston, MA, 2002.

Sacks, Alvin M., *Residential Water Problems*, NAHB Home Builder Press, Washington, DC, 1994.

South Carolina Residential Construction Standards, Residential Builders Commission of the South Carolina Department of Labor, 1997.

Standard Specifications for Tolerances for Concrete Construction and Materials (ACI 117-10), American Concrete Institute, Farmington Hills, MI, 2010.

Technical Notes on Brick Construction, Brick Industry Association, Reston, VA, 2002.

Tenenbaum, David J., *The Complete Idiot's Guide to Trouble Free Home Repair*, Alpha Books, New York, 2004.

Uniform Plumbing Code, International Association of Plumbing and Mechanical Officials, Whittier, CA, 2012.

Workmanship Standards for Licensed Contractors, Arizona Registrar of Contractors, Phoenix, AZ, 2009.